38-

Women and Deafness

Women and Deafness
Double Visions

Brenda Jo Brueggemann

Susan Burch

Editors

Gallaudet University Press
Washington, D.C.

Gallaudet University Press
Washington, D.C. 20002

http://gupress.gallaudet.edu

© 2006 by Gallaudet University

Published in 2006

Printed in the United States of America

Library of Congress Cataloging-in-Publication Data

   Women and deafness : double visions / Brenda Jo Brueggemann, Susan Burch,
   editors.
        p.   cm.
   Includes bibliographical references and index.
   ISBN 1-56368-293-1 (alk. paper)
      1. Deaf women—United States.   2. Deafness—Social aspects—United States.
   I. Brueggemann, Brenda Jo, 1958–   II. Burch, Susan.
   HV2545.W65   2006
   305.9′0820973—dc22

                                                                    2006014962

∞ The paper used in this publication meets the minimum requirements of American
National Standard for Information Sciences—Permanence of Paper for Printed Library
Materials, ANSI Z39.48-1984.

Contents

Introduction

Skirting the Issues
Women and Deafness

We began our work on this volume by skirting the issues. As early as 2000 we were having conversations with each other about the absence of published intersectional scholarship in Deaf studies generally. To our knowledge, no single volume of work and even very few articles or essays existed that blended, compared, or complicated what it meant to be deaf and female. Whatever the many and complicated reasons might be, gender studies has typically skirted deafness even as Deaf studies has largely skirted gender.

If Deaf studies has typically skirted (gone around) gender, then what would it mean to put a skirt on (feminize) Deaf studies? And if women's studies had traditionally not given "voice" (a common metaphor used in much feminist theory and women's studies scholarship) to deafness and Deaf identity, then what would it mean to give "Deaf eyes" to women's studies? These were the mirrored and twinned questions that generated this volume.

Martha Sheridan (1995) took up the double-bound absence of intersections between women's studies and Deaf studies, between Deaf identities and female identities, in her essay "Deaf Women Now: Establishing Our Niche." Sheridan discussed issues such as the "social status of deaf women"; the biases deaf women likely face with health care and other social services; the strengths of deaf women, including the 1982 formation of a women's caucus within the National Association of the Deaf (NAD) and an international organization, Deaf Women United (DWU), formed in 1985; the lack of research and theory in this intersected area (at the time she found "only four articles focusing on Deaf women . . . in the professional literature" (386); and how it is that "we can begin to transform the social inequities that Deaf women have endured" through various commitments to change.

This volume supports the commitment to change that Sheridan expressed. To encourage the intersections of these areas and to gauge how audiences might respond to such an intersection, over the past five years we put together several conference panels that focused on women and, or in relation to, d/Deaf identities, Deaf culture, or communities of deaf people. We skirted the issues first at four conferences: the March 2001 Gender and Disability Studies conference held at Rutgers University, the October 2003 Feminism(s) and Rhetoric(s) conference held at Ohio State University; the June 2003 Society for Disability Studies meeting; and the June 2004 National Women's Studies Association Conference. Interactions at these four key events—as well as in our own teaching and other academic arenas where we shared our work with historians, rhetoricians, language and literary scholars, and disability studies comrades—convinced us all the more of both the need and the potential for a book that would bring together *women* and *deafness*.

Our goals are three: first, to make use of and build further a bridge between women's studies and Deaf studies; second, to engage a wide and diverse audience of both scholars and students in those two fields; and third, to open up new territory for each of these two areas while also encouraging more traffic between them.

SEEING BRIDGES

This book places women and deafness in shared but also distinct frames because the two are not always one and the same thing (and we return to this point later). Deaf women—as well as women in relation to deafness—are represented and studied in this volume as blurred but distinguishable identities and experiences operating in complex spheres, sometimes complementary, sometimes conflicting. These complex spheres are political, public, personal, private, domestic, economic, institutional, linguistic, and relational. As an interdisciplinary volume, the

contents here represent research and methodological approaches from sociology, ethnography, literary/film studies, history, rhetoric, education,
and public health. In reflection of this disciplinary diversity, readers will
find that the chapters here employ different citation formats; stylistic
choices with text and tone also may vary across the disciplinary presentations. The sites—the spaces and places—for the studies gathered in this
particular collection are largely American (with the exception of Plann's
chapter on Spanish deaf education in the last half of the nineteenth century), and they range from around 1800 to the present day while also
locating their subject(s) in many different regional, local, economic, and
institutional settings.

We set out to explore the intersectionality of identities (as content or
subject area) as well as to employ interactionist approaches to scholarship
in identity studies (as method). With these intents, we have adopted and
adapted the thinking and approaches of a young feminist and disability
studies scholar, Alexa Schriempf (2001), and others who transcend "additive" or "pop-bead" identity studies frameworks "in which one theorizes
separate oppressions and identities and then adds them back together as
if that would explain the whole experience" (65). Unlike the large plastic
beads that preschool children are often given to pop-push together, creating either random or sometimes patterned sequences, this volume instead
represents an attempt to recognize that the terms (and bodies) of *women*
and *deaf* are more than just an additive kind of "doubling." Doubling
visions, we suggest, may do more than add; such visions may also multi-
ply, overlap, and refract one another. Doubling our visions can mean
many different ways of looking: as a potential mask, foil, mirror, or stand-
in for the other; as folding over the other, or even as one turning back
sharply on the other; as laid almost, but not quite, on top of, beside, or
behind the other. And finally, doubling visions can create parallel helical
chains similar but different, sequential yet always unique.

REACHING THE AUDIENCE

Appealing to a diverse audience has remained an important goal for this
volume. We hope that scholars, graduate students, and college faculty
alike will find this volume useful in part simply because there is no other

book like this in Deaf studies, disability studies, women's studies, or gender studies. A successful doubling of two fields and their operating subject terms, *women* and *deaf*, and the multidisciplinary and varied methodological approaches to these subjects required a collection of pieces that was accessible yet provocative for colleagues and scholars in these two fields as well as for students in either (or both) Deaf studies and women's studies. Deaf studies, disability studies, and women's studies all provide natural audiences for this collection. In fact, the expansion of these fields, particularly in the past decade, calls for a book of this kind as a basic progression of the academic understanding and new knowledge being created in these areas. This anthology shares many of the issues and central themes that are at the center of current scholarship in both Deaf and disability studies: (1) identities within (and alongside) identities; (2) the role of contextual studies; (3) multiple ways of reading texts, terms, subjects, events, and spaces; and (4) the role of agency—whether active, alleged, assigned, or subversive.

Women's studies and gender studies also call for a text like this one. Scholars in these fields often cut to the core issues of relationships, power, difference(s) and inequality, family, language, socialization, and the body. The authors in this collection share a keen interest in these factors and offer new interpretations and concepts that complement and complicate traditional women's studies research. Greater attention to minority populations as they are embedded in and intersect with "women's worlds" also broadens this book's audience.

Creating a work that undergraduates could access was a primary consideration for us. We believe that the emphasis on undergraduates as a vital audience for such a book is crucial for at least two interrelated reasons. A broader-based undergraduate education in disability studies (and Deaf studies alongside it) may have its greatest impact in the undergraduate liberal arts curriculum. As an issue, "disability" has long been attended to in graduate and professional schools where medical professionals, clinicians, service providers, and counselors (social work, legal, rehabilitation, employment, etc.) often learn how to work only *on* or *around* people with disabilities. Changing the way our culture perceives and responds to disability and people with disabilities constitutes a primary goal for most of the new disability and Deaf studies courses and programs that now appear on college campuses across the United States and Canada. This change will happen most successfully by educating undergraduates more broadly—using a liberal arts tradition—about the breadth and depth of identities, conditions, lives, experiences, languages, and communities that suffuse and surround the often flattened and falsely narrowed states of "deaf/deafness" and "disabled." Involving undergraduates in reading, writing, talking, and thinking about the cross-identity relationships of and in "deafness" (and "women," too) is an essential practice. For these interdisciplinary fields to evolve, scholars must encourage their students to conduct their own preliminary research in these areas. This kind of evolution and new scholarship developed directly from students will be an important part of the change in cultural attitudes and actual material conditions for many marginalized peoples (including women, deaf people, and individuals with disabilities) in both the present and future.

The importance of intellectual accessibility also demands that we produce scholarship that can be engaged by more than just specialists and holders of advanced degrees. New research in these areas should be made particularly accessible to students with disabilities. It has been demonstrated that the presence of strong identity studies programs (such as women's studies, Latino/Latina studies, African and African American studies, gay/lesbian and queer studies, and Asian American studies programs) promotes a welcoming and supportive environment for students who claim those identities. Such students are more likely to attend colleges that tangibly demonstrate that these identities are worthy of intellectual study. We hope for the same to happen for students who are deaf and/or disabled. The possibility of undergraduate students' access to and engagement with texts like this one can be an important part of establishing that welcoming environment and furthering intellectual study in these areas.

OPENING TERRITORY

Establishing, welcoming, furthering: these three moves stand behind our rationale for this volume. In short, we wanted this collection of essays to open up previously explored territories that were not yet very familiar to each other: *women* and *deafness*.

Yet even these two terms complicate matters. We must adopt them
even as we want to resist or remove them. Neither philosophers nor scientists have ever really been able to safely settle, finally define, or even carefully contain the shifting boundaries around *sex* or *gender*. Alongside those
contested boundaries lie equally shifting terms such as *woman/women*.
Seen as fallen souls by Plato and merely mutilated men by Aristotle in
Western philosophical tradition, women seem to have no identity or
definition other than that which is tethered to men. As such, the category
or term becomes only derivative, incapable of standing/meaning on its
own. Monique Wittig, for example, has worked philosophically to demonstrate that the class and character of *woman* is created only through/in
a relational appropriation by a man (1997).In its relational appropriation
and its derivative dependence upon *men*, what also troubles the term
women is its constructed nature. In *The Second Sex*, French essayist and
novelist Simone de Beauvoir famously posited, "One is not born, but
rather becomes, a woman" (1953). Three decades later, another feminist
critic and scholar writing about pornography, Andrea Dworkin, echoed
and expanded upon de Beauvoir's maxim: "Woman is not born: she is
made. In the making, her humanity is destroyed. She becomes symbol of
this, symbol of that: mother of the earth, slut of the universe; but she
never becomes herself because it is forbidden for her to do so" (1989).
More recently, Judith Butler (1993) and Donna Haraway (1991) have
written at some length about the trouble with terms that are associated—
largely through definitional acts—with *gender* and *sex*. In fact, Haraway
comes closer than probably any other feminist theorist of this century to
offering a nonderivative, original "definition" for *women* when she claims
in her introduction that "inhabiting these pages are odd boundary creatures—simians, cyborgs, and women—all of which have had a destabiliz-
ing place in the great Western evolutionary, technological, and biological
narratives. These boundary creatures are, literally, *monsters*, a word that
shared more than its root with the word, to *demonstrate*. Monsters signify" (2).

Deafness—as term and bodily condition—also has occupied a demon-
strative, monstrous, and boundary-like space. Deafness signifies. Much
like *woman* to *man*, *deafness* is most often only defined negatively in relation and appropriation to *hearing*. As a condition of failed senses (hearing,

and sometimes speech), deafness stands (or stumbles) like Plato's female "fallen souls." Typically recorded in our medical, scientific, and philosophical history as an aberration of linguistic normalcy, deafness marks a mutilation—much like Aristotle's women. It is an awesome, awful, monstrous condition demonstrating, on the lips of those who diagnose it, something akin to a lack, a loss, an absence, a difference, a deviance. In such constructions, deafness (and by extension, deaf people) echoes other terms, other "conditions," other people. *Listen*: deafness is not born; it is made. In the making, a deaf person's humanity is destroyed. She becomes symbol of this, symbol of that: innocent child forever thrust outside of language; savage silent beast; overcoming genius; gesturing ape related to, but still distant from, "human." But she never becomes herself because it is forbidden for her to do so.

Yet deafness, even conditionally (as a medical condition), signifies. This volume is not exclusively about deaf, or Deaf, women. (That volume surely still needs to be collected.) Rather it is a volume that includes essays about deaf women (the Allen Sisters and Helen Keller, for example) as well as pieces about Deaf women (Sarah of *Children of a Lesser God*, Robinson's activist-club president Annie Lashbrook, some of the ASL teachers Kelly interviewed in her ethnography) right alongside many chapters where the audiological/medical (deaf) or cultural (Deaf) dominance of identity is not altogether cut tidy and clear (the beauty-pageant queens Burch discusses; the subjects of Barnartt's educational/occupational/economic status research; perhaps even for Summer Crider, who is the central focus of Oliva and Lytle's essay). Additionally, it is a volume that features scholarship about not only deaf or Deaf women but also about people, often women, who are in relationship to them (and who may or may not be deaf)—women educators of deaf children, interpreters, and mothers of deaf children (as seen in the pieces by Lee, Plann, Winzer, Abel, Harmon, and Oliva and Lytle). Conditionally then, it could not be a volume about deaf women. The conditional term, *deafness*, in relation to the equally conditional term, *women*, was thus a difficult but deeply considered choice. In this case at least, it is less *deafness* or *women*, as the noun-states they are, that fail or fall—but language itself.

To be sure, however, this volume has certain limitations. Further scholarship is needed on racial, ethnic, geographical, economic, political, and age-based identities and experiences as they connect to either, or both, gender and deafness. Although we focus primarily on *women* in the (unclearly defined) gender arena in this volume, work also clearly needs to be done about the particular cross-constructions between *deaf* and the broader range of gendered identities beyond simply masculine/feminine. Even the way that all the service professions surrounding the condition of deafness and deaf people—those in the "field of deafness," as it is often strangely called—are predominantly occupied by women still needs to be seriously studied; we take such gendered "facts" for granted here in the globalized twenty-first century (at least in relation to the thing called "deafness"), yet the signification of female dominance in "service" to deaf people is a phenomenon that to deaf people remains an issue skirted by scholars, specialists, and activists alike. In addition, there is much critical work to do in considering how deafness itself can powerfully interrogate and even counter feminist theory's telling obsession with "voice" and its discomfort with "silence." By donning a pair of deaf eyes, women's studies might come to see its own language choices and philosophical positions differently. We hope the conversation has only just begun.

Works Cited

Butler, Judith. *Bodies that Matter: On the Discursive Limits of "Sex."* New York: Routledge, 1993.

De Beauvoir, Simone. *The Second Sex.* Ed. and trans. H. M. Parshley. New York: Knopf, 1953.

Dworkin, Andrea. *Pornography: Men Possessing Women.* New York: Plume, 1989.

Haraway, Donna J. *Simians, Cyborgs, and Women: The Reinvention of Nature.* New York: Routledge, 1991.

Schriempf, Alexa. "(Re)fusing the Amputated Body: An Interactionist Bridge for Feminism and Disability." *Hypatia* 16.4 (Fall 2001): 53–78.

Sheridan, Martha A. "Deaf Women Now: Establishing Our Niche." *Deaf World: A Historical Reader and Primary Sourcebook*, edited by Lois Bragg, 380–89. New York: New York University Press, 2001.

Wittig, Monique. "One Is Not Born a Woman." *Feminisms.* Ed. Sandra Kemp and Judith Squires. Oxford: Oxford University Press, 1998.

Part One

In and Out
of the Community

Editors' Introduction

This section generally assesses issues of female identity and specifically analyzes the influence of deafness on traditional interpretations of women's roles. By addressing both internal community relations and external influences on gender and Deaf cultural identities, these essays expose similarities and differences in the experiences of deaf and hearing women and examine what distinguishes Deaf women from their hearing and/or male peers. Studies of intimate and informal relations among women and girls in residential schools (Lee), role models (or anti–role models) such as Helen Keller (Nielsen), and women's organized activism (Robinson) demonstrate the flow and subtlety of female Deaf experiences. Likewise, the sociological study by Barnartt offers tangible evidence of the ways mainstream society demotes and marginalizes this doubly bound minority group.

In her essay, Lee carefully studies gender dynamics and role modeling within residential schools for the deaf, the traditional "home" of Deaf culture. She provides new insights into the social web of female dorm parents, teachers, staff, and students, while she also outlines previously neglected factors influencing Deaf women's historic identity. Like Lee, Nielsen critiques various educational forces—ones that shaped her subject's life—revealing significant and complicated cultural training. The profound influence of Keller's male role models offers a rich counterpoint to Lee's assessment of girls' family training in residential schools. Nielsen's reinterpretation of Helen Keller exposes factors that commonly placed Keller outside the actual and symbolic Deaf world, drawing our attention to the norms and boundaries of cultural communities that accepted or rejected individuals like Keller.

Extending beyond the school grounds, Robinson examines Deaf associations and clubs. Often seen as the center of an extended cultural family in the adult Deaf world, associations and clubs had a profound impact on community identity, specifically affecting gender roles within the Deaf world. This work reinterprets women's "separate sphere" by showing the ways Deaf female members negotiated their social roles and specifically promoted Deaf culture. Social tensions over gender, seen in the previous essays, provide a sharp lens in Robinson's piece, revealing fresh comparisons between Deaf women and their hearing peers.

Barnartt completes this section with a sociological study that examines patterns of education and labor force status from 1960 to 1990. Her study demonstrates that deaf and hearing women share similar experiences of inequality, yet the same is not true for deaf men. Raising important questions about the power of education and school, as well as of social expectations, Barnartt encourages us to reconsider the categories of "women" and "Deafness" as monolithic and unified. By focusing on economic status, she highlights the evolution of communities and, as Nielsen aptly describes it, the "complicated recipe of identity."

The authors of these four essays share an interest in the critical themes of education, economics, and social associations, while dealing diversely with the related concepts of training, patriarchal institutions, and community. Methodologically, these four chapters all emphasize context and describe both continuity and change over time. They focus on the ways gender complicates traditional views of deafness and vice versa. They break away from dichotomous definitions of identity, instead promoting concepts of identity that are more flexible and situational. They also address issues of agency, illustrating the variety of active roles deaf women assumed in their communities.

Some Questions to Consider

- How do these essays conceive of *community*? In these conceptions, what or who is inside or an insider and what or who is outside or an outsider?
- What distinguishes a deaf woman from her hearing and/or male peers?
- What are the relationships among school, work, and social associations for Deaf women?
- How do different *methodological approaches* to the question of context in these essays shape the *subject* of the study?

Family Matters
Female Dynamics within Deaf Schools

Jessica Lee

The apparent inferiority of woman's intellect is to be attributed to many restrictive circumstances. We are so accustomed to behold her in a state of development so far below her powers that we do not apprehend the full evil of these circumstances.
—*Agatha Tiegel, "The Intellect of Women," 1893*

Scholars in Deaf history commonly use the metaphor of home to describe Deaf residential schools because these institutes were the birthplace of Deaf culture.[1] Regardless of era or geographic location, residential schools served as surrogate homes for generations of Deaf people, fostering close relationships between students and staff. The structure of residential schools, in fact, intentionally echoed home and family life. Many deaf youngsters spent their childhoods there, learned important life lessons there, were acculturated there, built linguistic skill in a visual modality there, and developed lifelong relationships there. The schools' academic and social training made lasting imprints on the lives of their students. The representation and reproduction of the family in and through deaf education in the nineteenth and twentieth centuries also had a direct effect on America's Deaf community. However, scholars and Deaf leaders have generally overlooked the profound differences in educational experiences of Deaf people. Examining historical images of deaf education through a lens of gender highlights how these varied experiences are manifest in the structure of schools, faculty and administration roles, dorm life, vocational education, curricula, and extracurricular activities.

Studying the history of Deaf women in this area poses unique challenges. For example, few scholars have addressed women's experiences in the Deaf world, inside or outside the school grounds. Although a sizable amount of data is available from schools, including annual reports, yearbooks, student newspapers, and the like, sources from girls or women remain comparatively scarce and fragmented. Many Deaf people, for various reasons, tended to leave behind fewer written documents—historians' traditional source base—and Deaf women, more than men, left even fewer such documents. For multiple reasons, including some that are addressed in this essay, Deaf women have remained symbolically and literally behind Deaf men in historical studies. In this essay I seek in part to correct this oversight. Studying Deaf women and their training and experiences within residential schools sheds light on a significant population in the Deaf world. Additionally, I attempt to widen the scope of inquiry, encouraging a deeper understanding of disability, the lives of women, and concepts such as home and family.

Specifically gendered training distinguished girls' lives from boys' at residential schools. Through overt and sometimes covert means, educators trained deaf girls with narrow goals in mind: namely, for the girls to become wives and mothers. But individual educators did not act alone. Broader factors such as general educational programs, extracurricular activities, the physical isolation of residential schools, and the adult Deaf community's involvement all contributed to deaf girls' sense of place, status, and identity as workers and as community members. Ultimately, restricted gendered tracking in deaf residential schools resulted in fewer options for deaf girls than for their hearing peers, seriously undermining their economic independence and encouraging conservative gender roles. So although hearing women were receiving increased training in various vocations such as education, nursing, and secretarial work, deaf girls had less training and were encouraged to use marriage as a form of economic security.

Various external and internal factors promoted the domestic character of deaf schools. Parents had to be convinced that letting their young children live away from home in an institution for most of their children's developmental years was the best decision. Families with deaf children rarely had the resources to visit or bring their children home more than a few times a year. Extended separation, parents felt, might weaken familial bonds. Many already felt somewhat separated from their children because of language problems. Communication barriers often undermined parents' ability to instill appropriate behavior or attitudes in their deaf children. Commonly, deaf youngsters arrived at the residential schools with insufficient training to care for themselves or fully understand others. Superintendents and teachers explored strategies to address some of these problems through the curriculum. Schools had to assume the role of the traditional family in character development, living skills, and moral training. Structuring the school after the traditional family model helped in this endeavor. Promoting staff as motherly, dorms as homey, and superintendents as fatherly comforted parents and their children, who would be separated from one another for upward of ten months of the calendar year.[2] In addition, it gave the school "mothers" and "fathers" added authority to deal with the moral and social, as well as academic, development of their pupils. As in many traditional homes at the time, the "mothers" were primarily responsible for instilling moral values and proper etiquette.

Thus, throughout the nineteenth and early twentieth centuries, administrators predominantly hired women to tend to children, especially young children. Particularly in the "home inside the home"—the dormitories—women filled positions such as "house mother" and "dorm parents."[3] One such matron, Mrs. Willard, was described in 1890 as "the ideal matron; a woman of most exemplary Christian character, and in the largest sense of the word, a mother to the children under her charge."[4] An obituary in 1895 for another dorm employee, Elizabeth Fowler, exalted the kind lady:

> Her ability, fidelity to duty, and motherliness toward little children were so marked that Miss Garrett selected her for an "attendant" to the little deaf children in the "home." This office is one of peculiar responsibility, for the Attendant is not a mere nursemaid, but one who takes the place of a conscientious, intelligent and devoted mother, entering *con amore* into the little ones' lives

and leading them in wholesome ways, by pleasant paths, through all the waking hours when the children are not under a teacher's charge.[5]

Matrons such as Willard and Fowler oversaw much of the private lives of deaf children, profoundly shaping the lives of their wards. Judging whether to report poor behavior, doling out types of punishment and rewards, recognizing birthdays, and consoling or nursing those in need, dorm mothers often understood deaf pupils better than any other adults. They served an additional and vital purpose at the schools: as in regular homes, children had chores and responsibilities in the dorms as well as outside of them, and dorm parents coordinated with teachers and administrators to designate appropriate assignments. In part to save money, most residential schools expected students to provide some of the maintenance. Gender strongly informed labor divisions. Boys commonly did jobs that involved physical strength and that reflected masculine vocations: assisting with the school farms, building furniture, and providing grounds care. Girls remained in a domestic realm, cleaning rooms, cooking, and sewing clothing.[6] Some schools even established clubs to serve this purpose. As Stevens, an educator of the deaf, suggested: "Clubs could be organized among the girls in home-making projects. Taking charge of the dormitories, keeping them clean, fixing them attractively, and carrying out principles they have learned are all within the possibilities of every school. Instructing the smaller girls in bed making, dusting, and care of clothing could be some of the interests of the clubs."[7] Alice Terry, an alumna of State School for the Deaf in Fulton, Missouri, recalled, "It was custom for the older girls to take turns waiting on the teacher's table in the dining room."[8] "Good" girls such as Terry adopted the role of dutiful daughter, earning praise from the parental teachers, staff, and administrators.

Teachers—most of whom were women by the twentieth century—also served as mother figures. As one student reminisced in 1875, "Teachers would act not just as teachers but as surrogate mothers as well. A female faculty made the boarding schools appropriate places for children."[9] Another remembered teacher Kate McWillie Powers for her motherly kindness: "[she] never forgot the pupils, as every Christmastide many a heart of deaf children staying in school for the happy season was made bright and happy by the tenderness, sweetness and thoughtfulness of the gifted woman."[10] Faculty members such as Powers often felt additionally responsible for the children in their care. Like young people at any residential institution, deaf students were vulnerable, separated from their biological families, and in need of daily support. One student fondly thanked a female teacher: "We know of no teacher who did more for the happiness and welfare of those in her charge. Many a homesick child she soothed and cheered through the first hard days."[11]

By the turn of the century, women teachers dominated elementary deaf education and almost all courses having to do with speech and lipreading.[12] Their maternal reputation, along with various other factors, promoted this. In contrast to male teachers, who were commonly described as "master[s], commanding attention and obedience from all,"[13] females earned praise for specific maternal qualities. For example, Miss Wharton at the Mississippi Institute, according to one school report in 1915, "endeared herself to the little ones who sat at her knee, to those who grew into the estate of manhood and womanhood and never forgot her beautiful Christian teachings, and to her co-laborers on the faculty and institution staff."[14] The association between deaf girls and adult hearing women intensified by the early twentieth century, as female children outnumbered boys in oral classes.[15] Working one on one with deaf girls, hearing women oral instructors taught their pupils feminine etiquette as well as lipreading and speech, whereas male teachers taught deaf boys vocational or advanced academic subjects.[16] Gender expectations informed school policies, such as academic tracks for boys and girls. They also influenced how and what material was imparted to their students.

Overseeing the school family was a fatherly superintendent. Various factors colored the paternal cast of this position, including religion. The founders of deaf education in America were men of the church. They approached educating the deaf population as both an academic and a spiritual endeavor. Reverend Thomas Hopkins Gallaudet, the original principal of the first permanent school for deaf people in America, assumed the role of protector and provider. As one former student wrote of Gallaudet, "No more a father of the deaf and dumb is seen on earth."[17] His example clearly inspired generations of superintendents. Joseph Tyler, the president of the Virginia School for the Deaf, wrote to the parents of

Thomas Tillinghast in 1842: "Be assured, that your dear little boy will want for no attention in my power to bestow. My feelings toward all my pupils is, I think, warmer and more endearing than usual between teacher and pupil in ordinary schools, simply because my pupils are more helpless and more entirely dependent upon me."[18] Even as administration became more secularized in the late-nineteenth century, superintendents perceived themselves as spiritual and moral father figures for their "handicapped" wards. Although some viewed deaf children as especially dependent and deserving leniency, superintendents also doled out punishment when their children misbehaved. This served to enforce order and discipline in the schools at the same time it reinforced the men's paternal place in the school family. Females rarely assumed the head of such institutions. Management, long the domain of men, remained almost exclusively so in American deaf schools.[19]

Also of great importance was the fact that educators viewed their students as disabled. Common notions of disabled people as dependent, needy, weak, or simply inferior led many to coddle or infantilize the pupils. New Jersey Institute primary teacher Julia Foley was in charge of the academic, moral, and social training of two deaf girls who had arrived at the institute in 1895.[20] In her diary, Foley wrote about one of the girls: "Susan, in reality is a weakling. I am training her perception by touch and taste as well as smell."[21] On the social skills of the other girl, Mary, Foley reported: "She is not affectionate, not attractive: I suppose that accounts for her lack of affection. . . . [H]er affection has not been properly developed."[22] Another teacher, Laura Sheridan, wrote to her colleagues, "Deaf-mute girls . . . are not the independent beings their hearing sisters are, who through the ear and the press come in contact with every variety of mind in the world. All they know has been taught them, and what they read is often but imperfectly understood."[23] Educator W. H. Lloyd added in 1917, "The task of teaching the deaf is surely a trying one and of Herculean proportions. It includes intellectual, moral and physical training, while the measure of success actually attained depends on the willingness of the pupil to do as told."[24] Noting the "Herculean" problem of disability, educators defended their professional performance and validated their demands for more resources. Such rhetoric also distinguished them from "regular" teachers, confirming their familial obligation and authority within the deaf schools.

Perceptions of disability and gender affected relations within and outside of the classroom in other ways. Deaf girls often were required to know different subjects and were expected to understand less than their male peers. Boys from the New York Institution for the Instruction of the Deaf and Dumb in 1890, for example, were required to read twenty-six chapters of *History of the United States and Its People*; their female cohorts were required to read only nineteen.[25] When a board member of the school quizzed the pupils, he asked a young boy to "give a sketch of Alfred the Great, his reforms, laws, etc., and contrast the condition of the country on his succession, with the condition at this death."[26] More questions followed. "How did the science of chemistry originate?"[27] He then asked a female student, "Could you have had your choice, at what period of the early time in America would you have preferred to live, and why?"[28] He followed up: "Which is your favorite flower and why?"[29] The exchanges reveal common notions of appropriate gendered abilities. Boys were encouraged to be scholarly, whereas girls were encouraged to be personal and emotive. As this vignette demonstrates, girls generally needed to know only enough academic information for conversation, not more for future study. Their homework and public presentations reinforced this. Deaf girls, when writing in school newspapers or for samples printed in annual reports of institutions, described stereotypically feminine things. One school annual report quoted a sixteen-year-old female pupil's essay: "Botany is a description of flowers and plants, and please all people in the world especially those of the female sex because ladies seem to be more fond of flowers than gentlemen, and they are very fond of taking care of them in the summer months." The report continued, proudly quoting boys' letters to governors and mayors, highlighting their emerging sense of civic responsibility and leadership.[30] These gender disparities— intentionally as well as unconsciously encouraged—reflected and reinforced employment and social options for Deaf people after graduation.

Vocational training enhanced these differences. Deaf boys learned manual trades, such as shoe repair, carpentry, and printing, leading them to blue-collar work. Most eked out a living on their wages, achieving some financial independence and sense of accomplishment. Deaf girls, in contrast, were taught domestic arts, providing them primarily with skills to enhance their roles as wives and mothers. Such training offered women few employment options, and virtually no chance for economic independence. Thus, by design, vocational programs further reinforced girls' role as helpmate and dependent.[31] Educators rarely considered the implications of their choices. At professional conferences, discussion almost always focused on the education of deaf boys.[32] When attention did turn to girls, instructors emphasized the importance of training girls as homemakers. One from the Michigan school summarized in 1906: "Much of the energy the girls expend in useless waste of time could be utilized in well-directed home making. . . . One of our great economists has recently said: "the two greatest needs of America to-day are: The making of home makers and the training of a people to love their work.""[33] Another stated: "[a group of older girls achieved success by completing a course] in preparing meals, serving them and other household accomplishments. The girls take turns serving the meals in their Cottage-home. . . . [T]hey appear very sweet in their white caps and aprons, and many admiring glances are cast in their direction by the members of ball teams honored with invitations to dine at the school."[34]

The deaf girls at Michigan—and elsewhere—were prided on their combination of sewing, frugality, and beauty. Almost thirty years later in 1935, Amelia Brooks, another instructor from the school, outlined a vocational program for girls which would "help to develop in each girl the ability to do the right thing at the right time—to develop a wholesome character that will assist her throughout her life." Brooks then gave a litany of additional goals. Only the last one referred to industrial or vocational "adjustment."[35] One government official put it more directly: "It is better that a girl be taught to cook an egg right than to dig Greek roots." He continued, "The writer knows of many a case in the families of working people where the mother, father and all the other children have better cooked food and better clothing, both more economically purchased and prepared, as a result of having a seventeen or eighteen year old daughter out of a domestic science course."[36] Thus although hearing women increasingly entered the workforce as teachers, social workers, typists, and seamstresses during the Progressive Era, Deaf women, trained primarily in the beauty arts and domestic sciences, were encouraged to marry in order to find economic security.

Even language use and training inside schools reveal gender differences. Just as spoken English fostered a sense of commonality among children in mainstream schools, American Sign Language (ASL) unified Deaf people across the nation. Frequently denied full language until residential schools and stigmatized by their deafness among hearing family members and broader society, Deaf people felt particular affinity for their "language of the eye." Deaf children commonly communicated in signs with one another regardless of schools' communication policies, but girls commonly had less exposure to master signers; they also had restricted venues in which to express themselves in sign language. Often their use of sign was tied to dramatic performance. As Mary M. Williamson, a Deaf teacher, noted after a visit to the Michigan School for the Deaf in 1906, students presented a variety of performances for her, but the girls appeared only as dancers.[37] Williamson complimented the young ladies for the "piquancy of expression the dainty four maidens give to song."[38] Indeed, graceful, highly stylized signed performances by deaf girls had become a staple of deaf schools. Commencement ceremonies traditionally included groups of girls reciting poetry and hymns such as *Nearer My God to Thee*. Girls earned praise for their dramatic and artistic expressions, efforts that emphasized physical beauty and form with signing ability. Boys, in contrast, frequently honed their sign skills through public speeches and competition, displaying their command of sign language in debate teams or valedictorian addresses. They were encouraged to recite classic pieces of literature, to create their own work, for example, speeches, and to participate in debates and student government. In terms of sign language presentation, girls performed and boys communicated.

Other extracurricular activities carried gender training to the playground. Sports have always played a vital role in residential schools. Deaf school newspapers, often referred to as the Little Paper Family, regularly ran articles on athletic events, highlighting team unity as well as exceptional individuals.[39] Sports served as a unifying force for students as well as for the local adult Deaf communities. As with mainstream schools, the most popular sports focused on boys—football, baseball, and basketball. At such events, deaf girls generally assumed the roles of onlookers or cheerleaders. Their own athletic choices remained comparatively limited, underfunded, and overlooked.[40] Intentionally and unintentionally, girls thus were encouraged to assume feminine, supportive roles. These encouragements came in the form of less funding and fewer opportunities to perform, play, and practice. There was also constant praise for grace, style, and beauty, which are rarely characteristics of serious athletes.[41]

Did Deaf alumni encourage traditional gender roles at their alma maters? Typically, yes. Deaf adults maintained close ties with their local residential schools, reading and submitting letters to the institutes' newspapers. In one editorial, an observer described a postcard of students, noting that

> they appear a fine looking lot of young people, with the sexes about equally distributed. But scanning the bottom row in the picture there is evidence that the girls have slouched into masculine attitudes of the most unbecoming kind. Perhaps the gymnasium directress of the co-eds neglects her duty of teaching the necessary grace of poise and the proper manner of standing or sitting. Most growing young girls never give any thought to such things and need to be guided into correct habits. Anyway, there should be less gaucherie of manner among the co-eds.[42]

Closely scrutinized, "good" Deaf ladies earned praise for epitomizing feminine skills and behavior. As C. O. Dantzer, a prominent member of the Deaf community, claimed in a 1913 article about a ball, "the secret of the fine display, for fine it really was, which called forth the admiration of many a hearing person who was present at the ball, is the ladies were taught the art of dressmaking in this Institution and know how to make out of simple materials at little cost to them, beautiful and becoming dresses. Some of the gowns were quite simple, but—what is more attractive than a really beautiful woman?"[43]

For Dantzer and many other members of the Deaf world, a "successful" woman displayed domestic acumen. In this way, as Dantzer suggested, Deaf women impress Deaf spouses and also prove to the mainstream (hearing) world that they are "normal" citizens. Perhaps the 1917 poem entitled "A Girl's Complete Education" captures it best:

To be gentle.
To value time.
To dress neatly.
To keep a secret.
To learn sewing.
To be charitable.
To be self reliant.
To avoid idleness.
To study hygiene.
To darn stockings.
To learn economy.
To respect old age.
To learn how to cook.
To know how to mend.
To better the world.
To make good bread.
To keep a house tidy.
To be above gossiping.
To know how to buy.
To control her temper.
To make a home happy.
To take care of the sick.
To dress economically.
To take care of a baby.
To sweep down cob webs.
To know how to study.
To make a home attractive.
To be interested in athletics.
To marry a man for his worth.
To know the value of fresh air.
To understand the rules of diet.
To read the very best of books.
To be a helpmate to her husband.
To take plenty of active exercise.
To keep clear of trashy literature.
To understand character building.

To take an interest in the schools.
To understand emergency nursing.
To be light hearted and fleet footed.
To be womanly under all circumstances.
                                        —*N. C. R. News*[44]

The topic of girl's futures as housewives and mothers was a constant source of conversation in Deaf newspapers. Edward E. Ragna published two articles on the limitations of marriage, the first being "Limitations on the Marriage Market of the Young Deaf Girl" in 1921. He laments the issues in marrying both Deaf and hearing men and focuses on the high quality a young woman must be, specifically in domestic skills, to find a husband.[45]

The gender training received in school strongly informed Deaf people's identities even after they left the classroom. Upon reaching their maturity, deaf girls graduated from the role of dutiful daughters and supportive sisters to roles of wives and mothers. Most Deaf girls married classmates within several years of graduation.[46] Many likely agreed with Ragna, who confidently claimed in a popular Deaf newspaper, "It is unnecessary to speak of the desirability of marriage."[47] Deaf newspapers regularly broadcasted Deaf marriages and courtships, praising young couples and instructing readers to lead respectable lives. Marriage offered companionship and the respectable possibility of family. Deaf educators promoted these aspirations among students, in part because they believed that Deaf people deserved similar social opportunities as hearing people enjoyed. Success as a citizen, in this sense, depended in part on the ability to—and fulfillment of—marriage and family life. Yet school policies virtually dictated that Deaf girls marry. Limited vocational training seriously hampered the possibility of financial independence or career advancement. Deaf newspapers as well as professional publications conceded that Deaf women had few jobs available to them. And Deaf leaders, like Deaf educators, offered only meek advice for struggling single women.[48] More disadvantaged than their hearing peers, Deaf girls looked to marriage for economic security unavailable to them otherwise.

Family and home defined girls' lives, inside and outside the classroom. They were born in one family, attended and graduated from a second, and achieved success when they started one of their own. From the birth of American deaf education through the Great Depression, deaf schools provided deaf girls with specific gendered training, and limited choices. Although mainstream society increasingly recognized women's abilities in various professions, little had changed in the way of the roles and expectations of deaf girls. Women in the Deaf world—as in mainstream society—contributed to the character and success of their communities. But the uniquely potent imprint of residential schools on deaf individuals—girls and boys—fundamentally influenced how members interacted with one another, how they saw themselves, and how they expressed themselves.

The image of schools as a home responded to and embodied various mainstream notions about gender and disability. Although initially imposed from outside the community, the dynamics of family and home have resonated strongly within the Deaf world. In many ways, the emphasis on family fortified the Deaf community during decades of oppression and discrimination. As cultural kin, Deaf people demonstrated passionate connections to one another, from their formative school years until the end of their lives. At the same time, the model of deaf schools as home ultimately contributed to women's often inferior status as workers and as citizens in mainstream society. It also contributed to Deaf women's subservient place in the Deaf world, a position that remains little changed to this day. Through the structure of the schools themselves, the roles of faculty and administration, and the curricular and extracurricular options for deaf girls from 1817 to 1930, girls were transitioned from biological to educational families and into their futures, first as sisters and daughters and later as mothers and wives.

NOTES

1. See, for example, John Vickrey Van Cleve and Barry A. Crouch, *A Place of Their Own* (Washington, D.C.: Gallaudet University Press, 1989); Susan Burch, *Signs of Resistance: American Deaf Cultural History, 1900 to World War II* (New York: New York University Press, 2002); and Carol Padden and Tom Humphries, *Deaf in America: Voices from a Culture* (Cambridge, Mass.: Harvard University Press, 1988).

2. Burch, *Signs of Resistance.*

3. See, for example, Mary S. Garrett, J. C. Gordon, and Elizabeth I. Fowler, *Proceedings of the Fourteenth Convention of American Instructors of the Deaf* (1895), xcvii–xcviii; Warring Wilkinson, "Harriet B. Willard," *Report of the Proceedings of the Twelfth Convention of American Instructors of the Deaf* (1890), 342; Douglas C. Baynton, *Forbidden Signs: American Culture and the Campaign against Sign Language* (Chicago: University of Chicago Press, 1996), 65; and "Notes on the N.A.D. Meeting," *Mississippi Institute for the Deaf and Dumb Bulletin* 31, no. 1 (1915): 12.

4. Wilkinson, "Harriet B. Willard," 342.

5. Garrett, Gordon, and Fowler, *Proceedings of the Fourteenth Convention of American Instructors of the Deaf,* xcvii–xcviii.

6. W. H. Lloyd, "The Deaf in Their Relations with Others," *American Annals of the Deaf* 62, no. 2 (1917) and others write of the importance of deaf children making their own clothing and performing menial tasks to save money around the institute.

7. "Should the School or the Shop Teach Language?" *Conference of American Instructors of the Deaf* (1925), 106.

8. Alice Terry, "An Autobiography of My Childhood," *Silent Worker* (November 1920): 47–49.

9. Baynton, *Forbidden Signs,* 65.

10. "Notes on the N.A.D. Meeting," 12.

11. *Report from the Twentieth Conference of American Instructors of the Deaf* (Government Printing Office, 1914): 203–204.

12. Male teachers taught advanced academic courses. Baynton, *Forbidden Signs,* 56–57.

13. *Report of the Nineteenth Conference of American Instructors of the Deaf* (Washington, D.C.: Government Printing Office, 1911), 230.

14. Lula Edgar Wharton, *The Mississippi Institute for the Deaf and Dumb Bulletin* (December 1915).

15. See, for example, the research of Susan Burch, Douglas Baynton, Robert Buchanan, and Margaret Winzer.

16. Robert M. Buchanan, *Illusions of Equality: Deaf Americans in School and Factory 1850–1950* (Washington, D.C.: Gallaudet University Press, 1999), and Burch, *Signs of Resistance* (New York: New York University Press, 2002), 71.

17. J. O. D, Letter about the death of T. H. Gallaudet, *Directors of American Asylum Thirty-Sixth Annual Report* (Hartford, Conn.: Tiffany and Company, 1852), 28.

18. Joseph D. Tyler, Letter to Tillinghast family, November 1842, quoted in Van Cleve and Crouch, *A Place of Their Own*.

19. See, for example, the annual reports for American Asylum for the Deaf, 1817–1949, and New York Institute for the Instruction of Deaf and Dumb, 1879–1891, and reports from the Conference of American Instructors of the Deaf, 1915–1935.

20. Julia A. Foley, "Two Deaf Girls," *Silent Worker* 8 (October 1895): 11–12.

21. Foley, "Two Deaf Girls," 11.

22. Foley, "Two Deaf Girls," 11.

23. Laura C. Sheridan, "The Higher Education of Deaf-Mute Women," *American Annals of the Deaf* 20 (October 1875): 249.

24. W. H. Lloyd, "The Deaf in Their Relations with Others," *American Annals of the Deaf* 62, no. 2 (1917): 119.

25. "Report of the New York Institution for the Instruction of the Deaf and Dumb" (1890).

26. "Report of the New York Institution for the Instruction of the Deaf and Dumb," 35.

27. "Report of the New York Institution for the Instruction of the Deaf and Dumb," 39.

28. "Report of the New York Institution for the Instruction of the Deaf and Dumb," 35.

29. "Report of the New York Institution for the Instruction of the Deaf and Dumb," 38.

30. American Asylum of the Deaf and Dumb, *Board of Director's Forty-Sixth Annual Report* (Hartford, Conn.: Lockwood and Company, 1862), 44.

31. Gillett, *Conference of American Instructors of the Deaf* 19 (1911): 191. Gillett discusses the two basic vocational skills that are taught to deaf girls: housework and sewing.

32. H. M. McManaway, "The Proper Training of Shop Teachers as the Solution of Most of Our Problems," *Conference of American Instructors of the Deaf* 24 (1925): 106, as well as a significant portion of the *Twenty-Ninth CAID Report of Proceedings* (1935) discussed how, overall, education at residential schools left women to meet their postgraduation lives with a strong sense of family, a strong set of domestic skills, and real expectations, which prepared them for a lifetime of limited opportunity. See also Driggs, "Declaration of Principles," *American Annals of the Deaf* 72 (1927): 253.

33. Kelly H. Stevens, "Freehand Drawing and Applied Art: Their Place in Vocational Training," *Conference of American Instructors of the Deaf* 24 (July 1925): 106–10.

34. Mary M. Williamson, "Glimpses around the Michigan School," *Silent Worker* 18, no. 8 (1906): 113–14.

35. Amelia Brooks, "Reorganization of the Girls' Vocational Course of Study," *Report of Proceedings of the Twnety-Ninth Convention of American Instructors of the Deaf* (1929), 250–53.

36. "Some Thoughts on Education,"*Mt. Airy World* (1912): 53.

37. Williamson, "Glimpses around the Michigan School," 114. There is also mention of female performances in Baynton, *Forbidden Signs*, 82.

38. Williamson, "Glimpses around the Michigan School," 114–15.

39. The papers of the Little Paper Family are considered by many as a vector for group cohesion. Published as a vocational training exercise, they quickly spread across the United States, providing cultural and political information to their audience. See Van Cleve and Crouch, *A Place of Their Own*, Burch (2004), and Buchanan, *Illusions of Equality*.

40. Silent Worker (extracurricular file) and Burch, *Signs of Resistance*.

41. Girls' teams were almost always underfunded, and girls were more often praised for their other roles, for example, annual exhibitions and beautiful costumes, as well as their roles on the sidelines. See Nell M. Bergen, "The Girl's Athletic Association," *Silent Worker* 30, no. 4: 66; Arthur Wenger, "Distinctive Features of Schools for the Deaf," *Silent Worker* 33, no. 4: 111; and Warren Robinson, "Girl's Basketball Teams, Wisconsin School for the Deaf," *Silent Worker* 24, no. 9.

42. *Silent Worker* 20, no. 6 (1908): 109.

43. C. O. Dantzer, "Deaf at Home," *Mt. Airy World* (1913): 167.

44. "A Girl's Complete Education," *Silent Worker* 30, no. 3 (1917): 53.

45. Edward E. Ragna, "The Limitations of the Marriage Market of the Young Deaf Girl," *Silent Worker* (1921): 214.

46. Ohio School for the Deaf published an eighty-year record on the post-baccalaureate lives of their alumni. Most women were married and very few to hearing men. "Graduation Classes of the Ohio School for the Deaf 1869–1949," Gallaudet Archives, Washington, D.C.

47. Ragna, "The Limitations of the Marriage Market of The Young Deaf Girl," *Silent Worker*, 214.

48. "What Girls May Do: Is Deafness a Bar to Photo-Engraving?" *Silent Worker* 27, no. 2 (1914): 37.

Was Helen Keller Deaf?
Blindness, Deafness, and Multiple Identities

Kim E. Nielsen

Helen Keller remains, even more than thirty years after her death, the world's most famous "out of the closet" person with a disability—most certainly the most famous female with a disability. The Alabama native lost both her sight and hearing as the result of an illness at nineteen months of age and became an international star at seven years, but primarily lived and is remembered as an advocate for blind people. The identity she embraced and lived in public was that of a *blind* woman whose civic interests and knowledge revolved around *blindness*.

A major irony of Keller's primary identification with blindness is that several times throughout her life she repeatedly voiced the sentiment that deafness was more debilitating than blindness. For example, in 1929 she wrote in her autobiography *Midstream* that she felt "the impediment of deafness far more keenly than that of blindness."[1] In 1936 she echoed the sentiment:

> Lack of hearing has always been a heavier handicap to me than blindness. Sealed ears render more difficult every path to knowledge. The deaf are as hungry for a word as the blind are for a book under their fingers, yet it is harder to find people who will talk with the deaf than people who will supply the sightless with embossed books. . . . Regretfully I perceive the impossibility of working for both the blind and the deaf as I have often longed to do.[2]

Without conscious irony, because her article was about her work on be-half of blind people, she repeated the same sentiment in a 1938 *Good Housekeeping* article.[3]

A further irony of Keller's primary identification with blindness is that a wide array of political and social issues interested her deeply. Joining the Socialist Party of America in 1909, she became an advocate of female suffrage, a defender of the radical Industrial Workers of the World, and a supporter of birth control and the unemployed. She criticized World War I as a profit-making venture for industrialists and urged working-class men to resist the war. She supported striking workers and jailed dissidents and expressed passionate views about the need for a just and economically equitable society. She followed international politics closely, never failing to form strong opinions on international matters, and became one of the nation's most effective but unofficial ambassadors, visiting more than thirty countries.

Despite these many interests and pulls of identity, Keller's concerns remained primarily tied to her identity as a blind woman. Her single-minded public identity as a blind person—not deaf, Deaf, disabled, or female—emerged for institutional and cultural reasons.[4] This "choice" carried consequences for her. And because she remains a preeminent cul-tural figure of disability, this "choice" carries consequences for our con-temporary understandings of identity. Exploring these reasons illustrates the vital importance of including disability alongside and as part of gen-der, race, class, and sexuality as an analytical tool.

THE PUSH TO BLINDNESS

Why, then, did Keller choose to spend most of her life energies and the public capital generated by her fame focused on advocacy for *blind* peo-ple? More specifically, why did she advocate for the American Foundation for the Blind (AFB)? She declared in 1929 that she dedicated her life to this advocacy because she "heard the call of the sightless."[5] More accu-rately, the individuals and institutions of Alexander Graham Bell, Bos-ton's Perkins School for the Blind, and eventually the American Foundation for the Blind vigorously reinforced the call. Once pushed in this direction, Keller found it difficult to follow other life paths.

Keller's first step toward our shared cultural memories, and toward her identification with blindness, came when Alexander Graham Bell first heard of the six-and-a-half-year-old child in 1886. From their hometown of Tuscumbia, Alabama, her parents sought assistance with the young girl they loved, for they felt increasingly incapable of parenting her. Responding to a letter from Helen's mother Kate, Bell, already famous as an inventor of the telephone and as an educator of deaf people, met with Helen, her mother, and her father, Captain Arthur H. Keller. Bell forwarded them to Perkins School for the Blind in Boston but remained an active presence in Keller's life. He was, in Keller's characterization, "a wise, affectionate, and understanding friend." She vacationed with the Bell family and considered him a father figure. He always, she said, "considered me a capable human being, and not some sort of pitiable human ghost groping its way through the world."[6]

Bell is a controversial figure in the history of culturally Deaf people. He believed signing to be a primitive and subhuman form of language. In concert with others, he led the campaign to suppress the use of sign language among deaf people. He thus insisted that teaching lipreading and oralism (oral speech) to deaf people was the "greatest of all objects."[7] Keller agreed, characterizing oralism as "one of the divinest miracles of the nineteenth century."[8] In marriage, in education, and in social life, Bell therefore encouraged separating deaf people from one another in order to make sign language and Deaf culture nearly impossible. Many Deaf people, reveling in the rich Deaf culture made possible by American Sign Language (ASL) and the communities developed around Deaf institutions, resisted organizationally and personally. Many were, and are, antagonistic toward Bell and Keller for their endorsement of oralism. Using ASL, several generations of deaf children had grown to literacy and public success. Forced to use primarily oral techniques of communication rather than sign, literacy and education levels fell in the late-nineteenth century.[9]

ASL is a language in which individuals use facial expressions and hand and arm motions to signify entire concepts, just as spoken or written words signify concepts. It has its own sentence structures, verb forms, and conjunctions. Educated in an oral system and an advocate for it, Keller didn't use ASL but generally fingerspelled English. She described finger spelling: "I place my hand on the hand of the speaker so lightly as not to impede its movements. The position of the hand is as easy to feel as it is to see. I do not feel each letter any more than you see each letter separately when you read. Constant practice makes the fingers very flexible, and some of my friends spell rapidly—about as fast as an expert writes on a typewriter. The mere spelling is, of course, no more a conscious act than it is in writing."[10]

Bell considered Keller's fingerspelled English to accord with his educational views. He thought the same of her steadfast efforts to learn and use spoken English. Thus, though known as an educator of deaf people, he pushed her toward Perkins School for the Blind because he believed educators of deaf people could do little for her—indeed, might even harm her by encouraging her to use a signed language. He also endorsed Perkins because its staff had taught fingerspelling to one deaf-blind child: Laura Bridgman. Bell ignored or rejected the possibility of the American Asylum for the Deaf (now the American School of the Deaf) in Hartford, Connecticut, which had taught deaf-blind Julia Brace sign language. Bell may have sought to keep Keller away from institutions embroiled in debates about oralism.

In the mid–nineteenth century, an immense theological, educational, and philosophical debate raged about the relationship among speech, intellect, and the soul. Without speech or oral input, many believed that a child would never cultivate intellect or soul—indeed, might even lack them. Teaching such a child was generally thought impossible.

Boston reformer and Perkins School for the Blind Director Samuel Gridley Howe searched for a deaf-blind child suitable to explore these issues and establish his fame. Finding seven-year-old Laura Bridgman in 1837, he immediately brought her to Perkins. Bridgman, like Keller many years later, had lost her sight and hearing at a fairly young age as a result of illness and had appeared a bright and creative child. Howe's success at teaching her language, and his perhaps even greater success at publicizing her, made Howe, Perkins, and Bridgman nearly world famous. Charles Dickens visited the child, chronicling her in *American Notes* (1842). Her fame reportedly surpassed that of any other woman except the queen of England. Learning of Bridgman by reading *American Notes* prompted Keller's mother to seek an education for her daughter. At the American

Asylum for the Deaf, however, Julia Brace had learned sign language approximately twelve years before Bridgman. Howe considered her as a possible student before he met Bridgman but believed her, at eighteen, too old to learn. Perhaps the fact that Brace did not embrace language with the same enthusiasm and skill of Bridgman was because she lost sight and hearing at four and a half and then was not encouraged to use a signed language until she was older.[11] A major and consequential difference between the two young women and their institutions is that the American Asylum for the Deaf did not pursue publicizing Brace, nor did it use students and the display of students to raise funds, as Perkins did so skillfully. For Keller's parents and for Alexander Graham Bell, the school where Laura Bridgman, by then elderly, still lived was the only place to even consider when seeking an education for young Helen.[12]

When young Helen's parents contacted Perkins, they corresponded with Samuel Gridley Howe's son-in-law Michael Anagnos. Howe was dead, but his reputation and that of Perkins continued under Anagnos' care. Within months Anagnos arranged to send the school's star pupil, Anne Sullivan (later Anne Sullivan Macy), to the couple's Tuscumbia, Alabama, home.

Not long after Sullivan taught language to the young Helen, she convinced Arthur and Kate Keller that their child would be best served *at* Perkins. The pair moved to Boston in 1888. Like Howe with Laura Bridgman, Anagnos devoted intense efforts toward publicizing her successful education. If there was a doubt before, Perkins became the nation's premier school for blind children, with Helen Keller and Anne Sullivan Macy forever linked to it.

After Perkins, Keller and Sullivan spent several years at New York's Wright-Humason School for the Deaf, a leading oralist institution and proponent of oralism, attempting to develop her lipreading and oral speech. Her brief flirtation with a deaf institution was for the sole purpose of existing and succeeding in the hearing world. Her ambition was starkly apparent. To her, success meant attending the best mainstream college. After several further years of preparation at the Cambridge School for Young Ladies, she entered the prestigious female counterpart of Harvard, Radcliffe, in the fall of 1900 and graduated in 1904. By choosing college and Radcliffe, despite the vigorous opposition of many, and by apparently not even considering Gallaudet, Keller took further steps away from deafness and the Deaf community.

Upon her graduation from Radcliffe in 1904, Keller believed her most viable and important public role to be advocacy for both deaf and blind people. She already had addressed both the Massachusetts and New York legislatures on behalf of bills funding manual training for blind people. She felt that with additional education she could accomplish great things, and included deafness within that scope: "If these workers and philanthropists in Massachusetts and New York thought that I, a junior in college, could help hundreds of unfortunate men and women, how much greater must my chances of usefulness be when I comprehend more fully the needs of the deaf and blind! . . . I must follow where the good cause leads."[13]

The "good cause" led to various fundraising and lobbying efforts throughout the 1900s and 1910s. Keller's first appeals were intensely emotional and echoed earlier fundraising displays of Perkins students by Samuel Gridley Howe.[14] Just a recent college graduate, she sought money for existing institutions such as the New York Eye and Ear Infirmary and the New York Association for the Blind. She emphasized the responsibility of able-bodied people to give: it was "a sacred burden," a "blessing to the strong to give help to the weak." At most events she was the featured attraction. As Alexander Graham Bell or Sullivan Macy relayed her words, crowds stared at her through lorgnettes (similar to opera glasses). According to the *New York Times*, women cried and men "coughed uneasily." Keller's appeal—"I do not wish to be a beggar, but I hope this basket will be filled with checks"—filled the basket repeatedly.[15] This philanthropic model matched practices used by institutions for and of blind as well as d/Deaf people.

By the time Keller entered the 1920s she sought continuance of a meaningful public life, but she also dearly needed adequate financial support for personal stability. The publication of *The Story of My Life* in 1903 was a success, and she considered herself a professional writer. Yet the money she earned was not enough to support her household in the fashion she desired, so she depended on the philanthropy of the wealthy. Simultaneously her political interests expanded and radicalized. She increasingly wanted to write on subjects other than her own disability, such as economic inequalities and Socialism, but editors tended to be uninterested.[16] Money was a constant stress.

The newly created AFB supplied both an income and a meaningful public life, becoming the center of her and Anne Sullivan Macy's lives. Founded in 1921, the AFB united a coalition of the American Association for the Instruction of the Blind and the American Association of Workers for the Blind. Its founders knew the AFB needed Keller and Macy if it was to have national impact, for they were already leading national figures of philanthropy, blindness, and disability in general.[17] Keller's employment with the AFB cemented her public identification with the cause of blindness, removing her further from deafness, the Deaf community, and other causes nearly exclusively. In just three years she and Macy had lectured about blindness and advocacy of blind people to more than 250,000 people at 249 meetings in 123 cities. The AFB became the dominant organization pertaining to blindness in the United States, and Keller remained affiliated with it for the rest of her life.[18]

Keller's public persona made her an incredibly effective fundraiser and lobbyist. As AFB President M. C. Migel noted, "Only a heart of stone could fail to respond to an appeal from Helen Keller." Legislators were "spellbound," wept, and reportedly "adjourned temporarily to greet her."[19] In the 1930s and 1940s she either visited or wrote targeted letters to at least eighteen weepy state legislatures, most often encouraging funding for or creation of state commissions for the blind. Other causes included funding for educational institutions for blind people, bills to allow blind persons to travel with a guide on public transportation for one fare, funds for talking books (records), and funds for Braille books. Sometimes the AFB initiated the visits, sometimes local organizations wrote to the AFB seeking her assistance, and sometimes local organizations wrote her directly. In almost every case, the AFB was eventually involved. The numerous letters of thanks she received testify to her effectiveness. She also lobbied, occasionally in person but most frequently via telegram or letter, the U.S. Congress and U.S. presidents.[20]

By the time Keller reached adulthood, "the blind" had become her primary public focus. The identity she somewhat reluctantly embraced in public after the mid-1920s was that of an apolitical and guileless *blind person* whose civic interests and knowledge revolved around *blindness*. Her primary cultural representation remains that of a young deaf-blind girl who overcame tragedy to become a benevolent international purveyor of goodwill for blind people. The early institutional efforts of Bell, the legacy of Howe and Bridgman, and the continued efforts of Anagnos and Anne Sullivan Macy all pushed her in that direction. Keller's need for an income, and her subsequent lobbying and fundraising efforts on behalf of the American Foundation for the Blind, strengthened the move.

FLIRTING WITH DEAFNESS

Institutions for blind people, namely Perkins and the AFB, dominated Keller's institutional relationships. In both omission and practice, however, she maintained personal relationships with d/Deaf people, d/Deaf institutions, and issues of importance to Deaf people. From the time she became a public figure, the d/Deaf community followed her and claimed her as one of its own. These relationships existed but remained erratic and complex; they offer ambiguous and contradictory, but perhaps thus deeply human, evidence of Keller's thoughts on deafness, deaf people, and people with disabilities in general.

For example, because Keller vacationed and corresponded intimately with the family of Alexander Graham Bell, she clearly knew and spent some time with his deaf wife Mabel. Her letters frequently included greetings to Mabel as well as the rest of the Bell family. A. G. Bell assumed a paternal role in Keller's childhood and early adult life; living away from her mother, knowing that Mabel was deaf, Keller might have hoped to develop a maternal relationship with the older woman. Mabel Bell, however, forbade people to call her deaf, refused to use sign language or fingerspelling, and resented her husband's financial and personal investment in deaf education. She apparently avoided the household when Keller was present. Clearly there was no close relationship or assumption of a shared experience of disability or deafness between the women. To the child and young adult Keller, Mabel Bell modeled deaf adulthood as rejecting deafness as an identity.[21]

As an adult, some of Keller's stances also created a hostile distance between herself and the Deaf community. Her oralist stance and use of oral
speech made many Deaf activists deeply hesitant about her. Reports on
Keller in the *Silent Worker*, the leading newspaper of the Deaf community, placed her squarely in the debate about oral speech and the oral
teaching method. For example, after Keller spoke at the Library of Congress in 1907, one writer wondered about the usefulness of "oral speech
that had to have an interpreter" and noted that the audience sat for an
hour listening to "Helen's unnatural utterances without understanding
anything."[22] A California reporter harshly criticized Keller's oral lecture
tours: "no other public demonstration ever worked greater injury to the
deaf as a class" because the public interpreted Keller as proof of the superiority of oralist teaching, despite the fact that Keller was not initially educated in the oral method.[23]

Another example is her public stance on eugenic questions. At the
height of her involvement in radical politics, she supported eugenic and
euthanasia policies to prevent the birth and sustenance of children with
significant impairments. Though she later changed her mind, and though
this position accorded with the eugenic thought of both radicals and con-
servatives of her era, it was a stance deeply feared by the Deaf community.
Rightly so, many Deaf people feared the possibility that eugenic ideologies would be put into practice against them (for example, with laws
against deaf people marrying).[24] Though Keller never publicly included
deaf people in her eugenic discussions, her adoption of eugenics in general
would have caused many in the Deaf community to regard her with suspi-
cion or anger.

One piece of isolated historical evidence suggests that the potential for,
and perhaps the reality of, other possibilities existed in Keller's life. In
July 1919, the year before she accepted employment with the AFB and
twenty years after her brief stint at Wright-Humason School for the Deaf,
she awoke one morning to a "complete, overwhelming surprise." Expect-
ing to find one person downstairs, she found "an avalanche of handshakes
and good wishes from twenty-seven friends—deaf people who had come
to spend the afternoon with me." Who these people were and from where
Keller knew them is not clear. What is certain, however, is that Keller

delighted in the surprise birthday party on the lawn of her Wrentham, Massachusetts, home. As she wrote, "everyone seemed thoroughly happy."[25] In this case Keller clearly enjoyed the company of these twenty-seven deaf friends.

Keller, however, spent the majority of her life relatively isolated not only from deaf people but from anyone with a disability. The *Silent Worker* followed her when she became a public figure in her childhood, originally claiming her proudly as part of the Deaf community. Once an adult, however, expressions of frustration appeared. In 1915, while complaining of Keller's oralism, one columnist wrote, "I sincerely hope that she will yet condescend to form a real acquaintance with us."[26] In 1916 the paper recorded a "universal complaint" that Keller did not visit schools for the deaf while traveling but encouraged understanding of Keller's busy schedule.[27] In 1925 the newspaper noted that while in Los Angeles Keller had been invited to "a luncheon of a club of Los Angeles deaf ladies" but had not even responded to the invitation—despite the fact that "it was by means of the Manual Alphabet of the Deaf that the light" first reached her.[28] Others criticized her decision to go on the vaudeville stage, calling it, for example, "a most deplorable thing" that challenged the dignity and pride of all deaf people.[29]

None of Keller's seemingly close friends were disabled, perhaps the only exception being Japanese educator Takeo Iwahashi (who was blind). Her isolation stands in sharp contrast to the politicized groups of people with disabilities that existed during her lifetime, based in friendships and social networks formed in educational institutions. Though it is unlikely that Sullivan or other supporters such as Alexander Graham Bell, Perkins's Michael Anagnos, or AFB leader M. C. Migel would have volunteered knowledge of such networks, Keller apparently did not seek it. Though she frequently disregarded the opinions of her advisers on other issues (such as female suffrage, radical politics, and religion), she seems to have made no inquiries or efforts to learn about disabled professionals, disabled tradespeople, or other adults with disabilities living on their own. This includes blind networks such as the American Blind People's Higher Education and General Improvement Association, the turn-of-the-century network of blind professionals and intellectuals of her own generation who published the advocacy journal the *Problem*.[30] She linked neither with the blind school alumni associations nor with the next generation of organized blind activists, who formed state associations in the 1930s and the National Federation of the Blind in 1940. She certainly left no lasting relationships with deaf people and d/Deaf organizations.

THE PULL OF THE CULTURAL FIGURE

The institutional push of Alexander Graham Bell, Perkins School for the Blind, and the American Foundation for the Blind influenced Keller's public identity as a gendered and disabled person. The figures of blindness and deafness pervasive in popular culture and literature were equally influential in creating her public identity of gender and disability—but certainly more difficult to trace.

Historically, in cultural and literary consciousness, "the blind person as seer is the central figure of the literature of blindness."[31] In recent centuries the innocent and compelling young blind girl has appeared as an incredibly popular cultural trope, building upon and regendering the much earlier figure of the blind visionary.[32] Her blindness is both metaphorical and literal. It is a gift that shields her from all sin; her lack of sin becomes a gift she can then share, either as a cultural figure or as an author herself, with those morally burdened by sight. It allows her to serve as both "an object of desire and as a moral exemplar."[33]

Keller intimately knew of and employed the figure of the innocent blind girl. There is no doubt that she read widely in the literature of the Western tradition. She wrote, "Literature is my Utopia. Here I am not disfranchised. No barrier of the senses shuts me out from the sweet, gracious discourse of my book-friends."[34] She sprinkled her own writings liberally with references to other literature. From the moment she became a world-renowned figure as a young child, she received praise for all she did to embody the trope with which she was so familiar. As both a child and an adult, she employed the representation to her own personal benefit and to effective fundraising. First and foremost, after all, she sought an active public life of political and social effectiveness. To forge this public life as an adult, she manipulated a very compelling cultural symbol into a powerful tool—building upon the blind young virginal girl but twisting her profoundly to include an element of political and economic power.

Equally compelling cultural and literary representations of deafness were not available to Keller. Though in the eighteenth century the best-known deaf people were male, by the nineteenth century deafness and sign language had become feminized in popular cultural and in schools for deaf people.[35] After the 1820s Laura Bridgman became the dominant representation of deafness to the U.S. public. She was both deaf and female, and her fame "helped forge the link between the ideal of feminine silence and the actual speechlessness of the deaf."[36] By the supposed silence of her deafness she literally embodied the ideals of Victorian femininity. Changing public and institutional attitudes toward signing by the late nineteenth century (such as those held by Alexander Graham Bell), however, stigmatized gestural language as primitive and unseemly. As Elisabeth Gitter argues, "the destruction of Sign and signing institutions coincided with the devaluation both of the traditional literary figure, the silent redemptive heroine, and the living embodiment of that figure, Laura Bridgman."[37]

Unlike Bridgman, Keller came to womanhood in the age of the New Woman, in which female silence, once praised, was "often portrayed as symptomatic of mental disease, anger, of malevolence"—and in which Sign served as the primary marker of both deafness and inferiority.[38] Keller's embrace of oral speech differentiated her from *inferior* deaf people, female representations of deafness, and deafness in general. The disappearance of positive cultural and literary representations of deaf female figures and the oralist marginalization of Sign decidedly pulled her away from a public identity as a deaf person and toward a public identity with blindness.

THE TUG-OF-WAR OF COMPETING IDENTITIES

When Helen Keller spoke in the 1930s of her decision to work for the AFB she lamented "the impossibility of working for both the blind and the deaf, as I have often longed to do."[39] Several years later she continued, saying, "Reluctantly, therefore, I have confined my activities almost exclusively to the dwellers in the Dark Land."[40] She voiced a similar sentiment when she told her friend Jo Davidson that she would not be able to put energy into the 1944 Henry Wallace presidential campaign because she could not carry on "two or more diverse kinds of work at once."[41] Like all of us, she had limited energies, and like many of us, she felt she had to select a "trump" identity.

As so many feminist theorists have resolutely argued for a strong academic generation, all of us live multiple and intersecting axes of identity. The tug-of-war between Keller's seemingly competing identities and interests did not serve her well. She was never *only* a woman, *only* blind, *only* political, *only* a white U.S. citizen. She embodied a particularly complicated social location. She was deaf-blind. She loved dogs. She was a single white female who embraced many aspects of traditional femininity but was denied many of the privileges of that normative femininity because of ideas about disabled women as asexual and unfit for reproduction. Her primary emotionally intimate relationships were with women. She cared about racial and economic inequalities. She lived a privileged class life but depended upon the charity of others for many years. She experienced disability differently than disabled men because of her gender. She experienced femaleness differently than women with normative bodies because of her disability. Her fame made her experiences of both disability and gender atypical. As Susan Wendell wrote about being a woman with a disability, "these different experiences create the possibility of different perspectives which have epistemic advantages with respect to certain issues."[42]

These complex realities gave Keller unique but sometimes limited insights. At other times she intrinsically and compassionately understood these multiple and intersecting identities. For example, her arguments on behalf of expanding the Social Security Act reflected awareness that class, disability, multiple disabilities, and race frequently intersected to exacerbate social disregard. In 1944 she urged that the Social Security Act support "the particular needs of the poorer blind." Her testimony before the House Labor Committee highlighted the circumstances of "the colored blind" and "the deaf-blind." These were, she said, "the hardest pressed and least cared-for" among her "blind fellows."[43] None of these groups found widespread acceptance and support within either the Deaf or blind community during Keller's lifetime.

Asserting that all of us reside at social locations of long and complicated addresses is not new. Perhaps Helen Keller's contribution to the discussion of the axes of identity is an insistence that we—as feminists, scholars, activists, and individuals—pay further attention to the complicated recipe of identity. All of us have bodies that differ. The bodily differences of people with disabilities, however, are considered not only of greater consequence than the bodily differences of others but also deeply socially discrediting. People with disabilities have had and continue to have lower educational rates, lower incomes, and less social influence than those not considered disabled. People with disabilities have been and frequently continue to be denied access to public space and participation in public events. Historically, laws have denied people with disabilities marriage, education, children, employment, citizenship, and the right to be in public. People with disabilities faced and do face discrimination as a social grouping. Disability alone, however, is not a satisfactory tool of analysis—just as gender alone is not, just as race or class alone is not. Building on the words of Rosemarie Garland-Thomson, to understand Keller it is clear that our analyses must include "the ability/disability system—along with race, ethnicity, sexuality, and class."[44] Including disability is not only important because of its often invisible but constant inclusion in identity but also because "the identity category of disability can pressure feminist theory to acknowledge bodily particularity and history."[45]

Keller, however, lived a complicated life—and complicates everyone's theoretical arguments about identity and disability. The realities of her life—and of deaf and Deaf politics—remind us insistently that *neither disability nor deafness is a historically consistent or unified category*. "The disabled community" rarely if ever existed as a concept, much less a political and identity constituency.[46] People with multiple disabilities have found themselves further disenfranchised. Organizations of and for people with disabilities sometimes have, or feel themselves to have, competing interests and priorities. People with disabilities are of different races, classes, sexual orientations, and ideologies and have immensely different bodily experiences. Analyses of the multiple and intersecting axes of identity fail when we assume disability to be a monolithic category. The failure to acknowledge differences among women weaken(ed/s) feminist organizing; so can the assumption that all deaf women experience deafness similarly.[47]

The public and internal identity Keller wrestled with was not that of merely a woman with a disability or that of merely a deaf woman: it was that of a blind woman. She and many others saw, and some continue to see, no commonality between blind people, d/Deaf people, people with mobility impairments, or others with a disability. Keller's visits to World War II veterans with disabilities show some acknowledgement of a parallel group experience, but the purpose of her visits was to inspire the veterans to personally "overcome" their disability.[48] For her to have argued that disability comprised a political category comparable to class, or that the myriad of disability experiences resulted in a shared public identity, would have been truly revolutionary—and difficult. Despite her resistance against it, she found advocacy for blind people and deaf people to be a dichotomy in which she had to choose one over the other. She lamented this choice, and the exclusion of other possible choices outside this dichotomy, but ultimately felt it necessary to forge a public identity—a "trump" identity—almost exclusively devoted to one aspect of the multidimensional identity that all of us live.

Activist and scholar Corbett O'Toole recently argued that "studying disability without looking at the intersections of multiple identities results in a very limited perspective about who disabled people are and what they need."[49] The ways Keller was pushed and pulled to claim a primary public identity of blindness make it difficult for us to examine all that she was. Forcing Deaf or deaf-blind women today to claim a primary public identity makes it difficult for us to examine all that they are. Our historical understandings of Keller will be enriched if we can undertake a fuller examination of the multiple axes of her identity, recognizing and including all of them. So also will our contemporary understandings of gender and deafness be enriched if we recognize and embrace the enriching complications of multiple identities.

NOTES

1. Helen Keller, *Midstream: My Later Life* (New York: Greenwood Press, [1929] 1968), 248.

2. Helen Keller, *Helen Keller's Journal* (London: Michael Joseph, Ltd., 1938), November 17, 1936, 31–32.

3. Helen Keller, "She Is Not Dead," *Good Housekeeping*, February 2, 1938, 144.

4. Small "d" deaf refers to people who are deaf. Capital "D" Deaf refers to people who are deaf culturally; that is, they are part of and identify with Deaf culture.

5. Keller, *Midstream*, 75.

6. Keller, "If You Have Friends You Can Endure Anything," *American Magazine*, September 1929, 62. See also Robert V. Bruce, *Bell: Alexander Graham Bell and the Conquest of Solitude* (Boston: Little, Brown & Company, 1973), chap. 30.

7. Douglas C. Baynton, *Forbidden Signs: American Culture and the Campaign against Sign Language* (Chicago: University of Chicago Press, 1996), 55. See also Richard Winefield, *Never the Twain Shall Meet: Bell, Gallaudet, and the Communications Debate* (Washington, D.C.: Gallaudet University Press, 1987).

8. Keller, "If You Have Friends You Can Endure Anything," 63.

9. For information on the history of deaf people and the Deaf community, see, for example, John Vickrey Van Cleve and Barry A. Crouch, *A Place of Their Own: Creating the Deaf Community in America* (Washington, D.C.: Gallaudet University Press, 1989); Harlan Lane, *When the Mind Hears: A History of the Deaf* (New York: Vintage Books, 1989); Robert M. Buchanan, *Illusions of Equality: Deaf Americans in School and Factory, 1850–1950* (Washington, D.C.: Gallaudet University Press, 1999); Susan Burch, *Signs of Resistance: American Deaf Cultural History, 1900 to WWII* (New York: New York University Press, 2002).

10. Helen Keller, *The Story of My Life* (New York: Dover Publications, [1903] 1996), 32.

11. Gary E. Wait, "Julia Brace," *Dartmouth College Library Bulletin* 33, no. 1 (November 1992); Edward J. Waterhouse, "Education of the Deaf-Blind in the United States of America, 1837–1967," in *State of the Art: Perspectives on Serving Deaf-Blind Children*, ed. Edgar Lowell and Carole Rouin (Washington, D.C.: United States Department of Education, 1977), 5–17; Lane, *When the Mind Hears*, 255–60.

12. Keller describes meeting Bridgman in *Midstream*, 245–47. See also Ernest Freeberg, *The Education of Laura Bridgman: First Deaf and Blind Person to Learn Language* (Cambridge. Mass.: Harvard University Press, 2001); Elisabeth Gitter, *The Imprisoned Guest: Samuel Howe and Laura Bridgman, the Original Deaf-Blind Girl* (New York: Farrar, Straus and Giroux, 2001).

13. Helen Keller, "My Future as I See It," *Ladies Home Journal*, vol. 20, November 1903, 10–11.

14. Gitter, *The Imprisoned Guest*; Freeberg, *The Education of Laura Bridgman*.

15. *New York Times*, May 12, 1903; January 16, 1907.

16. For more on this, see Kim E. Nielsen, *The Radical Lives of Helen Keller* (New York: New York University Press, 2004), chap. 2.

17. Joseph Lash, *Helen and Teacher: The Story of Helen Keller and Anne Sullivan Macy* (New York: Addison-Wesley, 1980), chap. 29.

18. Lash, *Helen and Teacher*, 530–31; Keller, *Midstream*, 232.

19. Address by M. C. Migel, November 14, 1932, M. C. Migel folder, Helen Keller Archives, American Foundation for the Blind, New York.

20. For more on this period of Keller's life, see Nielsen, *The Radical Lives of Helen Keller*, chap. 2.

21. Bruce, *Bell*, 247, 295, 321, 380, 397.

22. E. F. L., "Stray Staws,"*Silent Worker*, 20, no. 2 (1907): 25.

23. Alice T. Terry, "California," *Silent Worker*, 28, no. 2 (1915): 26. See also "Later On, Perhaps," *Silent Worker*, vol. 28, no. 10 (1916): 192; Alice T. Terry, "Sound—Why Not Leave It Alone," *Silent Worke*r, vol. 31, no. 7 (1919): 113.

24. For more on Keller and eugenics, see Nielsen, *Radical Lives of Helen Keller*, 11, 36–37, 40, 41. For more on eugenics and deafness, see Lane, *When the Mind Hears*, 353–61, and Burch, *Signs of Resistance*, 137–44.

25. Kim E. Nielsen, ed., *Helen Keller: Selected Writings* (New York: New York University Press, 2005), document 33.

26. Alice T. Terry, "California", 26.

27. "Later On, Perhaps,"*Silent Worker*, 28, no. 10 (1916): 192.

28. "Helen Keller and Mrs. Annie Sullivan Macy,"*Silent Worker*, 37, no. 9 (1925): 428.

29. Alexander L. Pach, "With the Silent Workers,"*Silent Worker*, 34, no. 7 (1922): 254.

30. Catherine J. Kudlick, "The Outlook of *The Problem* and the Problem with the *Outlook*: Two Advocacy Journals Reinvent Blind People in Turn-of-the-Century America," in *The New Disability History: American Perspectives*, ed. Paul K. Longmore and Lauri Umansky (New York: New York University Press, 2001), 187–213.

31. Naomi Schor, "Blindness as Metaphor," *Differences* 11, no. 2 (1999): 88.

32. James Emmett Ryan, "The Blind Authoress of New York: Helen De Kroyft and the Uses of Disability in Antebellum America," *American Quarterly* 51, no. 2 (1999): 385–418; Elisabeth Gitter, "The Blind Daughter in Charles Dickens's *Cricket on the Hearth*," *Studies in English Literature, 1500–1900* 39, no. 4 (1999): 675–89; Catherine J. Kudlick, "Should Blind Girls Marry? Thoughts on Gender, Disability and the Single Life in Modern France and America," unpublished paper in author's possession. Used with permission. For more on blindness and blind people in the nineteenth-century, see Ernest Freeberg, "The Meanings of Blindness in Nineteenth-Century America," *American Antiquarian Society* (2002): 119–52.

33. Ryan, "The Blind Authoress of New York," 396–97.

34. Lash, *Helen and Teacher*, 262; Keller, *Midstream*, 10; Keller, *The Story of My Life*, 53, 63.

35. Elisabeth Gitter, "Deaf-Mutes and Heroines in the Victorian Era," *Victorian Literature and Culture* 20 (1992): 179–96. Douglas Baynton makes a similar argument in *Forbidden Signs*.

36. Gitter, "Deaf-Mutes and Heroines in the Victorian Era."

37. Ibid., 181.

38. Ibid.

39. Keller, *Helen Keller's Journal*, November 17, 1936, 31–32.

40. Keller, "She Is Not Dead," 144.

41. Helen Keller to Jo Davidson, March 6, 1948, Papers of Jo Davidson, Library of Congress, Washington, D.C.

42. Susan Wendell, *The Rejected Body: Feminist Philosophical Reflections on Disability* (New York: Routledge, 1996), 73.

43. Keller and the AFB enthusiastically supported the Social Security Act. When it first passed in 1935, as the Wagner Economic Security Act, she allowed her name to be put on the amendment proposed by Senator Robert Wagner (NY, Democrat) to expand vocational training for blind people. Lobbying on behalf of the measure, she emphasized the amendment's economic as well as human benefits. Helen Keller's speech before the House Labor Committee Investigating Aid to the Handicapped, October 3, 1944, Legislation—Federal, Social Security Act—Title X, Helen Keller Archives, American Foundation for the Blind. See also *New York Times*, October 4, 1944.

44. Rosemarie Garland-Thomson, "Integrating Disability, Transforming Feminist Theory." *NWSA Journal* 14, no. 3 (Fall 2002): 2.

45. Rosemarie Garland-Thomson, "Feminist Theory, the Body, and the Disabled Figure," in *The Disability Studies Reader*, ed. Lennard J. Davis (New York: Routledge, 1997): 279–92, 284.

46. Some disability activists did make this argument during Keller's lifetime. The League of the Physically Handicapped protested employment discrimination in work-relief agencies and the Works Progress Administration (WPA) during the Depression and included people with a variety of disabilities. Paul K. Longmore and David Goldberger, "The League of the Physically Handicapped and the Great Depression: A Case Study in the New Disability History," *Journal of American History* 87, no. 3 (December 2000): 888–922.

47. In "The Other Body" Ynestra King relays the assumptions of others that she will befriend all women with disabilities because of her own disability. Ynestra King, "The Other Body: Reflections on Difference, Disability, and Identity Politics," *Ms* (Spring 1993): 72–75.

48. For more on these visits, see Nielsen, *Radical Lives of Helen Keller,* 77–79.

49. Corbett Joan O'Toole, "The Sexist Inheritance of the Disability Movement," in *Gendering Disability,* ed. Bonnie G. Smith and Beth Hutchison (New Brunswick, N.J.: Rutgers University Press, 2004), 297.

The Extended Family
Deaf Women in Organizations

Sara Robinson

D eaf organizations are the "extended family" in the adult Deaf world.[1] After exiting residential schools, Deaf people historically turned to the organizations to maintain their cultural connection with fellow Deaf people.[2] Associations specifically offered a place that welcomed signed communication, provided outlets for social and intellectual needs, introduced potential spouses and friends, fostered unity against external oppression, and created a home-like atmosphere for Deaf communities.[3] Of particular importance, American Deaf organizations were always self-governed, empowering Deaf citizens and countering widespread perceptions of Deaf people as dependent.[4] From the mid–nineteenth century through the Second World War, organizations by, for, and about Deaf people blossomed across the United States. In 1880, the formation of the National Association of the Deaf symbolically announced the existence of a national cultural Deaf community.[5] Many historians have included Deaf organizations in their research, but most have neglected the significance of gender relations within this "extended family." In this essay, I intend to correct this oversight. A gendered interpretation of Deaf organizations offers especially vivid evidence of women's agency and of their specific role in cultural transmission.[6]

Since the inception of the American Deaf community, its male leaders have held a conservative view of women, relegating them to restricted roles and options. Specifically, men dominated political and most public activities. Several factors promoted this. Virtually all members served voluntarily, receiving no pay for their organizational work. In general, only men who had financial means could afford to lead. Deaf women, however, had financial concerns as well as domestic concerns that included childcare, care of their homes, and often the approval of their husbands. Women also had to gain the approval of other community members. Many men—and women—preferred to follow male leaders rather than female leaders. All the members understood that successful administration depended heavily on their goodwill and support. Deaf organizations varied in size, purpose, and location, which also affected women's ability to participate. Not surprisingly, women had a greater chance of heading local clubs than larger state or national associations. In this essay, I focus on deaf women's participation in and leadership of social and political organizations that included both men and women.[7]

Male members encouraged female peers to participate actively only in social activities. Although they generally acquiesced, Deaf women contributed significantly to the development of associations and intentionally negotiated their place within them. Commonly, they turned men's view to their advantage, establishing their own roles and creating a niche of significance for themselves as social moderators and cultural promoters. Deaf women made themselves invaluable to the Deaf community by controlling the social expression of deafness, one of the most enduring and vital aspects of this cultural community.

Two organizations primarily represented the Deaf world on the national level—the National Association of the Deaf (NAD), founded in 1880, and the National Fraternal Society of the Deaf (NFSD), established in 1901. The former devoted much of its official resources to political and economic issues; the latter provided insurance and death benefits for its members.

Deaf women attended NAD conventions and claimed membership in the organization from its earliest years. Individual females were elected to the board, usually as vice presidents and as officers of social committees.[8] Their participation in the political sphere, however, was limited, and the chief executive position remained exclusively male until the late-twentieth century. Proceedings from NAD conventions depict colorful debates and passionate speeches about pressing topics throughout the late-nineteenth and early-twentieth centuries. Yet few women's voices are captured in these pages, suggesting that women served a more passive role within this "male" sphere of politicking or that their expressed opinions were not deemed significant enough to document.

Conservative male leadership in the NAD may have undermined women's opportunities for direct action in the public sphere, but women found other valuable avenues within the organization. As cultural and social matrons, women gained both influence and recognition. One of the primary examples was their role in the biannual convention. NAD conferences provided several days of public Deaf celebration and socializing as hundreds of members flocked to host cities for daytime meetings and nighttime banquets. Women commonly joined in the opening celebrations by performing/signing patriotic songs. At the NAD convention in Atlanta in 1923, for instance, a "charming young woman from Florida, Miss Crump, gave a sign rendition" of two songs.[9]

Women took charge of community social activities, an immense undertaking. Convention and event reports frequently thank various women for their substantial contributions to the success of the event. Social events, which ranged from casual picnics and outings to large balls at state and national conventions, offered opportunities for socialization, communication in sign language, and physical space for friends to reunite. Here, Deaf people could boast about their normalcy and middle-class status to mainstream society, promote their reputation, and foster social ties. They were places to vent and to relax after heated debates about deaf education, driving bans, job discrimination, and the lack of insurance access. Social events also promoted networking that could lead to job opportunities and romantic interests. Before the days of the TTY, Internet, and pagers, social gatherings represented the primary place where Deaf people shared news and gossip.

Although the NAD limited women to the social realms, the NFSD (or "Frat") flatly denied admission to women. Committed to insurance benefits for Deaf male workers, NFSD leaders expressed concern that women were not in an economic position to fulfill the required financial obligations. Some women publicly rejected these claims, noting that they, too, needed the protection Deaf men enjoyed. Female membership, however, did not occur until 1951.

Unwilling to yield fully to their exclusion, groups of Deaf women attempted to redefine their relationship with the Frat by proposing a national organization of OWLS (a secret female society at Gallaudet College) or an auxiliary to the National Fraternal Society of the Deaf. Beginning in 1909, proponents depicted their female society as a national forum for social uplift, combining social, educational, literary, and philanthropic work. Modeled on efforts already under way at the local level, the national women's group would be designed to provide independent relief work while relying on men for financial support.[10] In an effort to assist with this, women proposed fund-raising activities that additionally would serve as social functions for the Deaf community. Simultaneously echoing and expanding their traditional role in the Deaf community, these women claimed to be the moral and social guide of Deaf people while asserting an independent and potentially powerful separate space.[11]

After considerable debate and negotiation, Deaf women established Ladies Auxiliaries and immediately began using them to achieve their own agenda. These women, especially Gertrude "Pansy" Nelson and Augusta K. Barrett, successfully exploited traditional views of women as gentle tamers and protectors of the hearth, and their participation in the NFSD had tangible results. When women started hosting social functions, members' attendance markedly increased. Women also helped recruit for the Frat, increasing numbers and funds. Male members candidly admitted that they used their auxiliaries to assist in recruiting.[12] Women's "special touch"—their homemade refreshments and desserts as well as their pleasant company—attracted many single Deaf men who worked in relatively isolated environments. Jay Cooke Howard in 1923 stated,

> [I]f you judge of the work accomplished so far in raising funds for the entertainment of the delegates and visitors at the Frat convention in St. Paul, the Auxiliary Committee is the tail that wags the dog. It is a fact that the attractive force of these seven charming ladies has been such that there has been a steady stream of contributions and earnings into the coffers and it is not necessary to refer to what these girls are going to do. We can point with pride to what they have done as an indication of what they will do. They are real lookers and go-getters.[13]

Underscoring that only men could be full members, leader Tom Anderson claimed that when "we don't want the women around . . . we cleverly manage to keep them in the ante-room until our August ritual is satisfied" but recognized that "we never fail to put out the old welcome sign to the ladies when there is work to be done at Frat socials or conventions. The dear things work their fingers to the bone for the Frat."[14]

Anderson's paternal comments nevertheless acknowledged that women actively sustained the organization, serving a vital role in its success. Women had a two-pronged approach—they demonstrated their value and benefited from the social connections. By doing this, they were able to press the issue of full membership, reminding the men that women were vital in the success of the Deaf organization and of NFSD in this particular case.

State associations offered more varied opportunities—and sometimes restrictions—for women. New Jersey's Association of the Deaf, for example, denied women outright,[15] and North Dakota quietly omitted leading members such as Olga Anderson, who was its first president in 1916, from its history.[16] New York and California associations, in contrast, enjoyed female presidents Annie Lashbrook and Alice Terry, respectively, in the 1920s.[17]

What enabled women like Lashbrook and Terry to lead significant state associations of the Deaf when national organizations became more male oriented? Several factors help to explain this. After the death of her husband, Charles, in 1909, Annie Lashbrook took over his job as a printing teacher at the Rome School for the Deaf. The widow tightened her bonds with the school and her fellow graduates, overseeing the publication of the *Rome Register*, training several master printers, and becoming an active member of the Rome Alumni Association.[18] She served the executive committee as secretary-treasurer of that association. By 1912 she became the secretary of the Empire State Association of the Deaf (ESAD). Demonstrating special ability as an administrator, she was elected second vice president of the NAD in 1913. After her term ended two years later, she ran for the presidency of the ESAD. In 1919, Lashbrook took the helm of the ESAD.[19] By all accounts, she was a well-respected leader. Her involvement in the local Deaf community and establishment of an alumni association for the school built a solid résumé for her as a committed advocate and mother figure to her community; her involvement with the NAD as a second vice president gave her clout and a network on which to draw. These earlier successes probably sparked her interest in the presidency of the ESAD.

The landscape in New York proved more fertile for women with aspirations like Lashbrook's. As early as 1867, the ESAD had admitted female members.[20] The association also heavily emphasized its social purpose, which drew many women. New York State Deaf conventions, advertisements proclaimed, were not merely political affairs. They fostered rich social opportunities for its members. Before and after the biannual meetings, Deaf newspapers ran articles on the festivities, detailing the fanfare that distinguished Deaf New Yorkers from others in less urban and affluent states.[21] In addition to general socializing, the group also advocated aid for elderly Deaf citizens, as well as charity work for underprivileged Deaf people. Because the ESAD actively funded and managed various "feminine" efforts of social uplift, it seemed uniquely open to elect a capable female administrator like Lashbrook. Moreover, the group's strong interest in Deaf schools may have enhanced Lashbrook's appeal, because she had direct ties to the Rome school. Her role as a printing teacher—a "male" vocation—probably also helped her candidacy. That she was heavily engaged in social work, was a founder of a social meeting place for the local Deaf community, and had worked for the NAD distinguished her from many of her male competitors. New York, during this era, was indeed more liberal than the Midwest and the South, and its members would have been more accepting of variants in social roles. Lashbrook, having established her status as a good wife, could take advantage of her widowhood and lack of children to utilize her time and financial resources to support voluntary leadership roles. Indeed, some may have seen her participation in organizations as compensation for her own domestic circumstances, adopting the Deaf community as a substitute for a husband and children. Annie Lashbrook clearly boasted exceptional attributes by any standard. It appears that Lashbrook was an exception in the ESAD, too. Although she served as president and eventually become a trustee, Lashbrook had almost no female peers or successors in the organization before the 1950s.[22]

Alice Terry's story shares certain similarities. Terry, a graduate of the Missouri School for the Deaf, moved with her husband Howard to California in 1910 after marrying in 1901 and having three children. She became very active in the California Deaf community in the mid-teens, when her children were teenagers. With children old enough to look after themselves and with a supportive husband, she was able to devote her energy to the Deaf community and to writing. Both she and her husband were gifted writers, and Alice Terry distinguished herself from her female peers by publishing numerous editorials in several Deaf newspapers. When Berkeley, California, was chosen to host the 1915 NAD convention, Alice Terry joined the social committee to help plan the event. Young, attractive, and articulate, Terry impressed members of the organization, who then asked her to speak at the convention. Her activities in the NAD dwindled after the convention, in part because later conferences were hosted by cities in other states and she preferred to be involved in the local and state organizations.

Supported by her husband, Terry continued to write, and she established herself as a feisty commentator on Deaf politics and as an advocate of Deaf clubs. Like Lashbrook, Terry had many assets to promote her candidacy in state-level Deaf politics: a proven commitment to various Deaf clubs, her financial situation, and a professional network. Both Terry and Lashbrook worked in fields dominated by men—printing and journalism. Terry likely reminded her friends at the local Los Angeles Silent Club (LASC) of this unique asset, promising to advertise the LASC in her articles and thus maximize its potential as a social center for the Deaf community. Members elected her president in 1920.[23] Terry quickly expanded the LASC's membership and social activities. With her husband's active encouragement, Terry also ran for the executive position of the state association for the Deaf in 1920. She won it easily and ultimately served two terms as president. Several factors enhanced her candidacy. Although a large and popular state for Deaf people, the California Association of the Deaf (CAD) had struggled in the years before Terry assumed its presidency. It needed a leader who had enough financial security to devote considerable volunteer time to its causes. Terry not only had this advantage but also brought the support of a large Deaf community in Los Angeles to her aid. Moreover, she had a national reputation from her articles. Her effective leadership contributed to her reelection. As CAD member and famous artist Douglas Tilden proclaimed, "Mrs. Terry was the only president C.A.D. ever had."[24]

For Lashbrook and Terry, hard work and earned respect at the local level and involvement with the NAD preceded their rise to state organization presidencies. At the local level, they performed generally "feminine tasks," promoting social events. Through this work, they gained leadership abilities and insights that enabled them to lead statewide organizations in 1919–20. Local clubs served as stepping stones for women who aspired to leadership posts in larger organizations. Both had reputations for being highly moral, educated, and able to handle "male" work and were either widowed or had supportive husbands. Those characteristics made them acceptable to the communities they served. Their election to statewide presidency happened around the same time that general mainstream women accomplished suffrage by winning the right to vote in 1920 and succeeded in passing the temperance amendments, showing women's increasing political power and skill. Those social changes may have contributed to the political atmosphere in the already liberal states of New York and California, which allowed Deaf women to gain top leadership positions.

The examples of Lashbrook and Terry demonstrate the possibilities for Deaf women leaders at the state level. But they also reveal the limitations. State organizations throughout the nineteenth and first half of the twentieth centuries varied considerably in regard to policies, character, and leadership. Like national associations, state organizations served dual purposes: as political organs and social facilitators of the Deaf community. Because they met more frequently and had close geographic ties, the latter factor was stronger in state groups. The ESAD proclaimed its objective was "to promote the welfare, in every respect of its members and other deaf mutes. More particularly it is designed to cultivate feelings of friendship among the members, and form a bond of union, and afford an organization whereby they may act together for the common good."[25]

Most women who joined state associations participated within a distinctly "separate sphere." Women's involvement in the Pennsylvania Society for the Advancement of the Deaf (PSAD) highlights the options and opportunities available to rank-and-file female members. The organization's reports also reflect common attitudes toward female participation and membership, as well as toward leadership in the Deaf community.

The PSAD was established in 1887, and it was a vibrant, active organization well into the twentieth century. Through the PSAD, male leaders combated driving bans, employment discrimination, and deaf peddlers as well as engaged in philanthropic activities. In all of these endeavors, men dominated the committees, discussions, meeting agendas, and decision making. Women did not engage in these overtly "political" activities. Only in campaigns that directly involved social outreach or social celebration did women directly participate. Indeed, in this sphere, women led.

The most visible expression of social work supported by the PSAD was its Home for the Aged and Infirm Deaf. Founded in 1902, the home symbolized the "extended family" created by the intergenerational bonds among culturally Deaf people. Women were very involved in the governance of this institution. They served as officers, advisory committee members, and volunteer workers. Officially, men oversaw admissions and financial and other administrative issues; in reality, women had responsibility for the day-to-day management of the home. They cared for residents, addressed entertainment and dietary needs, and oversaw the grounds maintenance. They kept records of events and expenditures and actively sought ways to keep the home financially solvent. Exploiting their culinary skills and social popularity, women hosted bazaars. These events not only raised money for the home but also recruited new members to the PSAD and to their cause. Undertaking the enormous task of caring for elderly deaf people earned female PSAD members respect and praise. The work also empowered them by giving them an opportunity to manage a significant program in the organization, to directly affect the lives of the residents, and to create a lasting symbol of the PSAD's strength.

PSAD women expressed their active support in other social venues, usually by hosting social events or undertaking community functions. Women also generally managed the enrollment committee. Recruiting fell to the women in part because men viewed them as alluring, possessing persuasive powers, and gifted socially. In short, feminine stereotypes created a niche within the organization for women to work, collaborate, and sustain the organization. Commonly, women also chaired the resolutions committee. More official than political, this committee issued thanks, recognized contributing individuals, and officially encouraged affiliations with other organizations. As with membership and banquet committees, the resolutions group emphasized mostly social and ritual traditions within the organization.[26]

PSAD women performed other rituals. Convention invocations usually included ministers offering thanks and prayers, followed by the women singing/signing the national anthem. In 1938, for example, Jane Greenfield "beautifully sang" the flag song. Deaf publications, including the PSAD newsletter and national papers such as the *Silent Worker*, consistently praised women for their "generous character," "work ethic," "beauty," and "ability to execute social functions."[27] The ladies of the PSAD hosted Donation Day to raise funds to support the Pennsylvania Home for the Aged and Infirm Deaf. "The handsome sum of $63.32 was raised on the last Donation Day for the Home through the efforts of Mrs. J. A. Dunner and her lady aides. They were tendered the thanks of the branch."

This ability to execute social functions was important to the Deaf community because social activities were the primary attractions of state and national conventions and served as powerful recruiting tools for potential members. Increased membership allowed organizations to pursue greater activities and goals. Social events fostered a sense of unity among members, provided space for exchange of ideas and beliefs, and energized the group, motivating them to become more politically active. These social events benefited the women, too, by providing a network of friends and a place to share advice and opinions. The exchange of ideas on issues that affected their cultural identity as well as their gendered identity was particularly important. This had added meaning for Deaf women. Before the advent of technology such as TTYS and the Internet, Deaf women especially were isolated from mainstream society. Relying heavily on face-to-face interaction for recent news, women acutely understood the importance of social events and eagerly attended them. These "family gatherings" allowed women the opportunity to discuss issues that hearing women commonly shared as well (but with fewer communication barriers)—courtship and marriage, the challenges of motherhood, employment, and daily news. In addition, club meetings provided space for Deaf women to boast of their homemaking skills, bringing skills from the home into the extended family. Spouses and male peers praised their handiwork, profiting in part by their affiliation with women who exemplified middle-class American values. In this way women received recognition and praise for their roles both in the private home and in their "extended family."

Local organizations, because of their geographic base and access as well as their primarily social purpose, afforded women the greatest opportunities for leadership and influence. Social events and meetings were frequent. Often located in large cities or towns, local clubs usually drew a comparatively more diverse membership than state organizations. Dues were less than for state and national organizations, which allowed working-class as well as elite members, women as well as men. These smaller organizations also provided members with immediate and tangible benefits—dances, card games, barbeques, and general fun on weekends and holidays.[28] Members looked to clubs as places for causal meetings to vent, discuss politics and their day-to-day jobs, meet people, find spouses, and share in the feeling of belonging to a community. Club leaders generally had narrower responsibilities than leaders of state and national organizations: they primarily managed funds and oversaw social events and membership drives.

Because clubs cost less to join and maintain and demanded fewer intensive commitments, women who had domestic responsibilities such as husbands and children were able to participate without detracting from their familial duties. The highly social character of clubs further promoted female membership and oversight. With larger numbers, women members gained more influence in general in clubs than they did in state or national associations.

They also had more opportunity to lead. Hypatia Boyd Reed, for example, established the Paul Binner Club in Milwaukee in 1920.[29] Reed single-handedly organized this group and became its president. Described as "partly social and partly literary," the Paul Binner Club allowed talented women like Reed to gain power by fusing the so-called feminine activities of social planning with general club management. Reed, for example, gained recognition for entertaining her peers, for example, by performing the role of deaf heroine Sophia Fowler Gallaudet in plays. She and her female peers also provided the refreshments at club gatherings.

Reed clearly delegated duties, but mostly to female members, thereby upholding superficial gender codes while exerting her power.

In the same year that Reed established her group, Alice Terry ascended
to the head of the LASC. Like Reed, Terry managed an organization committed to social interaction. Reforming what she saw as masculine traits
in the group, she implemented moral reforms, such as banning card playing. For Terry, improving the club's image would promote virtue among
the Deaf world and draw more members. She hoped that her "civilizing"
influence would help them eventually achieve their dream of purchasing
property for the club. In her many articles in the *Silent Worker*, Terry
emphasized the group's successes and, in so doing, promoted herself as an
able leader.

The *Silent Worker* provides consistent examples of women in leadership
positions throughout various regions of the country. Men were comfortable with female leadership at the local level because the Deaf community
knew that the local clubs had one primary purpose: they were social in
character, regardless of the mission and nature of the club. As a tool for
socialization and community development, it was acceptable for the
women to assume the leadership because of their expertise and nature.
The women took advantage of the leadership in the clubs and the social
and charitable characters of such local clubs to create a niche for themselves in the Deaf community and to make themselves invaluable to their
male counterparts, who would not want to make do without their company, or their delicious refreshments, or their tireless labor.

Economic status also played a role in determining who became involved in club activities. The spouses of middle-class men may have been
more able to participate in the leadership of local clubs because their husbands could support their families. The Terrys of Los Angeles are good
examples of this. Although the local clubs were for Deaf people of all
economic statuses, those who did not have to work because of their
spouses' earning ability were able to stay "home" both at the club and at
their domiciles and pursue projects more to their liking. Those women
took over the leadership of the local clubs because they had the time,
energy, and financial resources to do so, whereas most men had to work
to support themselves and their families.

In contrast to state and national associations, local clubs elected women to their boards with little comment, suggesting that it seemed "normal" to do so. Women participated as equally as men did in the social venues. Both men and women participated in the entertainment by giving plays and recitals and by planning the logistics of outings; they socialized without separation of the sexes and without consideration of gender. Photographs of various social events hosted by the clubs provide evidence that women served as social catalysts.[30]

Before the 1950s, women in Deaf organizations generally functioned in a separate sphere, attending to social rather than political issues. It would be easy to consider this gender tracking as a clear example of women's inferior status in the Deaf world, but such an oversimplified interpretation neglects important factors. Deaf men and women—in newspapers, organization reports, and oral histories—consistently praised women's organizational roles, highlighting the value of social affairs. Indeed, Deafness was and is commonly celebrated as a social identity. As mainstream society intensified its attacks on this minority group, cultural preservation and social outlets took on added meaning. Responsible for planning virtually all social events, from the local to national level, deaf women played a recognized and vital role in the survival of the Deaf community.

Club membership was particularly important for women because between the 1880s and the 1950s mainstream society increased its direct discrimination against Deaf people. Scientific advancements intentionally and unintentionally contributed to this, including eugenic research and policies, telephone, radio, and sound films. Automobile bans, civil service and New Deal employment bans, and the rise of strict oral policies served to undermined Deaf people's cultural and citizenship status. Organizations provided Deaf people with a respite from these impending challenges. Although traditional gender roles dominated, Deaf women in the clubs drew power from performing on par with hearing women and being seen as normal and culturally valuable within the club environment. Their social and domestic service in clubs challenged pervasive mainstream stereotypes that marked Deaf women as dependent, defective, and pitiful. Responsible for planning virtually all social events from the local to national level, Deaf women played a recognized and vital role in the survival of the Deaf community.

Admittedly, many Deaf men expressed chauvinist attitudes, and many parlayed these ideas into organizational policies. In most state organizations and both of the national organizations, Deaf women were denied full access to participate and shape their society. These official organs focused more on typically "male" issues—politics, education, economics, and civil rights; social support played a smaller role. In contrast, local clubs—the primary social outlet for Deaf people—represented an arena for greater female influence and expression. In all of these organizations, however, women demonstrated self-advocacy, creativity, and tenacity. In so doing, they formed important relationships between and among women and men, fortifying social links that sustained their culture. Many Deaf women cherished this role in part because they keenly understood the social barriers to mainstream society caused by auditory deafness. By excelling as matrons in the "extended family," Deaf women challenged mainstream views of Deaf people and promoted equality for Deaf women within Deaf society.

NOTES

1. John Vickrey Van Cleve and Barry A. Crouch, *A Place of Their Own: Creating a Deaf Community in America* (Washington, D.C.: Gallaudet University Press, 1989), 59.

2. Edwin A. Hodgson, *Proceedings of the Fourteenth Convention of the Empire State Association of the Deaf* (New York: Deaf-Mutes' Journal Print, 1891), 24–25.

3. Susan Burch, *Signs of Resistance: American Deaf Cultural History, 1900 to World War II* (New York: New York University Press, 2002), 3.

4. Thomas Francis Fox, "Social Status of the Deaf," in *Proceedings of the Second Convention of the National Association of the Deaf* (New York: New York Institution for the Instruction of the Deaf and Dumb, 1883).

5. *First Proceedings of the National Deaf Mute Convention, 1880* (New York: New York Institution for the Instruction of the Deaf and Dumb, 1880).

6. *Proceedings of the Eighteenth Convention of the Empire State Association of the Deaf* (New York: Fanwood Press, 1891), 67–68.

7. The *Silent Worker* is a good place to start. In its pages, the reader can find blurbs, comments, and articles about a wide variety of Deaf organiza-

tions including mission aid societies, church auxiliaries, literary societies, sewing circles, and local single-sex organizations such as the Ladies Aid Society of Chicago.

8. Jack Gannon, *Deaf Heritage: A Narrative History of Deaf America* (Silver Spring, Md.: National Association of the Deaf, 1981), 428.

9. Alexander Pach, "The Atlanta Convention," *Silent Worker* 36, no. 1 (October 1923): 11.

10. Gertrude "Pansy" Nelson, "Ladies' Auxiliary: A Gentle Appeal to Deaf Women of the United States," *Silent Worker* 21, no. 9 (June 1909): 158.

11. J. F. Meagher, "Nadfratities," *Silent Worker* 32, no. 4 (January 1920): 103.

12. Alice T. Terry, "Funds and Funds: Funds for Everything but the Right Thing," *Silent Worker* 30, no. 8 (May 1919): 136.

13. Jay Cooke Howard, "The Minnesota Auxiliary Committee," *Silent Worker* 33, no. 8 (May 1923): 328.

14. Tom L. Anderson, "The Forum," *Frat* (April 1929): 2.

15. New Jersey has a complex history of Deaf associations. The New Jersey Society of Deaf Mutes was organized in 1894, and there is no evidence that it had women. The New Jersey Association of the Deaf was established in 1896, functioning side by side with the New Jersey Society of Deaf Mutes. Documents from the New Jersey Association of the Deaf shed no light on female membership, but local newspaper accounts describe women's involvement in social activities at the conventions as early as 1904. The earliest mention of full membership for women in the New Jersey Association of the Deaf was made in 1918. The *Silent Worker* also mentions a New Jersey Branch of the National Association of the Deaf. Later, the New Jersey Association of the Deaf, Incorporated, was founded. There is no evidence directly linking each of these organizations.

16. North Dakota School for the Deaf, "Our Seventy-Five Years 1890–1965," Devils Lake, North Dakota, [1960?].

17. In North Dakota, Olga Anderson helped organize, draft a constitution, and found the North Dakota Association of the Deaf in 1916, only three years before Annie Lashbrook became president of the ESAD. Anderson became the first president of the organization only to be completely omitted from the history books half a century later. She was accompanied by two other women who served as a vice president and treasurer during her administration. "Deaf Launch Association at Meeting," *Fargo Forum*, June 1916, 2.

18. Schaltro, "Deaf Printers of the Triangle Cities," *Silent Worker* (October 1919): 3.

19. The ESAD had a period of dormancy from 1919 to 1936. In 1936, Annie Lashbrook continued in the role of president until the convention in Binghamton, New York, where James M. Lewis was elected president. The call for a convention of the ESAD came in the April issue of the *Deaf Mute's Journal*, which described how the state wanted to limit or revoke the rights of Deaf drivers after a car accident involving a Deaf driver. Someone wrote a letter saying that they needed a strong state association to fight for the rights of Deaf people in New York State. With this letter, Annie Lashbrook appointed William Lange as treasurer, appointed new officers to the executive committee, and operated the ESAD from April to August, when the convention was held. The specific reasons for dormancy are not identified in the *Deaf Mute's Journal* but it hints at several causes: one possible cause was that there were too many state schools in New York. In most states, there is only one school, so there is a strong centralized Deaf population. The school would hold its reunion at same time as the convention. In New York, this was not the case. There were many centers of Deaf population, no single reunion, and no "need" for a state gathering. A second possible reason is that the NAD and NFSD had great conventions that were very social and very political, and those who attended the NAD and NFSD conventions did not feel the need to spend more money on going to a state convention. A third possible reason is that "the deaf of New York" were too well organized. There were many, many local organizations in cities. For portions of the state of New York, many Deaf people felt that their local clubs were serving their needs and that there was no real reason to continue the ESAD. When it was revived in 1936, it was because of a statewide decline in the rights of Deaf people, in particular the threat to revoke driving licenses. At this time, the ESAD also agreed to become affiliated with the NAD.

20. "Rome Alumni Association," *Silent Worker* 32, no. 9 (June 1920): 241.

21. "Proceedings of the Second Biennial Meeting of the Empire State Association of Deaf-Mutes, held on the 28th, 29th, and 30th of August, 1867," *Forty-Ninth Annual Report and Documents of the New York Institution for the Instruction of the Deaf and Dumb* (Albany, N.Y.: Van Benthuysen and Sons' Steam Printing House, 1868), 153.

22. Lashbrook was definitely president for at least one term. ESAD proceedings stop in 1899 and do not indicate how long Lashbrook was president or for how many terms.

23. Burch, *Signs of Resistance*, 68.

24. Kinda Al-Fitanyi, "Alice T. Terry: The Fight against Oralism in Deaf Education" (paper presented at the Fourth International Conference on Deaf History, Washington, D.C., June 29, 2000); Howard L. Terry, "Alice in Silentland," *Silent Worker* (November 1950): 5.

25. "The Empire State Association of Deaf-Mutes," *Social Programme* (1888): 14.

26. Ibid.

27. Thomas F. Fox, "Our Prominent Deaf Women," *Silent Worker* (April 1912): 130; Augusta K. Barrett, "Our Prominent Deaf Women: Agatha Tiegel Hanson," *Silent Worker* 23, no. 9 (June 1911): 163.

28. The local organizations varied in character from religious to literary to charity and philanthropy to sewing and social clubs. Some local clubs were single sex and some were coed. They varied depending upon the size and the interests of the local Deaf community. "The Home Club of Delavan, Wisconsin," *Silent Worker* 36, no. 7 (April 1924): 335.

29. Hypatia Boyd Reed, "Birth of Milwaukee Public School Night for the Adult Deaf," *Silent Worker* 33, no. 1 (October 1920): 34.

30. One example is the outing of San Diego's Club El Sordo. In the photographs, the men and women are intermingled eating and standing under a live oak for a photograph. Ruth C. Hesley, "San Diego, Cal.," *Silent Worker* 36, no. 8 (May 1924): 382.

Deaf Women and Inequality in Educational Attainment and Occupational Status
Is Deafness or Femaleness to Blame?

Sharon Barnartt

R esearch on the effect of disability on socioeconomic status has shown
that workers with disabilities are disadvantaged compared to workers
without (Berkowitz and Hill 1986; Burkhauser and Haveman 1982;
Weaver 1991). Additionally, a substantial amount of evidence suggests
that women with disabilities are disadvantaged when compared to men
with disabilities as well as when compared to women without disabilities.
Disadvantages for women with disabilities have been reported in socioeconomic status variables such as education, labor force participation rates,
occupational status, and income (Altman 1982, 1985; Barnartt 1981;
Barnartt and Christiansen 1985; Baldwin and Johnson 1995; Christiansen and Barnartt 1987; Deegan 1981).

Deaf workers have shown similar disadvantages in most studies (Christiansen and Barnartt 1987; Barnartt 1986), although Altman and Barnartt's 1997 study of workers with hearing losses, not just deaf workers,
shows that those workers have slightly higher incomes than workers without impairments.[1] Socioeconomic disadvantages have been reported for
deaf women when they are compared to deaf men. The incomes of deaf
female workers were substantially lower than those of deaf male workers
in the early part of the 1900s. Deaf women's salaries were reported to be
42 percent of deaf men's salaries in 1910 and 45 percent in 1920 (Best

1943, 249). The U.S. Department of the Interior (1936, 73) found deaf women's salaries to be 76 percent of deaf men's. In 1956, 75 percent of deaf women workers earned less than $3,000, whereas almost 75 percent of deaf men earned more than $3,000 (Lunde and Bigman 1959, 27). In the early 1970s, female college graduates earned only 74 percent of the salaries of male college graduates (Winakur 1973).[2]

The period of time between the early 1970s and the early 1990s is important for research on gender for a number of reasons. Major civil rights legislation prohibiting gender discrimination in various aspects of employment was passed in the mid-1960s. The 1963 Equal Pay Act and the 1964 Civil Rights Act were two of the most important pieces of legislation. Additionally, the feminist movement was actively involved in fighting for women's rights in the 1960s and 1970s (Freeman 1975; Katzenstein and Mueller 1987).

The period is also of interest to research on people with disabilities, including deaf people. Although the most important piece of civil rights legislation for people with disabilities was passed in 1990, several important pieces of legislation had been passed in the late 1960s and early to mid-1970s, including the Architectural Barriers Act of 1968, the Rehabilitation Act of 1973, and the 1975 Education for All Handicapped Children Act (now called the Individuals with Disabilities Education Act).

Thus, examining changes during this period helps us to examine the ways in which gender-driven processes, disability-driven processes, and demographic and other societal-level changes interacted. In this essay, I examine how those changes affected two socioeconomic variables for both genders of people with and without hearing impairments.

METHODOLOGY

Data for this article come from several data sets. These include the 1972 National Census of the Deaf Population (NCDP) and the 1990 and 1991 National Health Interview Surveys (NHIS). The NCDP began its sampling procedure by attempting to identify and locate all prevocationally deafened people in the United States, using membership lists of Deaf organizations as well as other sources. From this list of approximately 400,000 people, a final sample, stratified on the basis of age and sex, was drawn (Schein and Delk 1974). Although its focus was on prevocationally deaf people, the study ended up surveying all household members in the chosen households, so the final sample also included people with less severe hearing losses as well as people with later-onset hearing losses. Although it cannot be assumed that the family members who were interviewed were located by any sort of acceptable sampling strategy, this study does include the only data available for that time period on both prevocationally deafened adults and those with other hearing losses. More than 5,400 people were interviewed in total, of whom more than 1,400 were older than twenty-five and had some hearing loss; they are referred to here as "HH/deaf."[3] There are about 1,000 in the same age category who indicated that they had no hearing loss; they are labeled as being "hearing."

Data for 1990 and 1991 come from the NHISs done in those years. Conducted by the U.S. Department of Health and Human Services, the NHIS is an annual survey of health status, which samples approximately 46,000 households. The 1990 and 1991 surveys included a screening question that asked whether the person had any "hearing difficulty." Supplementary questions were then asked to those people who acknowledged having problems with their hearing. The present analysis includes about 4,000 respondents older than twenty-five who had some degree of hearing loss and about 12,000 in the same age range who did not.

The two surveys used here included the same or similar questions on educational and occupational attainment and degree of hearing loss, and they either used the same or compatible categories. Educational attainment was coded into four categories: "less than high school," "high school graduate," "some college," and "college graduate or more." Occupational attainment was coded into three categories: "White-collar" jobs include professional and technical, sales, and clerical jobs; occupations in this category range from doctors, lawyers, and computer programmers to salespeople, secretaries, and file clerks. "Blue-collar" jobs include manufacturing, transportation, and farming jobs, such as factory workers, truck and bus drivers, and farmers or farm workers. "Pink-collar" jobs include service jobs, many of which are traditionally female, such as waitresses, barbers or beauticians, child care workers, and janitors (Howe 1977).[4]

Hearing status was coded into two categories. People who were categorized as HH/deaf ranged from those who indicated they had "some hearing problems" to those who indicated that they had "a lot of trouble" or were "deaf" in one ear or both ears.

EDUCATION

1972

Table 1 shows the educational levels for males and females, both hearing and HH/deaf, in earlier and later years. For males, there were large differences in the percentages that had not completed high school but smaller differences in the other categories when the two hearing status groups were compared. About 48 percent of hearing males but more than 55 percent of HH/deaf males had not completed high school. About 31 percent of both groups were high school graduates. Less than 10 percent of both groups (about 9 percent of hearing males and about 5 percent of HH/deaf males) had attended some college, and about 12 percent of hearing males but less than 8 percent of HH/deaf males had graduated from college or more.

Among the females, the numbers were quite similar. About 45 percent of hearing females, compared to about 55 percent of HH/deaf females, had not graduated from high school. About 35 percent of each group (37.5 percent of hearing females and 34 percent of HH/deaf females) had graduated from high school. Hearing females were more likely to have attended some college (10 percent versus 6 percent) or to have graduated from college or more (7 percent compared to 4 percent), but the differences are not huge.

When the sexes are compared within each hearing status, we see that among hearing respondents the women were more likely to have graduated from high school (38 percent of females versus 31 percent of males) or attended some college (10 percent of females versus 9 percent of males), but men were almost twice as likely to have graduated from college or had postbaccalaureate education (12 percent of males versus 6.8 percent of females). Among the HH/deaf respondents, there were fewer gender differences, but they were in the same direction as those for hearing respondents. About the same percentage of both sexes (55 percent) had not graduated from high school. As with the hearing respondents, slightly more women than men were high school graduates only (34 per-

TABLE 1: Educational Attainment by Hearing Status by Sex, 1972 and 1990–91 (Age 25 +)

	1972		1990–1991	
	Hearing	HH/Deaf	Hearing	HH/Deaf
Males	N = 497	N = 799	N = 7086	N = 3187
Less than high school	47.9%	55.2%	26.7%	43.1%
High school graduate	31.0	31.7	35.9	31.8
Some college	9.1	5.4	17.5	13.0
College grad or more	12.1	7.8	19.9	12.1
Females	N = 541	N = 782	N = 4820	N = 1082
Less than high school	45.5%	55.4%	32.6%	44.7%
High school graduate	37.5	34.1	36.9	32.0
Some college	10.2	6.3	15.9	13.1
College grad or more	6.8	4.2	14.6	10.2

SOURCES: 1972 National Census of the Deaf Population; 1990 and 1991 National Center for Health Statistics, National Health Interview Survey.

cent of females versus 32 percent of males) or had attended some college (6 percent of females versus 5 percent of males). As with hearing respondents, males were almost twice as likely as the women to have college degrees or more (7.8 percent of men compared to 4.2 percent of females).

Overall, we see that, at this time, the vast majority of all adults, whether with hearing losses or not, were only high school graduates or had not even graduated from high school. Less than 20 percent of any group except hearing males had attended some college or had graduated from college or more—and even for hearing males, the percentage was only 21 percent. Women were less likely than men to have had any college background.

1990–91

With the passage of almost twenty years we see large improvements in the educational attainments of all adults. Among males, the percentages that had not finished high school decreased to about 26 percent among hearing respondents, although it was still at 43 percent of HH/deaf respondents. Hearing males were slightly more likely to have graduated from high school (36 percent compared to 32 percent), attended some college (18 percent versus 13 percent), or obtained a college degree or more (20 percent versus 12 percent). Thus, among males in 1990–91, there appear still to be large differences by hearing status, with the majority (almost 75 percent) of HH/deaf males likely either not to have graduated from high school or only to have graduated from high school but not attended college.

Among the women we see similar improvements but smaller differences by hearing status. About one third (32 percent) of hearing females, compared to almost 45 percent of HH/deaf females, did not graduate from high school. Slightly more than one third (37 percent) of hearing females, compared to a little less than one third (32 percent) of HH/deaf females, graduated from high school. Hearing women were more likely both to have attended some college (16 percent versus 13 percent of HH/deaf women) and to have graduated from college or more (15 percent versus 10 percent) than were HH/deaf women.

Comparisons

Table 2 presents percentage differences so that we can more easily identify the magnitude of the differences. When we examine the 1972 comparisons, we see that there are fairly large differences by hearing status for both males and females. That is, for both sexes, hearing respondents had larger percentages in the higher educational categories ("some college"

TABLE 2: Comparisons of Educational Status, by Hearing Status[a] and Gender[b]

1972	Hearing % - HH/Deaf % (Males)	Hearing % - HH/Deaf % (Females)	Male % - Female % (Hearing)	Male % - Female % (HH/Deaf)
Less than high school	−7.3	−9.9	2.4	−0.2
High school grad	−0.7	3.4	−6.5	−2.4
Some college	+3.7	3.9	−1.1	−0.9
College grad or more	+4.3	2.6	5.3	3.6
1990–91				
Less than high school	−16.4	−12.1	−5.9	−1.6
High school grad	+4.1	+4.9	−1.0	−0.2
Some college	+4.5	+2.8	+1.6	−0.1
College grad or more	+7.8	+4.4	+5.3	+1.9

and "college graduate or more"), whereas the HH/deaf respondents had larger percentages in the "less than high school" category and for the females in the "high school graduate" category. The third and fourth columns show the sex differences but that they are larger for hearing respondents than for HH/deaf respondents. That is, HH/deaf adults show

a. A positive result indicates that the HH/deaf group has higher percentage; a negative result indicates that the hearing group has a higher percentage.
b. A positive result indicates that males have a higher percentage; a negative result indicates that females have a higher percentage.

very small sex differences: the largest is in the "college graduate or more" category, in which HH/deaf males are 3.6 percent more likely than HH/ deaf females to show up. For hearing respondents, however, females are 6.5 percent more likely to graduate from high school and about 1 percent more likely to have some college, but they are more than 5 percent less likely to have finished college or continued on for postgraduate education.

When we examine the 1990–91 comparisons, we see that large differences by hearing status remain. That is, HH/deaf respondents were much more likely not to have graduated from high school, whereas hearing men and, to a lesser extent, hearing women were much more likely to have attended some college or to have graduated from college or more. The differences by hearing status are larger than they were in 1972 for both sexes, although the differences are more pronounced for men than for women. For men, hearing status made a very large difference in educational attainment, with HH/deaf men showing a considerable disadvantage when compared to hearing men. For women, the educational disadvantage related to being deaf or hard of hearing is much smaller.

OCCUPATIONAL STATUS
1972

Table 3 shows occupational distributions for the groups for the two time periods. It shows that in 1972, 37 percent of hearing men worked in white-collar jobs, whereas only about 21 percent of HH/deaf men worked in such jobs. Although a majority of both groups of men (53 percent of hearing men compared to more than 70 percent of HH/deaf men) worked in blue-collar jobs, a small minority (about 10 percent of hearing men compared to about 9 percent of HH/deaf men) worked in pink-collar jobs.

Among the women, a majority of hearing women (about 57 percent) but only about 38 percent of HH/deaf women worked in white-collar jobs. Only 18 percent of hearing women but 49 percent of HH/deaf women worked in blue-collar jobs. About 25 percent of hearing women but only about 14 percent of HH/deaf women worked in pink-collar jobs.

When we compare the sexes, we see very large differences. Women in both hearing status groups were more likely to hold white-collar jobs than

TABLE 3: Occupational Attainment by Hearing Status by Sex, 1972 and 1990–91 (Age 25 +)

	1972		1990–91	
	Hearing	HH/Deaf	Hearing	HH/Deaf
Males	N = 398	N = 715	N = 4495	N = 1261
White collar	40.2%	21.8%	44.3%	37.5%
Blue collar	51.8	71.0	48.3	53.6
Pink collar	8.0	7.1	7.4	8.9
Females	N = 217	N = 376	N = 1776	N = 499
White collar	53.5	36.0	65.9	61.9
Blue collar	21.2	49.7	14.4	15.2
Pink collar	25.3	14.3	19.7	22.8

SOURCES: National Census of the Deaf Population (for 1972 data) and National Center for Health Statistics, National Health Interview Survey (for 1990–91 data).

were their male peers of the same hearing status, whereas the males were much more likely to hold blue-collar jobs than were their female peers. Hearing women were also much more likely to hold pink-collar jobs than were hearing men, but this is actually likely to indicate much lower incomes for the women, because pink-collar jobs tend not to pay very well. HH/deaf women were less likely to hold pink-collar jobs than hearing women, probably because many of these jobs involve extended interactions with people.

1990–91

As in education, the almost twenty-year time span produced large changes. For males, there were increases in the percentages holding white-collar jobs (to 44 percent for hearing men and to 38 percent for HH/deaf men) and decreases in the percentages holding blue-collar jobs (to 48.3 percent for hearing men and to 54 percent for HH/deaf men). The percentages holding pink-collar jobs remained fairly stable and low (7 percent for hearing men and almost 9 percent for HH/deaf men.)

For women, the percentages holding white-collar jobs also increased, to 66 percent for hearing women and to 62 percent for HH/deaf women. The percentages holding blue-collar jobs decreased slightly for hearing women to 14.5 percent but massively for HH/deaf women to 15 percent. Percentages for pink-collar jobs decreased for hearing women to about 20 percent but increased for HH/deaf women to 23 percent.

Overall, although the percentage distributions changed substantially during this time period, the large sex differences remained. This can be seen when we examine the comparison table.

Comparisons

Table 4 shows that were large percentage differences between hearing and HH/deaf workers of both sexes in 1972. These were largest in the blue-collar category, in which HH/deaf men were 19 percent more likely to work than hearing men but in which HH/deaf women were almost 29 percent more likely than hearing women to work. The differences were also large in the white-collar category, in which hearing workers were about 18 percent more likely to work than were their same-sex HH/deaf peers. Overall, at this time, the females were more different by hearing status than males were, primarily because of the blue-collar differences.

There were also large differences by sex. Women at this time were more likely to hold white-collar jobs than were their male peers, and men were much more likely to hold blue-collar jobs than their female peers. At this time, gender was a very strong determinant of the type of job a person held. The prototypical jobs held by HH/deaf men were either factory or post office work, whereas those for HH/deaf women were factory work, especially in clothing factories (Greenberg 1972).

The comparisons for 1990–91 show that the magnitude of differences by hearing status was much smaller than it had been in 1972, and this was true for both sexes. The largest difference was the 6.8-percent greater likelihood that hearing than HH/deaf men would hold white-collar jobs. However, sex differences are, if anything, even larger than they were in 1972. Women were 22–24 percent more likely than their male peers to

TABLE 4: Comparisons of Occupational Status, by Hearing Status[a] and Gender[b]

1972	Hearing % - HH/Deaf % (Males)	Hearing % - HH/Deaf % (Females)	Male % - Female % (Hearing)	Male % - Female % (HH/Deaf)
White collar	18.4	+ 17.5	− 13.3	− 14.2
Blue collar	− 19.2	− 28.5	+ 30.6	+ 21.3
Pink collar	+ 0.9	+ 11.0	− 17.3	− 7.2
1990–91				
White collar	+ 6.8	+ 4.0	− 21.6	− 24.4
Blue collar	− 5.3	− 0.8	+ 33.9	+ 38.4
Pink collar	− 1.5	− 3.1	− 15.0	− 13.9

hold white-collar jobs, whereas men were 34–38 percent more likely than their female peers to hold blue-collar jobs.

OVERALL RESULTS

Overall, then, sex differences in education were not very large for either hearing status group in either time period, although they were larger for the hearing group than for the HH/deaf group. Hearing women still show a slight educational disadvantage compared to hearing men. For HH/deaf people, gender does not make much difference.

But educational differences by hearing status remain, and they appear to have increased somewhat across the time periods, especially for men. The biggest area of difference is in those who have not graduated from high school. This is the area in which the percentages of HH/deaf are

a. A positive result indicates that the HH/deaf group has higher percentage; a negative result indicates that the hearing group has a higher percentage.
b. A positive result indicates that males have a higher percentage; a negative result indicates that females have a higher percentage.

larger than the percentages of hearing people, and this is true for both sexes.

Patterns of occupational status for the sexes changed in a slightly different way than did educational status. Hearing status became a much weaker determinant of occupational status in 1990–91 than it had been in 1972, but sex as a determinant of occupational status remained very strong and even increased its strength by 1990–91. By this time, HH/deaf women's occupations were quite similar to those of hearing women. For men, the hearing status differences were a little larger than for women, such that hearing men were more likely to hold white-collar jobs whereas HH/deaf men were more likely to hold blue- or pink-collar jobs.

DISCUSSION

How do we explain the ways in which hearing status and gender were important in producing these changes in educational and occupational status? And were there other factors that could explain the changes shown here?

Educational Attainment

There has been a trend toward increasing educational attainment in the general population, which has continued from the beginning of the twentieth century. It is likely that this increase also affected HH/deaf people, because some of the increase in educational attainment in the overall population is attributed to the spread of schooling to groups traditionally disadvantaged by the educational system (Mare 1995, 156).

For HH/deaf people, legal changes regarding education occurred during the period in question. The Education for All Handicapped Children Act mandated education in the least restrictive environment and is often cited when educational changes for children with disabilities are discussed. However, the Individuals with Disabilities Education Act (IDEA) was intended to change *where* children attended school rather than how much school they attended. By itself, then, it did not increase the amount of education HH/deaf children had, and so we see that large percentages of HH/deaf respondents still had not completed high school in 1991.

The discrepancy is larger for men than for women, especially in attending college and in graduating from college or continuing to graduate school. (Of course, that law could only have affected a small proportion of people who were older than twenty-five by the time of the 1990 or 1991 NHIS surveys and so might have been included in the present sample.)

However, it is in fact likely that if IDEA did not directly affect the educational attainment of HH/deaf children, it did so indirectly, at least at the postsecondary level. The number of postsecondary educational programs for HH/deaf students did increase markedly from 1970 to 1985 (Schroedel and Watson 1991). This expansion of opportunity, probably at least somewhat related to the legal changes, is likely to be at least partly responsible for the increase seen in the percentages of both sexes of HH/deaf people who attended some college, because most of the new programs were at the community college or vocational/technical level rather than at the bachelor's level or beyond. Thus, legal changes may have built upon the general societal trends to produce increases in education for HH/deaf people.

There are only small gender differences to be seen among the HH/deaf respondents; there was a slightly larger gender difference in the educational attainment of hearing respondents than there was for the HH/deaf respondents in 1972. These did not disappear by 1990–91. The discrepancy is seen in the relatively higher college-completion rates of hearing men than women and the higher rates of women than men not completing high school. It is likely that cultural pressures arising from gender role expectations are at least partially responsible for this difference.

Occupational Status

In the occupational sphere, there has been a clear lessening of the effect of hearing impairment over the time period in question. Gender-driven labor force processes overtook disability-driven labor force processes in importance. HH/deaf women came to look quite a bit more like women without hearing losses and HH/deaf men came to look a little more like men without hearing losses than they did in 1972.

One facile explanation for these results is that laws that outlaw discrimination based upon disability are effective. These laws include the Rehabilitation Act of 1973 and the American with Disabilities Act (ADA) of 1990, which forbids employment discrimination in all sectors of the labor force except under very specific conditions. However, the Rehabilitation Act forbade discrimination only by government contractors, and ADA regulations had not even been put into place by the time the 1991 data were collected. So, it seems unlikely that legal changes can explain the lessening effect of hearing status on occupational status.

Rather, there were other social structural or demographic changes at the societal level that seem likely to have affected the occupational status of both hearing and HH/deaf respondents. One of the most important of these is the decline in the blue-collar sector of the economy, especially in factory work (Levy 1995). Because blue-collar jobs employ men dispro-portionately, gender differences result from this social structural change.

Progress made in occupational attainment is related to progress made in educational attainment—this is true for people with as well as without hearing losses. The largest change in the occupations of workers of both sexes is seen in their increasing participation in white-collar jobs. This movement into white-collar jobs by women and hearing men is likely to have occurred at least partially because of improvements in educational attainment. People with more education are better prepared for work in white-collar jobs than are those with less education. Thus, the improve-ments in educational attainment that occurred during this period posi-tioned some workers well for the changes that were occurring in the labor force as a whole.

However, we also need to consider the effect of sex segregation of occu-pations on these changes. Sex segregation means that women are chan-neled into certain jobs—those considered to be "female" jobs—and away from other jobs—those considered to be "male" jobs. For men, the re-verse is true (Hall 1994; Tomaskovic-Devey 1993). Sex segregation de-creased slightly in the two decades at issue here, although it remained true that more than half of all workers would have had to change jobs to achieve equal representation in all occupational categories (Bianchi 1995).

Traditionally female jobs include teaching, librarianship, social work, nursing, clerical work, the types of factory work that require smaller movements, and pink-collar work such as child care work, cosmetology, and waitressing. Many of the traditionally female white-collar jobs (which are lower status and lower income than are male white-collar jobs) such as nursing, secretarial work, and clerical work are likely to require high school degrees or some college education and to provide on-the-job training rather than to require college or graduate degrees (Oppenheimer 1976). Women in general have little representation in higher status white-collar jobs or in blue-collar jobs because those are traditionally male occupational categories.[5] Traditionally male jobs that require high levels of education include those in medicine, law, academia, and executive positions, whereas those that do not require high levels of education include factory work that requires large movements or strength, construction work, driving trucks or buses, and farming.

Two processes were occurring for HH/deaf workers during this time period: First, changes in educational attainment permitted some to take advantage of changes in labor force structure. However, because of sex segregation of occupations, this trend primarily worked to the benefit of women. In 1972, it appears that HH/deaf workers of both sexes were more strongly affected by segregation based upon their hearing status than that based upon their sex. This segregation put the largest group of HH/deaf workers of both sexes into blue-collar jobs, and it made HH/deaf women look quite different from hearing women. By 1991, because of improvements in educational attainment, HH/deaf women were more likely to have adequate educational preparation for traditionally female white-collar jobs. Although HH/deaf women still had an educational deficit compared to hearing women, they were more likely than in the past to have had sufficient educational preparation to work in many white-collar jobs, especially technical, clerical, and administrative support jobs.

Because of occupational segregation by sex, women with lower educational attainment levels tend to work in pink-collar or service, rather than blue-collar, jobs. In 1972, HH/deaf women who had less education than hearing women were most likely to have worked in blue-collar jobs. But because some HH/deaf women still had less education than hearing women, by 1991 they had higher participation rates in pink-collar jobs than did hearing women.

Overall, then, by 1991 HH/deaf women's occupational status came to be more similar to that of women without hearing losses than was true in 1972. This occurred because increased levels of educational attainment meant that some HH/deaf women had adequate educational preparation for traditionally female white-collar jobs, and so occupational segregation by sex worked to channel them into jobs quite similar to those of hearing women.

The same cannot be said for HH/deaf men. By 1991, both hearing men and HH/deaf men became more evenly split between white-collar and blue-collar jobs, and both groups remained unlikely to work in pink-collar jobs. However, HH/deaf men were still much more likely to hold blue-collar than white-collar jobs, whereas the reverse is true for hearing men. In part, this is a reflection of HH/deaf men's lower proportions in the "some college" and "college graduate or more" categories and much higher proportion in the "less than high school" category. Men with some college or less cannot work in male white-collar jobs, such as those in medicine, law, business, or academia, because they lack the level of education necessary. Nor do they work in traditionally female white-collar jobs that require lower levels of education, because those are female jobs. Instead, they work in blue-collar jobs, which are traditionally male but which require less education than male white-collar jobs. The larger percentages of HH/deaf men still working in blue-collar jobs reflects the larger number of those men who did not complete high school or who completed high school but did not begin postsecondary education.

We see, then, that the educational attainments of HH/deaf women improved enough so that they could move from blue-collar jobs into traditionally female white-collar jobs. For HH/deaf men, though, improvements in educational status were not enough to move them into traditionally male white-collar jobs. Instead of moving into traditionally female white-collar jobs, they remained in blue-collar jobs in large numbers. Unlike HH/deaf females, they could not even move into pink-collar jobs, because those, too, are traditionally female.

Thus, patterns of occupational segregation interacted with changes in educational attainment to produce, by the early 1990s, the fact that HH/deaf women in the labor force looked substantially like women without hearing losses. For HH/deaf men, gains in educational attainment were not enough to put them into the position of being treated like men without hearing losses, although they have made some gains.

These results suggest an improvement in the overall socioeconomic *status* of HH/deaf women but they cannot be interpreted to mean that the women's relative *income* position vis-à-vis HH/deaf men has improved. During the time period in question here, the income position of women in the general population improved compared to that of men (Bianchi 1995). Although it seems likely that the income position of HH/deaf women would have improved compared to hearing women, it is not clear how it would have changed compared to HH/deaf men. Blue-collar jobs have tended in the past to pay better than traditionally female white-collar or pink-collar jobs (although that is less true today). This suggests that the income position of HH/deaf women vis-à-vis HH/deaf men would not have improved. However, the fact that the NHIS does not include personal income as a variable prevents that hypothesis from being examined here.

CONCLUSIONS

Theoretical Implications

Sociologists use the term "master status" to refer to a status (position in society) that affects all other statuses the person has. Gender and race are often mentioned as master statuses in which the members of the socially devalued category (in the United States, females and blacks) experience negative consequences in many or most or all of aspects of their lives as a result of being a member of that category. Others, including this author (Barnartt 2001), have suggested that disability is also a master status. This appears to be true attributionally, as in "Oh, she's blind and that's why she does not make her bed," as well as relating to identity (Goffman 1963). Although gender and race, on the one hand, and disability, on the other, may be similar master statuses in the social structure, they do not have the same interpretation legally (Barnartt and Seelman, 1988). (See also Barnartt 2001 for a comparison of these master statuses.)

This article suggests that, at least with regard to educational attainment and occupational status, deafness is not *the* master status. Rather, gender is. It is, perhaps, the "master" master status. Yes, hearing status does differentiate workers, but this is more true for men than for women. Overwhelmingly, the labor force treats people as members of their gender first and then, perhaps, as members of a disability category.

Practical Implications

The strength of occupational segregation by sex must be taken into account when either the educational attainment or the occupational status of HH/deaf workers is discussed. Amount of education has strong implications for types of jobs that are available, but occupational segregation by sex does, also.

For women of any hearing status, higher status white-collar jobs have been becoming more available, but only if levels of education past the baccalaureate degree are received. Lower levels of education above high school permit women access to lower white-collar jobs, which do not have high salaries but which remain plentiful in the economy. For women with the lowest levels of education, pink-collar jobs are available and likely to be increasing (although their levels or pay and benefits make them undesirable for many workers).

For men with lower levels of education, the lack of a high-paying alternative may begin to cause serious problems, and these may become worse for HH/deaf men than for HH/deaf women. HH/deaf men, as well as hearing men, will increasingly be pushed out of blue-collar jobs as those jobs disappear. Until the educational levels of HH/deaf men increase, without retraining they have few alternatives. For HH/deaf women with lower levels of education, the situation is similar, but there is one important difference: they need fewer years of education to be able to move into white-collar jobs. Thus, educators of HH/deaf children need to take occupational segregation by sex and its implications into consideration as they teach and advise HH/deaf children about their futures.

NOTES

1. This essay does not enter the debate about whether deafness is a disability, but interested readers should see Foster (2001) and Lane (2002) for discussion of this issue.

2. However, this was also the gender differential between the salaries of hearing college graduates at that time.

3. HH denotes hard of hearing.

4. This is unlike blue-collar jobs, which are traditionally male, hence the designation "pink" collar (Howe 1977).

5. However, the categories being used here do not permit us to examine the distribution of either sex within these occupational categories.

Works Cited

Altman, B. 1982. Disabled women: Doubly disadvantaged members of the social structure? Paper presented at the annual meeting of the American Sociological Association, San Francisco, Calif.

Altman, B. 1985. Disabled women in the social structure. In *With the power of each breath: A disabled women's anthology*, ed. S. Browne, D. Connors, and N. Stern, 69–76. Pittsburgh, Pa: Cleis Press.

Baldwin, M., and W. Johnson. 1995. Labor market discrimination against women with disabilities. *Industrial Relations* 34 (4): 55–77.

Barnartt, S. 1981. The socioeconomic status of Deaf women workers. Paper presented at the annual meeting of the Mid-South Sociological Association, Shreveport, La.

———. 1986. Disability as a socioeconomic variable: Predicting Deaf workers' incomes. Paper presented at the annual meeting of the American Sociological Association.

———. 2001. Using role theory to describe disability. In *Exploring theories and expanding methodologies: Where we are and where we need to go*, ed. S. Barnartt and B. Altman, 53–75. London: Elsevier/JAI Press.

Barnartt, S., and J. Christiansen. 1985. The socioeconomic status of Deaf workers: A minorities approach. *Social Science Journal* 22 (4): 19–33.

Barnartt, S. N., and K. Seelman. 1988. A comparison of federal laws toward disabled and racial/ethnic groups in the USA. *Disability, Handicap and Society* 3 (1): 37–48.

Berkowitz, M., and A. M. Hill. 1986. *Disability and the labor market: Economic problems, policies and programs*. Ithaca, N.Y.: ILR Press.

Best, H. 1943. *Deafness and the Deaf in the United States*. New York: Macmillan.

Bianchi, S. 1995. Changing economic roles of men and women. In *State of the union: America in the 1990's, vol. 1: Economic Trends*, ed. R. Farley, 107–54. New York: Russell Sage Foundation.

Burkhauser, R., and R. V. Haveman. *Disability and work: The economics of American policy*. Baltimore, Md.: Johns Hopkins University Press.

Christiansen, J. B., and S. N. Barnartt. 1987. The silent minority: The socioeconomic status of deaf people. In *Understanding deafness socially*, ed. P. Higgins and J. Nash, 171–96. Springfield, Ill.: Charles C. Thomas.

Deegan, M. J. 1981. Multiple minority groups: A case study of physically disabled women. *Journal of Sociology and Social Welfare* 8 (2): 274–95.

Freeman, J. 1975. *The politics of women's liberation*. New York: David McKay.

Goffman, E. 1963. *Stigma*. Englewood Cliffs, N.J.: Prentice Hall.

Greenberg, J. 1972. *In this sign*. New York: Avon.

Hall, R. H. 1994 *Sociology of work: Perspectives, analyses and issues*. Thousand Oaks, Calif.: Pine Forge Press.

Howe, L. 1977. *Pink collar workers: Inside the world of women's work*. New York: G. P. Putnam's Sons.

Katzenstein, M., and C. M. Mueller. 1987. *The women's movements of the United States and Western Europe*. Philadelphia: Temple University Press.

Levy, F. 1995. Incomes and income inequality. In *State of the union: America in the 1990's, vol. 1: Economic trends* ed. R. Farley, 1–57. New York: Russell Sage Foundation.

Lunde, A. S., and S. K. Bigman. 1959. *Occupational conditions among the deaf*. Washington, D.C.: U.S. Government Printing Office.

Mare, R. D. 1995. Changes in educational attainment and school enrollment. In *State of the union: America in the 1990's*, vol. 1: *Economic trends* ed. R. Farley, 155–213. New York: Russell Sage Foundation.

Oppenheimer, V. 1976. *The female labor force in the United States: Demographic and economic factors governing its growth and changing composition*. Westport, Conn.: Greenwood Press.

Schein, J. D., and M. T. Delk, Jr. 1974. *The deaf population of the United States*. Silver Spring, Md.: National Association of the Deaf.

Schroedel, J., and D. Watson. 1991. Postsecondary education for students who are deaf: A summary of a national study. *OSERS News In Print* 4 (1): 7–13.

Tomaskovic-Devey, D. 1993. *Gender and racial inequality at work: The sources and consequences of job segregation.* Ithaca, N.Y.: ILR Press.

U.S. Department of the Interior. 1936. *The deaf and the hard-of-hearing in the occupational world,* Bulletin 1936 no. 13. Washington, D.C.: U.S. Government Printing Office.

Weaver, C. 1991. *Disability and work: Incentives, rights and opportunities.* Washington, D.C.: AEI Press.

Winakur, I. 1973. The income determinants of Gallaudet College alumni. PhD diss., American University.

Part Two

(Women's) Authority
and Shaping Deafness

Editors' Introduction

The issue of authority is a central theme in both Deaf studies and women's studies. Throughout American history, both Deaf people and women have had to fight for civil liberties against a domineering society. Citizens who happened to be deaf *and* female experienced a double share of discrimination: once from society in general and another from their own cultural group. For example, although all deaf people in several states were prohibited by law from driving automobiles in the 1920s and 1930s, at the same time all American deaf women were also denied membership in a leading advocacy organization, the National Fraternal Society of the Deaf (NFSD). Women were not even admitted to the NFSD until the 1950s and were not permitted to vote in the other prominent organization, the National Association of the Deaf, until 1964.

The authors of the essays in this section call attention to the evolution of empowerment, self-definition, and the contested boundaries between and within these two "minority" populations. In these essays, they expand the analysis of authority to include concepts of influence, maternal roles, conformance, and rebellion. They consider the dynamics of relationships and assess how relations enhance what is seen as disabling: deafness and gender. Although scholarship in Deaf studies shares some common characteristics with women's studies, the combination of the two disciplines in these essays offers perspectives on empowerment and authority that modify the traditional views of both disciplines.

The methodology of this section emphasizes the close contextual framework of the subjects, illuminating the agency of women, both deaf and hearing, from different countries and centuries. Like in the essays in the previous section, in some of these works our contributors examine schools, but the perspective and foci differ. In this section, the broad impact of communication policy and the feminization of the teaching profession are generally examined while more specific attention is given to the role of hearing, female educators of deaf children.

This section begins with Plann's essay on Marcelina Ruiz Ricote y Fernández, a nineteenth-century teacher at the Madrid school for the deaf. Openly challenging common gender stereotypes, Ruiz Ricote criticized marriage, protested lower wages for women, and demanded education reforms to empower all female citizens. Plann's study transports us beyond the United States and provides a vivid example of feminism in an unfamiliar environment. In so doing, Plann demonstrates the powerful role of context and compels us to consider both continuity and change in Deaf and women's history.

Similarly, Winzer looks at single, hearing, female educators of the deaf and their struggle to create what Robin Muncy once called the "dominion of female reform." According to Winzer, skillful networking and labor transformations helped American women exploit gender stereotypes, enabling them to achieve professional success and economic stability. Her work offers a strong context for understanding the influence of gender on Deaf people's history, and she also examines the ramifications of these trends. By focusing on the challenges facing female educators of deaf children, these essays complicate the debate about communication in Deaf schools and further our considerations about that debate's impact on deaf children.

Turning from teachers to mothers, the chapters by Abel and by Oliva and Lytle offer a different, but sometimes similar, vantage point. Examining identity, communication, and gender from the perspective of mothers, Abel, Oliva, and Lytle unveil the early and intimate shaping of Deaf women's lives. Abel examines mothers of deaf children in the early 1900s, raising important questions about (women's) authority and (Deaf) education during this period. As Abel illustrates, oralists both entrusted mothers with enormous training responsibilities and assumed that they could easily and gracefully surrender even very young children to residential schools. Oliva and Lytle describe an evolving and multifaceted relationship between a deaf daughter and her hearing mother and demonstrate some of the challenges and options facing parents and deaf children in the late twentieth century.

Several overarching themes frame the essays in this section. Relations and relationships (including teacher-student and mother-daughter) appear as a common thread throughout these works, as does attention to the power of role models. The five authors in this section also raise important questions about ownership and control, and they expand the feminist critique of "separate spheres." They do this in part by contrasting gendered spheres of influence within and outside of schools, as well as between "masculine" authorities in school and society and "feminine" authorities—mothers and female instructors.

QUESTIONS TO CONSIDER

- How do these essays express comparable and contrastive ideas and experiences of *power* and *empowerment*?
- How do the authors interpret, and make use of, gendered concepts such as *relationships* and *role modeling*?
- Particularly in domestic and/or educational settings, how do Deaf/hearing women and girls challenge male and/or hearing *authority* and create their own authority?
- Consider the different vantage points of the subjects studied (students, teachers, mothers, daughters, Deaf, hearing, etc.). How similar or different are they? Why?

Marcelina Ruiz Ricote y Fernández
Nineteenth-Century Feminist Educator of Deaf and Blind Girls

Susan Plann

With a million women teachers like this one, . . . your country and the neighboring ones will be regenerated, ennobled, and spiritually enriched until the perfect social revolution is accomplished.[1]

—*Benito Pérez Galdós*, Realidad, *1889*

There is no essential difference between Man and Woman, and . . . the salvation of future generations of Humanity lies in the emancipation of Woman.[2]

—*Marcelina Ruiz Ricote, 1889*

During the last two thirds of the nineteenth century, the Madrid school for deaf and blind children employed a series of women

A longer version of this study, titled "In the Name of Woman: Marcelina Ruiz Ricote y Fernández," will appear in Susan Plann, *Portraits from the Spanish National Deaf-mute School: Nineteenth-Century Deaf Spaniards and Their Educators* (Washington, D.C.: Gallaudet University Press, forthcoming). I gratefully acknowledge the invaluable editorial assistance of Michael Sinisgalli in the preparation of this essay and the equally invaluable research assistance of Caryl Lee Benner.

teachers—all of them hearing—to instruct the girls in *labores*, which included sewing, embroidery, crochet, knitting, darning, and so on.[3] From 1869 to 1897 the job fell to Marcelina Ruiz Ricote y Fernández. As a single woman obliged to support herself, Ruiz Ricote recognized her students' need to prepare themselves not only for matrimony but also for the world of work, and she questioned the school's preference for homemaking over marketable job skills. Doña Marcelina expressed her thoughts on women's education when she delivered the graduation address in June of 1889, becoming the first woman teacher to speak at this event. The position she espoused was radical for the day, and she was no doubt out of step with many of her colleagues at the staid, male-dominated school. Her belief in women's right to a meaningful education were comparable to those of her most progressive feminist contemporaries, and she alone seems to have applied these ideas to the instruction of deaf and blind girls.

BACKGROUND

Spain's first state-sponsored school for deaf children opened in Madrid in 1805. Originally known as the Royal School for Deaf-Mutes, in 1852 the establishment's name was changed to the National School for Deaf-Mutes and the Blind, to reflect its expanded function.[4] The first deaf pupils were all boys, but in 1835 deaf girls were admitted as day students, and in 1852 they were finally admitted as boarders.

The fact that formal instruction of deaf girls did not begin until several decades after that of deaf boys was part of a larger trend: during the 1800s the education of Spanish girls lagged consistently behind that of Spanish boys, and this was true of deaf and hearing children alike. Fewer girls than boys attended school, and there were fewer schools for them. The Madrid deaf school posed no exception to the rule, and throughout the nineteenth century the boys educated there always outnumbered the girls.[5]

A GROWING INTEREST IN WOMEN'S EDUCATION

Marcelina Ruiz Ricote began her career as a teacher of deaf and blind girls shortly after the triumph of the 1868 revolution, known as *la gloriosa*, "the glorious one." The ensuing *sexenio revolucionario* (1868–74) was marked by a spirit of reform and renewal and a concern for education. Its effects were soon felt at the National School, where improvements included reorganization of the curriculum, expansion of vocational classes, acquisition of instructional materials, and revival of the teacher-training class, as well as much needed repairs to the physical plant. Enrollment too increased considerably, from 130 students in 1868 to 180 in 1870–71 (including 51 girls, 38 of them deaf and 13 blind).[6]

With *la gloriosa* also came the first real interest in women's education, which was now seen as an important instrument of social reformation. One of the first initiatives was a series of Sunday conferences held at the Universidad Central in Madrid. The intent was both to promote women's instruction and to arouse public interest in the subject. It is an open question whether Ruiz Ricote attended any of these conferences, but as a resident of the Spanish capital she was doubtlessly aware of their existence.

During these years, concern for women's instruction also led to the establishment of the Academy of Conferences and Public Lectures (Academia de Conferencias y Lecturas Públicas), the Governesses' School (Escuela de Institutrices), the Women's Artistic and Literary Club (Ateneo Artístico y Literario de Señoras), and the Association for the Teaching of Women (Asociación para la Enseñanza de la Mujer). Momentum generated during the *sexenio* continued under the restored monarchy, and the final decades of the 1800s spawned an important series of pedagogical congresses: in Madrid in 1882, in Barcelona in 1888, and again in Madrid in 1892. The congresses furthered discussion of women's instruction, their right to higher education, and their place in the workforce, and the National School was among the participants.[7] It is within this context of heightened interest in women's education and the concomitant debates on the topic that Ruiz Ricote's career as an educator of deaf and blind girls must be viewed.

THE SITUATION OF YOUNG WOMEN AT THE NATIONAL SCHOOL

Despite the growing awareness of the importance of women's education, for female students at the National School day-to-day life continued to present numerous challenges, not the least of which was the physical environment. At the time Ruiz Ricote joined the faculty, Spain's premier institution for deaf and blind children was in a deplorable state. Over the years, successive directors had petitioned the government for a new home for the school, but to no avail. Living conditions in the nineteenth century were not what they are today, and stuffy, overcrowded classrooms were the norm in Spanish schools, but the situation at the National School was bleak even for those times. Students were housed in a decrepit structure that dated from the seventeenth century and had once been a factory of official stamped paper, a place that a government-commissioned architect described as both "vile" and "wretched."[8]

Although conditions at the school were difficult for everyone, they were particularly difficult for the girls. Space was always at a premium, but although the boys at least had a small patio to play in, the girls had no recreation area at all. They passed their leisure time in a tiny parlor paved with ancient, dusty bricks,[9] and the only place they could catch a breath of fresh air was on the flat roof above the boys' section.[10] (The area led directly to the boys' dormitories, and the girls' presence there was cause for concern because it violated the Spanish ideal of absolute separation of the sexes.) As they languished in the cramped confines of the National School, the deaf girls' health suffered markedly, and learning too must have been affected adversely.[11]

Girls could begin their schooling between the ages of seven and fourteen, and their course of study lasted six years.[12] Their day started at 6:00 a.m. (5:00 a.m. in the summer), when they washed their hands and faces and put on their cotton dresses and white aprons. Once every two weeks they washed their feet with hot water, and on Sundays and holidays they cut their nails and changed their underwear. When personal grooming was completed, they attended mass and then had a light breakfast. Morning classes were followed by a midday meal of soup, rice or pasta, stew, and fruit for dessert. Then came the *siesta*. In the afternoon there were more lessons, a snack, and an hour and a half of playtime. After a dinner of stew or fish with potatoes or rice, the girls retired to their dormitory, where they slept on iron cots topped by corn-husk mattresses.[13]

For twenty-four hours each week the deaf girls were instructed in *labores* by Ruiz Ricote. (She was assisted in her efforts by two other women, a teaching assistant who helped out when class was in session and an aide

who looked after the girls the remainder of the time.) *Labores* formed
the core of the girls' curriculum, and the majority of their instructional
time was dedicated to these endeavors. Classes were held in a narrow,
poorly ventilated hallway that ran between the girls' dormitories and the
rest of their section of the building.[14] At the end of the corridor stood the
girls' only latrine, its foul odor heavy on the air. (The arrangement offered
a ready source of infection, the establishment's efforts at cleanliness
notwithstanding.[15])

Female students' instruction in homemaking was not limited to the
fancy needlework taught by Ruiz Ricote. They also made, mended,
washed, and ironed the school uniforms and washed and ironed the linen.
Older girls had the added responsibility of cleaning the premises and performing a variety of domestic chores. The stated objective was to teach
them to run a home, but because most were of humble origin, in all
likelihood they had already mastered these skills at their mothers' knee
before ever leaving the family home.[16] In a word, the girls provided the
establishment with uncompensated labor, and in turn they were prepared
for a life of drudgery. (The boys too supported the school with their un-
paid labor because they produced books in the print shop, furniture and
cabinets in the carpentry shop, and so on. But unlike the girls, in the
process they learned a trade with which they could earn a living after
graduation and perhaps even support a family: printers, for instance, were
the aristocracy of Madrid's working class.[17])

In addition to the twenty-four hours spent every week on *labores*, the
deaf girls dedicated eighteen hours to academic subjects, which were
taught, for want of classrooms, in the boys' section. (Girls' and boys'
classes were held at different hours and the school's authorities exercised
"the most exquisite vigilance," but the arrangement was still deemed im-
proper.[18]) Although deaf boys studied subjects such as Spanish grammar,
arithmetic, geography, history, and natural history, some of these subjects
were omitted from the girls' curriculum, sacrificed to *labores*, washing and
ironing, and instruction in running a household.[19] An additional six hours
per week of drawing, six of painting, three of penmanship, and four and
a half of gymnastics rounded out the girls' schedule of classes.[20] Their
intellectual formation was rudimentary at best, but at a time when many
Spanish children did not attend school at all and the vast majority of deaf

people received no education whatsoever, deaf girls at the National School represented an exceedingly small elite.[21]

Marcelina Ruiz Ricote y Fernández: An Exceptional Teacher and an Unconventional Woman

In 1869 Marcelina Ruiz Ricote y Fernández was hired to instruct female students at the National School for Deaf-Mutes and the Blind.[22] The third of ten siblings, she was born and raised in the village of Fuentidueña de Tajo, some sixty kilometers from the Spanish capital.[23] She had recently received the degree of teacher of lower primary education (*maestra de primera enseñanza elemental*) from the Escuela Normal Central de Maestras, the Women's Central Teachers' School.[24] The historical record does not reveal Ruiz Ricote's activities prior to attending teachers' school, but it is possible that she had worked previously as an uncredentialed teacher (there were many in her day). But be that as it may, Doña Marcelina began her career at the National School as first teaching assistant (*primera profesora auxiliar*), and before long she was promoted to the position of *labores* teacher.[25]

When she reported for work, Ruiz Ricote was still single and, at forty years old, she was considered long past marriageable age. That the new teacher should be middle-aged and single was probably viewed as an advantage by her employers at the National School. She was not likely to find a husband, so she could dedicate herself wholeheartedly to her job, and she could serve as a mother figure to the girls. But in the eyes of society her single status was not unproblematic. Most Spaniards believed women's purpose in life was to marry and raise a family, and nineteenth-century Spanish women were not trained to be self-sufficient. Marriage represented their only real career option, and marriages of convenience were not uncommon.

Settling into her new post at the National School, Ruiz Ricote continued to study on her own, and in January 1872 she earned the degree of teacher of upper primary education (*maestra de primera enseñanza superior*), which was conferred by the Provincial Junta of Madrid.[26] Although degree requirements were far from demanding by today's standards, at a time when Spanish illiteracy rates exceeded 80 percent for women and 60

percent for men, her achievement was to be commended.[27] Secondary
and university education would remain off-limits for women until the end
of the nineteenth century, but possession of the upper primary teaching
credential placed Ruiz Ricote in an elite cadre of female educators: in
1880 only 16 percent of them held this certification.[28] Yet despite her
intellectual merits, her job was to teach *labores*, because at the National
School academic subjects were the exclusive province of male teachers.

From the moment she began teaching, Doña Marcelina seemed to
excel at her work with deaf and blind girls. In 1870 she was officially
thanked for her role in the recent reorganization of the school, and she
was commended by the Office of Public Instruction (Dirección General
de Instrucción Pública) for her students' performance on their public ex-
aminations; the following year she was similarly recognized for her students' progress, and this time the commendation was issued by royal
order.[29] The historical record paints Ruiz Ricote as an active participant
at the National School, an educator who attended faculty meetings (her
name appears frequently in the minutes), voiced her opinions, and generally held her own. During her first two decades of employment there are
only indirect accounts of her presence and contributions, and one can but
imagine what her life at the school must have been like. Ruiz Ricote was
an unmarried, educated, independent female who was living at a time
when single women were seen as failures, learning in women was viewed
askance, and authority was assumed to rest naturally with males. The
National School was inherently hierarchical and traditional, and at least
some of its teachers were notoriously conservative in their views of
women. *La maestra* would have had to tread carefully in these patriarchal
halls.

RUIZ RICOTE'S THOUGHTS ON WOMEN'S EDUCATION

Much of what is known about Ruiz Ricote must be pieced together by
reading between the lines. Unlike some of her male colleagues, she wrote
no books on the education of deaf and blind children (she was probably
too busy teaching). But in a graduation speech pronounced on June 30,
1889, she expressed her thoughts clearly and for the record. For many
years the school's director had delivered the address, but for the previous

decade the distinction had rotated among the faculty—the male faculty, that is. But times were changing, traditional views on the education of Spanish women were being questioned and reevaluated, and women were assuming a more prominent role in the public discourse. Given this new awareness and Ruiz Ricote's own professional merits, it was entirely fitting that she should become the first woman in the history of the National School to speak on commencement day.

The ceremony was held in the school patio. On the platform were seated the president of the school's governing board, Manuel María José de Galdo, and three of its nine members, including the two female members, Carmen Rojo Herraiz, director of the Escuela Normal Central de Maestras, Ruiz Ricote's alma mater, and Casilda Mexía Sales, who was a teaching assistant there.[30] No doubt Rojo Herraiz and Mexía Sales had a special interest in hearing from the first woman ever to deliver the commencement address, and Ruiz Ricote, for her part, was most likely eager to make her case to them in particular.

The program opened with Ruiz Ricote's speech, and for the next few minutes Doña Marcelina exchanged her marginalized position as *labores* teacher for center stage. Setting forth her arguments in eloquent prose and eschewing the usual self-congratulatory remarks and pious platitudes to which educators of deaf and blind children were prone—clearly, this was no ordinary *maestra*—she brought the national debate concerning women's education to the corridors of the National School. This was her opportunity to enlighten the public and champion her students' special needs, and she was determined to make the most of it.

Before a large audience of both men and women, which included people from diverse social positions and walks of life, she began her address with all due modesty, protesting that she was unworthy of the honor that had been bestowed upon her and that she lacked the necessary talent. No doubt her protestations were a mere rhetorical device (none of her male predecessors had ever begun an address in such self-deprecating terms). But Ruiz Ricote's tactics were intended to disarm her listeners, gain their trust, and win them to her side. In selecting her to speak, Doña Marcelina continued, the school's governing board was in fact honoring all women. "I could and I should decline," Ruiz Ricote demurred, "citing my insufficiency and emphasizing the inferior level to which this act would be reduced, comparing myself to those who have spoken before me," but because she viewed this as a chance to secure a new right for others of her sex, she decided to accept "in the name of Woman."[31]

After thanking the board for honoring her, Ruiz Ricote cut directly to the chase, lobbying for women's rights in this most public of forums. Pleading "in the name of my sex in defense of women's educational abilities, and in the name of the beloved souls who receive the benefits of this establishment," she beseeched board members to increase the number of female teachers so it would at least equal that of males.[32] To avoid threatening male privilege, she reassured her listeners that this should be done without diminishing men's rights in the least and without decreasing their numbers.

The rights she alluded to were in fact considerable: throughout the nineteenth century female teachers constituted a minimal presence at the National School, and power was concentrated in hearing, male hands. At the time of Ruiz Ricote's speech there were seven hearing, male professors of deaf children and only one other woman—also hearing—on the faculty.[33] And although the girls' domestic training was left to female educators, their intellectual formation was entrusted to male professors.

Turning to the composition of the student body, Ruiz Ricote noted that to the necessary classification of the students in two groups, deaf children and blind children, could be added another division, the division between the sexes. Striking another blow for female and male equality, she asserted that many of the traditional distinctions between the sexes were disappearing, "since today, fortunately for the present civilization, there is no essential difference between Man and Woman."[34] Despite the changing views on women's place in society that characterized the last three decades of the nineteenth century, Ruiz Ricote's declaration was extremely radical for her day, and virtually none of her contemporaries would have conceded that there was no essential difference between women and men, much less that obliteration of these differences could be beneficial for civilization.

Expanding on her point, Ruiz Ricote averred that "the salvation of future generations of Humanity lies in the emancipation of Woman"— although she hastened to add that she was referring to women's emancipation "in the true and noble sense of the word" (no further explanation was provided).[35] Once again, her contention would have found exceedingly few supporters: the effects of the feminist movement, which had gained strength in England and the United States during the 1840s and 1850s, had not yet been felt in Spain (with the exception of isolated individuals).

Doña Marcelina's advocacy of women's rights extended to her students, whom she called "the persons I believe most worthy and with the most right to my love," and she affirmed that for their happiness she was "willing to sacrifice all I own and possess."[36] At sixty-two years old, childless and never married, the *labores* teacher had bonded deeply with her pupils, and she seemed to serve as a surrogate mother to the girls, most of whom were living away from their families for the first time.

Recognizing the need to prepare her charges to fend for themselves after graduation, Ruiz Ricote observed, "If woman, in general, is society's victim, because of her weakness, according to some, because of her ignorance and lack of resources, according to others, how much more propitiatorily must the deaf or blind woman surrender herself!"[37] Her language was indirect, as was required in the day, but the audience would have had no trouble grasping her meaning: because women were ill-prepared to take care of themselves, they were too often taken advantage of, and deaf and blind women, who were doubly disadvantaged, were even more vulnerable, hence, more likely to have to "surrender themselves"—perhaps to indecent demands or immoral propositions—to survive. And extending her considerations to hearing, sighted women as well, she asked rhetorically, "Does the woman who is truly ignorant cease perchance to be [deaf and blind]?" A woman who was uneducated was as much at risk of being victimized as one who was deaf and blind. These comments, she noted, applied to the familiar saying, the "product of some aberration of a man," according to which the best quality a woman could have was to be mute.[38] (*Aquella es buena que no suena*, "a good woman makes not a sound," proclaimed an old adage.[39]) And reflecting on whoever first gave voice to this popular saying, the *labores* teacher added acidly, "He was referring to his own wife, no doubt."[40]

Turning to the school's curriculum, Ruiz Ricote explained that pupils acquired the means to earn a living, and training was offered in trades such as drawing, lithography, painting, sculpture, and printing. At the time of her speech these classes were only for boys, but Doña Marcelina deemed such occupations equally suitable for women. (The conclusion followed logically from her claim that there were no essential differences between the sexes.) And the same could be said, she noted, of secretarial work or running a business office. The National School, she believed, should provide this instruction to deaf girls, so when they left the establishment they could find appropriate employment.[41] Although many still thought women should not work outside the home save in cases of extreme necessity, and then only in jobs considered proper for their sex, Ruiz Ricote recognized that her pupils, who came from the lower classes, were destined inevitably for the workplace. She knew the deaf girls would have to compete not only with boys and men but also with their hearing sisters, and she advocated training them for the best-paying jobs rather than limiting them to "women's work"—and women's miserable wages, which were always less than men's.

Continuing to describe the course of study, Ruiz Ricote explained that the deaf girls learned sign language and writing, along with some speech. But the major portion of the girls' training consisted of *labores*. Contrary to popular belief, Ruiz Ricote maintained, women were not the only ones suited to such work, for many men were also highly skilled at it. Equally erroneous, she said, was the notion that women should dedicate themselves solely to *labores*. Of course, they still needed to master skills such as simple sewing and mending, but with the advances in mechanized labor, "the more a woman is trained solely in *labores*," Doña Marcelina asserted, "the more she is impeded from acquiring useful, marketable knowledge"—and what was more, women's handiwork never commanded the price it rightfully deserved.[42]

On this subject too, many Spaniards begged to differ, and in another graduation speech delivered just a few years earlier, Miguel Fernández Villabrille, then the National School's director and first professor of the deaf students, had remarked that "modern educators"—no doubt he included himself among them—"lament that in the teaching of women, scientific knowledge takes precedence over homemaking." Villabrille thought the National School maintained a "suitable ratio" between domestic training and intellectual formation—a ratio that, as we have seen, favored stitchery and housework over academics.[43]

Yet Ruiz Ricote, while calling into question the school's emphasis on *labores*, did not oppose teaching her pupils these skills: "It is nevertheless evident that deaf girls can devote themselves perfectly well to all kinds of *labores* and apparel making," she stated. What she did oppose, however, was excluding them from the vocational training that could ensure their future, and she affirmed that "it is also evident that deaf girls can have the same aptitudes as deaf boys."[44] Doña Marcelina's belief that women should move beyond their traditional roles and work at jobs held exclusively by men was shared by other advanced thinkers of her day, but her suggestion that men might venture into women's sphere and take up the needle was virtually unheard of.[45]

Although Ruiz Ricote's call for a similar education for girls and boys was at odds with the convictions of most contemporaries, on the question of women's mission in life, she echoed the popular wisdom that it was to marry and have children.[46] But the *labores* teacher departed from the pack when she said that women's "natural, human, and social purpose" was to become the "head of a family"—a role her contemporaries reserved unfailingly for men.[47] Although it is not possible to say with certainty exactly what Ruiz Ricote had in mind, it is worth noting that the section "Obligations of the head of the family" in an 1883 girls' school manual referred unambiguously to the duties of the father, not the mother.[48]

Glossing over the fact that as a single woman she herself had, for whatever reason, neglected to fulfill woman's "natural, human, and social purpose," Doña Marcelina exhorted her audience, "We should see to it that the beings who concern us accomplish their mission with the least possible danger for society."[49] Women with no means of support—and unmarried women headed the list—did in fact pose a danger to society: there could be no social or economic stability, as one social critic explained, while "half the human race, if they do not inherit, receive support from their families, alms, or sinful gifts, goes hungry."[50] Speaking at a time when matrimony still represented women's best chance at financial security, Ruiz Ricote observed that even for a hearing, sighted woman the decision was difficult, as was the "manifestation of her will in such a transcendental act."[51] Girls reluctant to accept an arranged marriage might face considerable family pressure, Ruiz Ricote seemed to imply, and because they were unable to support themselves, they might be in no position to refuse.

For deaf or blind women, Doña Marcelina continued, the situation was even more difficult. (It could hardly be otherwise, because they had to compete on the marriage market with their hearing and sighted counterparts.) Thus, it was society's duty to "make up for their deficiencies," and this, she suggested, could be done by funding dowries, so that when they married they might better their social position and make their misfortune more bearable.[52] For deaf or blind girls from poor families, a dowry could indeed help even the playing field, and Ruiz Ricote's suggestion of setting money aside for such purposes was not without precedent: some twenty years earlier the National School had created savings accounts for those boys who labored most diligently in the establishment's workshops, monies they could take with them upon graduation, and charitable foundations provided dowries for impoverished hearing and sighted girls. Nevertheless, there existed no such arrangement for deaf and blind girls, whose need of assistance was even greater.[53]

Ruiz Ricote concluded her remarks by asking the audience to forgive her if she had failed to describe the National School's program well enough; in truth, she had described it all too well. Recognizing the opportunity to educate her listeners, including board members who might act on her suggestions, she had espoused the rights of women in general and her students in particular, insisting on the centrality of work to their well-being. She had outlined the deficiencies in the girls' education, identifying their actual needs and the importance of preparing them to earn a decent living, and she had underscored the desirability of hiring more women teachers. To put forth these views at a public gathering at which surely many did not share her perspective must have required great courage and resolve.

The historical record does not reflect the audience's response to Doña Marcelina's words, but we can suspect that at least some listeners reacted with surprise, displeasure, and even disbelief. At any rate, the ceremony continued with a musical performance by the blind girls and boys and the distribution of prizes to the students. The event ended with a speech by de Galdo, the president of the board, who used the occasion to announce that because of the government's financial difficulties, it would not be possible to continue repairs on the building or implement other needed reforms.[54] (Problems with the physical plant were never ending: not long before the president's speech, the wall separating the laundry room from the patio of the print shop had collapsed, and the remaining portion threatened to do the same.[55]) But despite this bad news, press accounts recorded that de Galdo's words were loudly applauded.[56] Newspapers reported no such response to Ruiz Ricote's speech, although one did allow that her delivery had been had been "stylistically correct."[57] The article also stated that the *labores* teacher, who was not mentioned by name, had explained the instructional methods used at the school and the changes needed to achieve better results, without providing further details.

Perhaps not surprisingly, Ruiz Ricote was never invited to give another commencement address. But in 1895 she spoke out once again for equal rights for women and men. This time she addressed the matter of equal pay for equal work, and the rights in question were her own. In a petition to the Ministry of Development she stated that she was the only woman teacher at the National School, and she respectfully asserted that she had "equal claim and rights to enjoy the same benefits as her fellow [male] professors," namely, a salary increase and regular raises every five years.[58] Although she had been on the faculty for twenty-seven years, she had not received the same financial consideration as her male colleagues, and at the time of her petition her salary stood at 1,500 pesetas. Calling attention to blatant gender discrimination, she observed that "as such an exceptional case" she found herself "unable to enjoy the same benefits as the other professors of this establishment."[59] At the National School the traditional differences between the sexes, whose gradual disappearance Doña Marcelina had lauded some years earlier, were still alive and well.

Ruiz Ricote's demands were entirely justified: in 1883 legislation had been passed that stated that men and women teachers should be paid the same. And not only was the letter of the law on her side, the school's governing board also supported her request, as did the Counsel of Public Instruction.[60] In response to her petition, a royal order granted the *labores* teacher five increases of 500 pesetas each, one for each five-year period she had been employed at the establishment, nearly tripling her salary.[61]

Doña Marcelina continued to teach at the National School until her death, at age sixty-seven, in April of 1897.[62] She passed away in her home at number 2 on the calle San Lorenzo and was laid to rest in the Sacramental de Santa María Cemetery; her demise was attributed to "cerebral congestion."[63]

The Impact of Ruiz Ricote's Efforts on Behalf of Her Students

Because her ideas were ahead of her time, the thoughts Ruiz Ricote expressed on graduation day in 1889 apparently had little, if any, immediate effect. Nevertheless, the tradition of allowing only men to deliver the commencement address had been broken, and three years later Consuelo Menéndez y García de Dios became the second woman to speak at the graduation ceremony.[64] But in contrast to her predecessor, Menéndez, who had been hired a few years earlier to teach the deaf girls artificial flower making, seemed perfectly content with the status quo. She had a more limited vision of her students' capabilities—one that was in accord with the school's curriculum. She believed deaf women could not compete with hearing women at many jobs, but she praised their skill at making artificial flowers, an occupation for which she considered her pupils ideally suited. Unlike Ruiz Ricote, Menéndez did not suggest that deaf girls learn trades traditionally practiced by men, and the National School continued to exclude them from such training.

In 1896 the curriculum was reorganized and the teaching of academics (never the school's forte) was further deemphasized in favor of vocational classes.[65] The goal was to enable graduates to earn a living: "Less intellectualism and more artistic-industrial training is what these students need," in the words of one (male) teacher.[66] In the early decades of the 1900s the school added numerous career options for deaf boys, and courses in photography, photoengraving, toy making, machine shop, fancy metalwork, and upholstery joined the establishment's long-standing classes in printing, bookbinding, basketry, carpentry, shoemaking, and tailoring. But the new opportunities were not available to girls, who continued to be taught skills deemed appropriate for their sex: sewing, knitting, embroidery, crochet, artificial flowers, and of course, domestic drudgery such as washing and ironing.[67] Suitable vocational training for the girls was cast as a "future project," but in the meantime, low expectations were the order of the day, and the emphasis remained on homemaking.[68] Thus, Ruiz Ricote's recommendation that girls learn lucrative, traditionally male-dominated trades came to naught—as did her suggestion that instruction in *labores* might be extended to at least some boys.

As for Ruiz Ricote's call for more female instructors at the school, the first woman professor of academic subjects was not hired until 1899 (two years after Doña Marcelina's death).[69] During the following decades, however, the number of women faculty increased gradually (the same was true at hearing schools as the teaching profession was gradually feminized). Dowries for deaf and blind girls, it seems, were never established.

Conclusions

Although Ruiz Ricote's thoughts on women's education and their place in society had little impact at the conservative, male-dominated National School, this forward-looking, unconventional woman was in step with—or ahead of—the most advanced thinkers of her era. We cannot know exactly what intellectual influences shaped her thought, but she was doubtlessly well aware of the debate about women's education that characterized her era—a debate to which she herself contributed. She may have attended public lectures and discussions on the topic, she was appraised of the important pedagogical congresses in which the National School participated, and she most likely read the works of progressive authors of her day. Although it is not possible to say which of these authors, if any, she was personally acquainted with, she surely knew Carmen Rojo, a staunch advocate of women's education, and Casilda Mexía, because both were affiliated with Ruiz Ricote's alma mater, both served on the National School's board of directors, and both were present the day of the *labores* teacher's groundbreaking speech. But leaving aside the question of possible influences and acquaintances, when it came to the rights of women and their instruction, Ruiz Ricote's ideas placed her in the company of a small and highly select intellectual minority that included her famous contemporaries Concepción Arenal and Emilia Pardo Bazán, as well as María Concepción Gimeno de Flaquer, Concepción Saiz, Leonor Canalejas, María Carbonell, Matilde García del Real, and Sofía Tartilán.[70]

There is, nevertheless, an important difference between Ruiz Ricote, on the one hand, and Arenal, Pardo Bazán, and other progressive figures of her time, on the other: most individuals who championed the rights of women and other socially disadvantaged groups did so from a position of relative comfort and privilege, but Doña Marcelina was writing from the trenches. She experienced gender-based discrimination firsthand, and she knew only too well the lot of women obliged to support themselves in an oppressive, patriarchal setting. Yet even as she herself confronted these circumstances on a daily basis, she enriched the lives of the students whose rights she proclaimed, teaching them and living among them for nearly three decades.

In upholding her pupils' right to meaningful instruction, Marcelina Ruiz Ricote y Fernández extended the call for women's education to some of Spain's most marginalized and neglected citizens, people who were disadvantaged both because of their gender and because of their deafness (or blindness), and she analyzed their needs within the framework and perspective of the ongoing national debate on women's education and place in society. Her concern for women's rights in general and the rights of deaf and blind women in particular earns this early Spanish feminist a place in Deaf history, as well as women's history and disability history.

NOTES

1. "Con un millón de maestras como ésta, . . . tu patria y las patrias adyacentes serán regeneradas, ennoblecidas, espiritualizadas hasta consumar la perfecta revolución social." (This and all subsequent translations are my own.)

2. "No hay diferencia esencial entre el Hombre y la Mujer, y . . . la salvación de la Humanidad venidera está en la emancipación de la Mujer."

3. In this study I do not observe the distinction between "Deaf" with an uppercase *D,* which refers to social groupings and cultural identifications resulting from interactions among people with hearing loss, and "deaf" with a lowercase *d,* which denotes the audiological condition of hearing loss. Although in Spain today a similar distinction is made between "*Sordo*" vs. "*sordo,*" no such usage occurred during the nineteenth century.

4. For the history of deaf education in Spain and the early history of the Madrid school, see Susan Plann, *A Silent Minority: Deaf Education in Spain, 1550–1835* (Berkeley: University of California Press, 1997).

5. During the 1873–74 academic year, for example, there were forty-one deaf girls and ninety deaf boys (Carlos Nebreda y López, *Memoria correspondiente al curso académico de 1873 á 1874* [Madrid: Colegio Nacional de Sordo-

mudos y Ciegos, 1875], 3–4). In 1889 there were 32 deaf girls and 73 deaf boys (Marcelina Ruiz Ricote y Fernández, *Discurso leído . . . en el día 30 de junio de 1889* [Madrid: Colegio Nacional de Sordomudos y de Ciegos, 1889], 27).

6. Carlos Nebreda y López, *Memoria . . . acerca del Estado del Colegio de Sordo-mudos . . .* (MS) [1868], Educación y Ciencia, leg. 3593, Archivo General de la Administración Civil de Estado (AGACE), Alcalá de Henares, Spain; Carlos Nebreda y López, *Memoria correspondiente al curso académico de 1870 á 1871* (Madrid: Colegio Nacional de Sordomudos y Ciegos, 1871), 40. In addition to the deaf and blind girls, in 1871 there were also 83 deaf boys, 45 blind boys, and 1 deaf-blind boy.

7. For information on the 1882 congress, see *Congreso Nacional Pedagógico . . . de 1882* (Madrid: Sociedad El Fomento de las Artes, 1883). On the 1892 pedagogical congress, see Rafael M. de Labra, *El Congreso pedagógico hispano-portugués-americano de 1892* (Madrid: Librería de la Viuda de Hernando, 1893). For details of the National School's exhibits and participation, see *Colegio Nacional de Sordo-mudos y de Ciegos. Exposición pedagógica . . . que celebrará dicho establecimiento . . . con motivo del IV centenario del descubrimiento de América . . .* (Madrid: Colegio de Sordo-mudos y de Ciegos, 1892).

8. "ruin," "mísero." Vicente de la Fuente, Informe acerca del estado del Colegio de sordomudos y ciegos en Madrid . . . [August 22, 1884], Educación y Ciencia, leg. 6245, AGACE.

9. Ibid.

10. Letter from Carlos Nebreda y López to the director general of Public Instruction, September 18, 1872, Educación y Ciencia, leg. 6244, AGACE.

11. Anastasio Menéndez, Proyecto de ampliacion y reforma para el Colegio Nacional de Sordomudos y Ciegos [June 19, 1873], Educación y Ciencia, leg. 6246, AGACE.

12. *Reglamento para el Colegio de Sordomudos de Madrid*, 1863, art. 62, art. 88, in Miguel Granell y Forcadell, *Historia de la Enseñanza del Colegio Nacional de Sordomudos* (Madrid: Imprenta del Colegio Nacional de Sordomudos, 1932), 334, 337. The *Reglamento* also contained provisions for an advanced course of study dedicated to either academics or vocational training and lasting an additional three years (art. 100–106, p. 338).

13. Francisco Escudero y Azara, Report to the Minister of Development [July 22, 1863], Educación y Ciencia, leg. 6243, AGACE.

14. Letter from Carlos Nebreda y López to the director general of Public Instruction, September 18, 1872.

15. Menéndez, Proyecto.

16. In 1903 the point was driven home by another woman teacher, Rafaela Placer de Monje, who advised, "I would do away with teaching them to wash clothes, since in view of the social class to which nearly all the girls belong, they already know how and they have excellent teachers in their own homes" ["yo surprimiría la enseñanza del lavado de ropas que dada la esfera social á que pertenecen casi todas las alumnas, ya la conocen y tienen excelentes profesoras en sus casas"] (Rafaela Placer de Monje, "Glosando un discurso," in Pedro Molina Martín, *IV Publicaciones de propaganda de las enseñanzas del Colegio Nacional de Sordomudos y Ciegos. Discurso leído el 18 de octubre de 1903* . . . [Madrid: Colegio Nacional de Sordomudos y Ciegos, 1903], 100, 98–103).

17. Raymond Carr, *Modern Spain 1876–1980* (New York: Oxford University Press, 1980), 39. In 1872 the National School had a print shop, locksmith shop, and bookbindery, along with shops for shoemaking, tailoring, carpentry, and cabinetmaking; lithography, weaving, and painting were also taught (Carlos Nebreda y López, *Memoria correspondiente al curso académico de 1871 á 1872* [Madrid: Colegio Nacional de Sordo-mudos y de Ciegos, 1872], 31).

18. *"la más exquisita vigilancia."* Letter from Carlos Nebreda y López to the director general of Public Instruction, September 18, 1872.

19. *Colegio Nacional de Sordomudos y de Ciegos. Instrucciones reglamentarias relativas al ingreso y permanencia de los alumnos sordomudos y ciegos* (Madrid: Colegio Nacional de Sordomudos y de Ciegos, 1873), 16–17. See also pp. 18–19 for further discussion of the curriculum.

20. Carlos Nebreda y López, *Memoria correspondiente al curso académico de 1872 á 1873* (Madrid: Colegio Nacional de Sordo-mudos y de Ciegos, 1873), 67. According to this same source, blind girls dedicated eighteen hours per week to academic classes and an equal amount to *labores*, plus six hours to music, nine to guitar and bandurria (an instrument similar to the lute), and four and a half hours to exercise.

21. In 1870, for instance, nearly half the children of school age (that is, between six and nine) were not enrolled in school (A. del Valle, "La Ley Moyano de 1857," in *Historia de la educación en España y América*, vol. 3, ed. Buenaventura Delgado Criado [Madrid: Ediciones Morata, 1994], 273, 261–78).

22. Ruiz Ricote's appointment at the National School is documented in her personnel file at AGACE in Alcalá de Henares, Madrid, Spain (Personnel

file of Marcelina Ruiz Ricote, Hoja de méritos y servicios, Educación y Ciencia, sig. 20193).

23. Ruiz Ricote was born on June 2, 1829 (personnel file of Marcelina Ruiz Ricote, certificate from the Escuela Normal Central de Maestras). Her sisters and brothers—five girls and four boys—were born between 1824 and 1842, Libro de bautismo no. 5, índice, Parroquia de San Andrés, Fuentidueña de Tajo). Her father, Casimiro Ruiz Ricote, and her paternal grandparents, Balentin Ruiz Ricote and Isabel Mora, were natives of Fuentidueña de Tajo; her mother, Antonia Fernández, and her maternal grandparents, Francisco Fernández and Josefa Cordón, were from the neighboring village of Estremera, which was eleven kilometers from Fuentidueña de Tajo (ibid., back of p. 205). I am grateful to Father Fernando José Gutiérrez Fernández of the parish of San Andrés, Fuentidueña de Tajo, for assistance in locating this document.

24. Ruiz Ricote's graduation from the Escuela Normal Central de Maestras is documented in the archives of the Universidad Complutense (letter from Ramona Aparicio to the rector of the Universidad Central, September 22, 1876, Archivo Histórico, Facultad de Medicina, Secretaría General, Caja 143, Escuelas Normales, Antecedentes, Exámenes, Madrid).

25. Personnel file of Marcelina Ruiz Ricote, Hoja de méritos y servicios.

26. Ibid.

27. In 1860 86 percent of Spanish women were illiterate, compared to 64.8 percent of Spanish men. In 1877 the figures stood at 81 percent and 62.6 percent, respectively (censuses of 1860 and 1877, cited in A. Viñao, "Escolarización y alfabetización," in *Historia de la educación en España y América*, vol. 3, ed. Buenaventura Delgado Criado [Madrid: Ediciones Morata, 1994], 392, 389–96).

28. Carolyn P. Boyd, *Historia Patria: Politics, History, and National Identity in Spain, 1875–1975* (Princeton, N.J.: Princeton University Press, 1997), 11. Although during the early decades of the nineteenth century many women teachers had no formal credentials, beginning in 1857 the Moyano Law required them to have a normal school degree that corresponded to the level they wished to teach (lower or upper primary school) and to have studied pedagogy and teaching methods. Women who had studied privately could also become teachers, provided they had completed two years of practice teaching (Moyano Law, art. 71, in *Historia de la educación en España*, vol. 2, [Madrid: Ministerio de Educación y Ciencia, 1985], 261–62). At midcentury there were in all of Spain only 4,066 women teachers, of whom only

1,871 had a professional degree (Mercedes Roig, *A través de la prensa: La mujer en la historia. Francia, Italia, España, S. XVIII–XX* [Madrid: Ministerio de Asuntos Sociales, 1989], 126).

29. Personnel file of Marcelina Ruiz Ricote, Hoja de méritos y servicios, Honores y condecoraciones.

30. Carmen Rojo Herraiz entered the Escuela Normal Central de Maestras in 1863 at age sixteen and completed her studies two years later; in 1873 she graduated from the Escuela de Institutrices. In 1881 she became director of the Escuela Normal, and in 1888 she was named to the governing board of the National School for Deaf-mutes and the Blind. For details of Rojo Herraiz's career, see Carmen Colmenar Orzaes, "Historia de la Escuela Normal Central de Maestras de Madrid, 1858–1914," vol. 2 (doctoral dissertation, Universidad Complutense de Madrid, 1988), 596–603. Casilda Mexía Sales was a teaching assistant (*profesora auxiliar*) at the Escuela Normal Central de Maestras from September 1889 through March 1890 (ibid., 657–58). Board president Manuel María José de Galdo was counselor (*consejero*) of Public Instruction and director of the Instituto del Cardenal Cisneros; other board members included Universidad Central professors Magín Bonet y Bonfill and José Montero Ríos, lawyer and publicist Eduardo Serrano Fatigati, and professor of the Escuela Normal Central de Maestros Agustín Sardá y Llabería, as well as Juan Gregorio Gutiérrez y Albornoz and the marquis of Hazas. On the day of Ruiz Ricote's speech, Bonet y Bonfill was also present, in addition to de Galdo and the two female board members ("En el Colegio de Sordo-mudos y de Ciegos," *El Magisterio Español*, July 5, 1889).

31. "Yo debía y podía declinar . . . aduciendo siquiera mi insuficiencia y apoyándola en el inferior nivel á que este acto iba á reducirse, relacionándome con los que me precedieron en el uso de la palabra," "en el nombre de la Mujer." Ruiz Ricote, *Discurso*, 4–5 (see n. 5).

32. "en nombre del sexo por las facultades educativas de [las mujeres], y en nombre de los queridos seres que en el Establecimiento reciben sus beneficios." Ibid., 5.

33. The other female teacher at this time was Consuelo Menéndez y García de Dios (see n. 58). In public schools for hearing children, 30.75 percent of the teachers were women in 1870; by 1885 their numbers had risen to 33.68 percent. In private schools, however, women constituted the majority of the teaching force: 55.26 percent in 1870 and 62.75 percent in 1885 (Narciso de Gabriel, "La mujer como maestra," in Sociedad Española de la Historia de la Educación, *Mujer y educación en España, 1868–1975, VI*

Coloquio de Historia de la Educación [Santiago: Departamento de Teoria e Historia da Educación da Universidade de Santiago, 1990], 437–48.).

34. "ya que hoy afortunadamente para la actual civilización no hay diferencia esencial entre el Hombre y la Mujer." Ruiz Ricote, *Discurso*, 7.

35. "la salvación de la Humanidad venidera está en la emancipación de la Mujer," "en el verdadero y noble sentido de la palabra." Ibid., 7–8.

36. "los seres creo más dignos y con más derecho á mi amor," "dispuesta á sacrificar cuanto valgo y poséo." Ibid., 12.

37. "Si la Mujer, en general, es víctima hoy de la Sociedad, por su debilidad, según unos, por su ignorancia y su falta de medios, según los más, ¡cuánto más propiciatoriamente no se entregará la Mujer ciega ó sordomuda!" Ibid., 8.

38. "¿Deja de ser [sordomuda y ciega] por ventura acaso la Mujer verdaderamente ignorante?" "producto de alguna aberración de un hombre." Ibid., 8.

39. Proverbs to this effect were numerous: *Las buenas callan y las malas parlan*, "good [women] are quiet and bad ones talk"; *la mujer y la pera, la que calla es más buena*, "women and pears, the one that doesn't make noise is best"; *mujeres y almendras, las que no suenan*, "women and almonds, [choose] the ones that make no sound"; and so on. But folk sayings occasionally contradicted the idea that women should keep quiet: *No te fíes de mujer que no hable, ni perro que no ladre*, "don't trust a woman who doesn't talk, or a dog that doesn't bark." (I am indebted to my friend and colleague Shirley Arora for assistance in locating these proverbs.)

40. "Su mujer querría decir, sin duda." Ruiz Ricote, *Discurso*, 8.

41. She advanced a similar argument concerning the blind girls, stating that they should be prepared for the same type of work as the blind boys, for example, for jobs playing in orchestras and bands and in cafés and places of amusement—occupations traditionally held by men (ibid., 8–9).

42. "Cuanto más á la mujer sólo se la dedique expresamente á labores, . . . más se le impide el adquirir conocimientos útiles y explotables." Ibid., 10.

43. "Duélense los modernos educadores de que en la enseñanza de la mujer predominen los conocimientos científicos á la educación familiar," "proporción conveniente." Miguel Fernández Villabrille, *Discurso leído . . . en . . . el día primero de julio de 1883* (Madrid: Colegio Nacional de Sordomudos y de Ciegos, 1883), 16.

44. "Es sin embargo evidente, que la sordo-muda puede perfectamente dedicarse á toda clase de labores y confección; pero también lo es que no está

excluída de las aptitudes de los sordo-mudos." Ruiz Ricote, *Discurso*, 10. The blind girls too learned sewing, crochet, and mesh making, and some even managed to embroider and make artificial flowers, but their limitations were obvious, and Ruiz Ricote urged that they be provided with instruction better suited to their needs and abilities.

45. Concepción Arenal (see n. 70), Ruiz Ricote's famous contemporary, advocated preparing women for the trades on numerous occasions. In 1884, for instance, she observed that "custom, without reason but with great obstinacy, shuts out women from the most lucrative occupations and trades, and even from those for which they are peculiarly fitted by nature," and she complained that "delicate mechanical arts which do not require strength, and other crafts which demand exactitude, patience, and assiduity are practiced exclusively by men" (Concepción Arenal, "Spain," in *The Woman Question in Europe*, ed. Theodore Stanton [New York: G.P. Putnam's Sons, 1884], 334). Another contempoary, María Concepción Gimeno de Flaquer (see n. 70), railed against men who held positions she believed should be reserved exclusively for women. In contrast to Ruiz Ricote's sugestion that deaf boys learn *labores*, she contended that "the needle and thimble are the patrimony of women, just as the sword is the patrimony of the soldier" ["la aguja y el dedal son patrimonio de la mujer, como la espada es patrimonio del soldado"], and she concluded that male dressmakers should be disallowed (María Concepción Gimeno de Flaquer, *La mujer española: Estudios acerca de su educacion y sus facultades intelectuales* [Madrid: Imp. y Librería de Miguel Guijarro, 1877], 120).

46. In this respect Emilia Pardo Bazán (see n. 70), one of Ruiz Ricote's best-known contemporaries, was ahead of the teacher of deaf and blind girls: at the Pedagogical Congress of 1892 she averred that "woman has her own destiny," "her first natural duty is toward herself," and the objective of her education should be "her happiness and personal dignity," but her view was shared by only a handful of Spaniards ["la mujer tiene destino propio," "sus primeros deberes naturales son para consigo misma," "su felicidad y dignidad personal"]. Emilia Pardo Bazán, "Conclusiones," in *La mujer española y otros artículos feministas*, ed. Leda Schiavo (Madrid: Editorial Nacional, 1976), 100, 99–102.

47. "el fin, natural humano y social de la mujer," "jefe de una familia." Ruiz Ricote, *Discurso*, 11, 12.

48. J. López y Candeal, ed., *Programas generales de Enseñanza* (Madrid: Estab. tip. de Felipe Pinto Grovio, 1883), 101–103, cited in Josette

Borderies-Guerena, "El discurso higiénico como conformador de la mentali-
dad femenina (1865–1915)," in *Mujeres y hombres en la formación del pensa-
miento occidental*, vol. 2, ed. Virginia Maquieira d'Angelo, Guadalupe Gómez-
Ferrer Morant, and Margarita Ortega López (Madrid: Instituto Universitario
de Estudios de la Mujer, Universidad Autónoma de Madrid, 1989), 300,
299–309.

49. "atender debemos á que los seres que nos ocupan cumplan su misión
con el menor peligro para la Sociedad." Ruiz Ricote, *Discurso*, 12.

50. "la mitad del género humano, si no hereda, ó es sostenida por la fa-
milia, ó recibe limosna, ó don pecaminoso, tiene hambre." Concepción
Arenal, *El pauperismo*, in *Obras completas*, vol. 1, t. 15 (Madrid: Librería de
Victoriano Suárez, 1897), 253.

51. "la manifestación de su voluntad en acto tan trascendental." Ruiz Ricote, *Discurso*, 12.

52. "compensar sus deficiencias." Ibid.

53. The boys' accounts had been established by royal orders of November
27, 1876, March 14, 1877, and March 9, 1887. By 1892 there also existed
monetary prizes for blind and deaf students of both sexes, although among
the deaf children preference was given to the boys (*Colegio Nacional de Sordo-
mudos y de Ciegos*, 13–14).

54. "Reparto de Premios en la Escuela de Sordo-mudos y ciegos," *El Liberal*, July 2, 1889, 5.

55. Communication from Miguel Fernández Villabrille [February 3,
1886], Educación y Ciencia, caja 32/8779, AGACE. Despite occasional attempts to shore up the decrepit structure, the building had continued to
deteriorate and decay rendered certain areas completely inaccessible. In 1884
disaster was narrowly averted when a deaf boy fell through the floor in an
isolated area cut off from the rest of the building; somehow he managed to
avoid landing in the water tank, where he might have drowned (de la Fuente,
Informe) [see n. 8].

56. "Reparto de Premios," 5. *El Magisterio Español* similarly described
Galdo's address as "an eloquent and justly applauded speech" ["un elocuente
y con justicia aplaudido discurso"] ("En el Colegio de Sordo-mudos y de
Ciegos," *El Magisterio Español*, July 5, 1889.).

57. "en correcto estilo." "En el Colegio," *El Magisterio Español*, July 5,
1889.

58. "igual título y derechos á disfrutar los mismos beneficios que sus com-
profesores." Petition from Ruiz Ricote [March 28, 1895], Educación y Cien-

cia, sig. 20193, AGACE. Starting in 1884 the National School also employed another woman to teach the girls to make artificial flowers (Manuela Díaz in 1884, Consuelo Menéndez y García de Dios beginning in 1886), but from Ruiz Ricote's affirmation that she was the school's only woman professor it is clear that her status was different from that of these two women (Granell y Forcadell, *Historia*, 424, 431).

59. "como caso tan excepcional," "sin gozar de los mismos beneficios concedidos á los demas profesores del referido Establecimiento." Petition from Ruiz Ricote [March 28, 1895] AGACE.

60. Personnel file of Marcelina Ruiz Ricote, communication from board president Baldomero G[onzález] Valledor [April 15, 1895]; communication from the Counsel of Public Instruction [May 18, 1895].

61. Her raise was granted on June 1, 1895 (personnel file of Marcelina Ruiz Ricote, notification from Minister of Development Alberto Bosch [June 1, 1895]).

62. Ruiz Ricote died on April 9, 1897, at 11:00 a.m. (personnel file of Marcelina Ruiz Ricote, letter from Manuel Blasco [April 10, 1897]).

63. "congestion cerebral." Death certificate, Marcelina Ruiz Ricote y Fernández, Registro civil de Madrid, t. 95–96, sección 3ª, folio 85.

64. Consuelo Menéndez y García de Dios, *Discurso leído . . . en el acto público de distribución de premios . . . el día 29 de junio de 1892* (Madrid: Colegio Nacional de Sordomudos y de Ciegos, 1892).

65. Pedro Molina Martín, *Instituciones españolas de sordomudos y de ciegos: Consideraciones sobre lo que son y debieran ser estos centros* (Madrid: Imprenta de Hernando y Compañía, 1900), 6.

66. "Menos intelectualismo y más enseñanza artístico-industrial es lo que se debe á los alumnos." Ibid., 25.

67. Ibid., 7.

68. "un propósito de futura realización." Ibid., 7.

69. In 1899 Granell includes a woman, Aurora Cuervo, among the professors of "general studies" ["estudios generales"] for the first time (Granell y Forcadell, *Historia*, 465).

70. Concepción Arenal (1820–93) was a Spanish writer and social critic whose many interests included education, penal reform, and women's rights. The author of more than twenty volumes, Arenal waged a lifelong campaign on behalf of the socially and educationally disadvantaged.

Emilia Pardo Bazán (1851–1921) was the author of some nineteen novels, twenty short novels, and more than five hundred short stories; she was also the founder of a book series and two magazines. In 1916 she became Spain's first female university professor.

María Concepción Gimeno de Flaquer, prolific author and journalist, defended women's right to an education. She asserted that women should receive the same intellectual and moral formation as men so that they might be useful to society, and she declared woman's mission in life to be "whatever she feels inclined toward" ["aquella hácia la cual se siente inclinada"] (*La mujer española*, 50–51, 52 [see n. 45]).

Concepción Saiz Otero, a graduate of the Escuela Normal Central de Maestras and of the Escuela de Institutrices, was a professor of the former institution from 1883 until 1909, when she joined the faculty of the Escuela Superior del Magisterio. A passionate defender of women's education, Saiz published widely on the subject.

Leonor Canalejas was a professor of the Escuela Normal Central de Maestras (1888–1904) and other schools under the direction of the Asociación para la Enseñanza de la Mujer and author of various articles on the situation of Spanish women.

María Carbonell Sánchez was an author and public school teacher in Valencia.

Matilde García del Real Mijares was an inspector of Madrid's municipal schools and author of numerous works, among them *La escuela de niñas* (Madrid: Lib. de Hernando y Cª, 1890) and *Nuestras escuelas de párvulos* (Madrid: Tip. del Asilo de S. Rafael, 1924).

Sofía Tartilán was an author, journalist, and director of *La Ilustración de la Mujer*. Her writings on pedagogy were, according to García Colmenares and Sánchez García, comparable to those of Concepción Arenal (Carmen García Colmenares and José Luis Sánchez García, "Sofía Tartilán: Autobiografía de una educadora desconocida," in Sociedad Española de la Historia de la Educación, *Mujer y educación en España*, 153, 153–60 [see n. 33]).

The Ladies Take Charge
Women Teachers in the Education of Deaf Students

Margret Winzer

E ducational historians have long been interested in gendered occupational structures; one critical strand is the meanings and tensions generated by the feminization of teaching. The multiple perspectives on the history of women as teachers, however, have tended to set the phenomenon in the context of the common schools.

Far less attention has been directed toward women teachers in the field of special education, whether they taught in institutional settings, day schools, or in special segregated classes. Historians have occasionally examined the lives and contributions of pioneers such as Leta Hollingworth, Elizabeth Farrell, and Caroline Yale, but have largely ignored the collective career paths of the women who formed the majority of those intervening with students with exceptionalities.

Women teachers catered to the needs of students burdened with a plethora of labels—deaf, hard of hearing, near blind, undernourished, academically maladjusted, mentally retarded, gifted, speech defective, tubercular, and so on (Palen 1923). Perhaps the most striking group emerged early in the field of special education—the female teachers concerned with the education of deaf students. The numbers were not large. In 1891 the total number of teachers employed in North American schools for the deaf was 686. Projecting from this and from figures published annually in the *American Annals of the Deaf (and Dumb)*, the women involved in the endeavor in the period 1867 to 1900 numbered somewhat less than

600. However, in contrast to their small numbers, these women teachers played significant roles in shaping the lives of deaf people, both from their direct influence as organizers in the campaign for the adoption of the oral system, and from their indirect cooperation in the process.

In the fifty years following the establishment of the first institution to serve deaf students in 1817, instruction through the language of sign—the manual mode—held sway. An opposing oral mode that stressed the centrality of speech and lipreading was not introduced until 1867. From that time on, educators assumed conflicting stances in regard to methodology that allowed no neutral or nonpartisan stance. Pursuing different avenues to the general goal of the intellectual and social development of the deaf child, teachers divided themselves into opposing camps of oralists and manualists.

The ferment about communication modes revealed clearly the differing aspirations and anxieties concerning deaf pupils so that pedagogical issues were pertinent to wider social values, implying differing viewpoints held by the oralists and the manualists relating to the role of deaf people in society. Manualists perceived deafness as a human difference, best accommodated through a special language; oralists saw it as a handicap to be overcome, with speech and lipreading allowing access to normal society. Hence, the controversy precipitated a debate not only on the techniques but also on the purposes and content of education. The quest for economic independence bounded manual school instruction; seeking greater social mobility determined oral curriculum.

The questions surrounding manualism and oralism, perhaps the longest-running issue in deaf education, are inherently interesting in themselves. Arguing from quite different philosophical bases, the ineradicable antagonisms between the two sets of players spilled over to affect, among other things, schooling for deaf students, the status of deaf teachers, the Deaf community, and the veracity of sign language.

Of the players, one team was chiefly women who advanced novel arguments and pedagogies. As they challenged the traditional diligent adherence to the manual modes of communication, they elevated oralism to the dominant ideology by the opening decades of the twentieth century, routed manualism, and ultimately altered the course of the education of deaf students for almost a hundred years.

Women's influence in the oral movement cannot be dismissed as just another example of the feminization of elementary education. Instead, under the tutelage of women, the oral reform expanded from a pedagogical technique to a philosophy that produced and reproduced gender-related meanings, behaviors, and orientations. As oralists battled relentlessly to achieve a radical new vision of the role in society of deaf people, they absorbed, to a marked degree, the question of professionalism. The oral teachers created a parallel profession with a unique curriculum and methodology, distinct institutional settings, rival facilities for teacher training, different licensing procedures, and competing professional associations. In doing so, they not only achieved numerical dominance but also leadership of the profession.

The period during which women assumed definitive educational leadership is relatively brief, spanning from about 1875 to 1910. Men soon enlisted in the oral cause once the fate of the manual methods was sealed. Gender as a proxy disappeared: the female numerical dominance persisted, but males took back the reins of leadership.

The complexities of the shifting gender ratios, so explicit in the second half of the nineteenth century, become murky as soon as the professional divide along gender lines dissipates. In the early decades of the twentieth century the problems plaguing the education of deaf students were not focused on the gender of the teaching corps but on whether there were teachers available at all.

Two major aims structure this chapter. The first is to make visible the manner in which the communication debate placed men and women teachers in separate spheres in the late-nineteenth century and the way in which women created a parallel profession of their own. The second is to visit, albeit briefly, a relatively unexplored period—the opening half of the twentieth century. This time frame saw men reassume pedagogical leadership within oral paradigms. The connecting theme lies in the persistent advance toward professional status, now embodied in the quest for teacher training and certification.

It is not reasonable to extract women from the history of education. The female dominance within the oral pedagogy cannot be understood in isolation; rather, it must be placed in context. Variables to consider include women's acceptance into the profession of teaching as a whole and the cracks that rapidly appeared in the ideology of the common schools, which led to the development of special segregated classes. Added to these are the complex and intricately meshed factors that underlaid women's oral domination, such as perceived expertise in speech teaching, novel school milieus, and modes of teacher training, which in turn generated unique professional identities among teachers.

THE DEBATE

As a prolog to discussion of the teaching corps, some distinctive characteristics of the communication controversy must be understood. A detailed analysis of the arguments would provide another complete essay; the following is a mere glimpse.

It was in mid-eighteenth-century Europe that the blurred outline of the debate was brought sharply into focus. Influenced by Enlightenment philosophies of language, the Abbé l'Epée in France perfected the manual or silent method, which focused on the supremacy of sign language and manual alphabets, with minor emphasis on the acquisition of mechanical speech. Simultaneously there developed in Germany an oral mode that eschewed manual forms entirely, adopting as its central tenet the superiority of speech and lipreading, supplemented with writing.

Thomas Hopkins Gallaudet, trained for the work in France, imported the manual system to the American Asylum for the Education and Instruction of Deaf and Dumb Persons. Later manual institutions, strikingly similar in philosophy and practice, all took their cues from the American Asylum and utilized the manual methods of l'Epée almost exclusively.

Within the founding institutions, patriarchal forms of governance operated. Schools were staffed and supervised by a tightly knit, male elite, predominantly members of the clergy, who elicited an entrenched conservatism in regard to methodology. Students' literary accomplishments were restricted and thought unnecessary, inappropriate, and tangential to moral development and the instillation of the traits of character and technical skills needed for upright living in an industrializing society. Four hours a day of academic work was generally all that was allotted to older students.

After Horace Mann and Samuel Gridley Howe toured European schools for the deaf in 1844, they concluded that the oral mode embraced in northern Europe was superior to other methodologies. Thereafter, Mann and Howe diligently stirred up educational and public opposition to the manual methods, speaking consistently in support of the advantages gained from oralism. Joining the battle were class-conscious parents who held more than an intellectual stake in the ideology of reform. They were concerned that their deaf children acquire the graces and be able to speak and understand the speech of others in normal society, thinking it equally undesirable that they be able to converse with only other deaf individuals.

The Clarke Institution at Northampton, Massachusetts, founded by Harriet Rogers in 1867, was built on the belief that oralism held the key to extended opportunities for deaf people and would produce better results than the traditional institutions. Shortly afterward, in 1869, Sarah Fuller opened the Horace Mann School for Deaf-Mutes, employing a curriculum and methodology known as the oral or articulation method. As the first day school within the system of public education, the Horace Mann School stimulated speculation about the capacities of deaf children and advanced the notion that these students were not deviant or dependent but rather worthy of an education identical to that provided hearing children. Pursuing the models of either Clarke or Horace Mann, eleven oral schools were operating by 1880 (Bell and Gillett 1884).

In one sense, the oral day schools served to advance the philosophy of oralism by creating novel environments for deaf children. Equally important, day schools and special classes reflected the early cracks in the ideology of the common schools. They institutionalized the tensions generated by great student diversity, including culture, language, behavior, and disability.

Horace Mann's vision for the common schools embraced all students. Yet, almost from the outset, the system was under stress as the expectations of the common schools proved less reliable than the rhetoric. Disorders and disabilities became boundary conditions that the public schools were remarkably reluctant to confront. Unable to maintain growing numbers of unruly, disabled, low-functioning, and immigrant children, the system embarked on a sustained effort to address the obstacles that diversity meant to the organizational and pedagogical structures of the schools. Seeking to maintain order, discipline, efficiency, and high standards, school districts created the community equivalents of institutions—special segregated classes. For example, New York opened classes for refractory and truant boys in 1874; Cleveland founded a class for incorrigible children in 1876 and one for the training of feeble-minded children in 1879. A class for crippled children opened in Providence, Rhode Island, in 1896; one opened for blind and partially sighted children in Chicago in 1899.

Furthering the advocacy for special classes were the voices of champions of services for the disabled, who were unwilling to restrict their facilities to the model of the common school. Major figures in the field of special education—notably Alexander Graham Bell, Samuel Gridley Howe, and Edward R. Johnstone, superintendent of the New Jersey Institution for Feeble-Minded Boys and Girls at Vineland—assiduously promoted segregated classes for all students with special needs. Howe was passionate in his assertions that "blind children can attend common schools advantageously, and be instructed in classes with common children" (Howe 1874, 119). Bell suggested that "the instruction of deaf children should go hand in hand with the education of those who can hear and speak in the public schools" (Ontario School for the Deaf 1884, 10). He further recommended "an exhaustive development of day schools" (Bell and Gillett 1884, 3). Wisconsin, Illinois, and Ohio passed laws by which the number of day schools could be increased indefinitely (A teacher 1902). Wisconsin created the largest system; by 1910, there were twenty day schools (Bush 1942).

By 1890, a menu of options existed for students with special needs—institutional settings, day schools, and segregated classes. Many of the early classes floundered: they existed without legislative underpinnings and, in most places, state reimbursements were negligible. Day schools for deaf students flourished. Almost entirely, the day schools and classes were staffed by women adhering to an oral methodology.

INSTITUTIONS AND COMMON SCHOOLS

At the opening of the nineteenth century, the notion of women as professionals was rarely entertained. Beginning in the 1830s, teaching developed as the province of women. When, as part of his reorganization of the Massachusetts school system, Horace Mann founded the first normal school in Lexington, Massachusetts, in 1839, he found that men were abandoning teaching for more lucrative opportunities; young women formed the bulk of the candidates. By the middle decades of the nineteenth century, the acceptance of women as teachers in the common schools was universal. From 1835 to 1850, for example, the number of women teachers in Massachusetts grew by 80 percent (see Clifford 1991).

The early educators of deaf students included no women. "As all privileged bodies are apt to make one mistake," wrote Fred De Land (1906), so did the founding institutions: they "omitted women from their system" (17). Women were not permitted to teach in the institutions for the deaf until 1852. The first female teachers of deaf students were hired by the New York Institution for the Deaf and Dumb in 1852 under rationales that mirrored those responsible for the deployment of women into the common schools.

The common schools, supported by taxes, were forced into thrifty housekeeping. School promoters, avidly seeking means to lessen expenditures and assuming that economy and improvement went hand in hand, hired women at about one third less than male teachers. For example, in 1868–69 male teachers earned an average of $111.23 a month; female teachers earned about $80.12 (Berkeley 1984). Lower salaries for women were justified on the basis that females did not have families to support; women were not expected to have job-related aspirations but were to look to eventual marriage; there were only limited purposes to be achieved in the schools; and the increased costs concomitant with the expanding school systems simply determined the lower rates for women.

The same economic forces were at work in institutional settings. "The appropriations now made for the institutions of the deaf and dumb," wrote Henry Barnard in 1852, "could be . . . more economically" and "more wisely applied, by the employment of well educated and properly trained female teachers" (*American Annals of the Deaf and Dumb* 1852, 196). Later, Edward Miner Gallaudet commented that women and institutional teaching merged "for the sole reason that their services could be had at low rates" (Gallaudet 1892, 5).

The imperatives of economy were further shaped by the demographics of a rapidly developing population, an expanding economy, the loss of available men to industrial and commercial enterprises, and, pointedly in schools for the deaf, a waning dominance of the clergy as teachers and leaders.

In both the common and the special schools, the educational capacities of women were soon "recognized to be far above those of men" (Seguin 1876, 48). Charming theories developed to explain women's expertise. Common wisdom held that women brought to the classroom the domestic virtues and piety that had previously made them teachers of their own children in their own homes. It was women's nurturing tendencies together with "the maternal instinct, the untiring patience" ("Seminary" 1831, 341) that qualified them peculiarly for the instruction of young children. Women teachers were thought to be generally kinder and gentler than men and more efficient for the work; for the first ten or twelve years of a child's life, female teachers were most preferable.

The school may have been a necessary institution, but it was not one that required extensive skills or great training on the part of the teacher. The ideology of women's sphere and their natural mission relegated them to elementary classrooms and a modicum of training.

For those aspiring to enter either general or special education, advanced training was reserved for men. For example, in 1857 Edward Miner Gallaudet accepted the superintendency of the newly established Columbia Institution for the Deaf in Washington, D.C., which became the National Deaf Mute College in 1864 and Gallaudet College in 1891. Consonant with traditional employment patterns in schools for the deaf, Gallaudet demanded that the faculty of the National Deaf Mute College be drawn from the most prestigious universities, preferably Yale. In turn, schools for the deaf throughout North America would be staffed with graduates versed in sign language. Within the manual schools, therefore, status became linked directly to academic achievement; advanced education was a prerequisite for upward mobility, and the pool of candidates was limited to those who could obtain the proper training. The gender bias emerges cogently in a 1903 report of 125 schools for the deaf that reported the name and qualifications of the principal. Of the sixty-three men, twenty-six (41 percent) had higher degrees as opposed to three (4.8 percent) of sixty-two women (Wing, "Statistics," 1902).

Denied higher training, women teachers of the deaf could exercise their presumed special talents with young children. Here they were deemed satisfactory because "no man has the patience to teach little children, deaf or hearing" (Wheeler 1920, 375). Strengthening the link was women's "fondness and tact in communicating knowledge, especially by means of oral methods," which rendered them "under all combinations, the best teachers, particularly of speech" (SeGuin 1876, 72). Further, as one wag noted in 1900, "their lips are more easily read—they have more practice, perhaps, and women do not wear beards" (Taylor 1900, 365).

By 1852 there were fourteen schools for the deaf in North America; only two of them employed the total of three women. By 1868 there were fifty-one women teachers, or 34 percent; in 1895 women made up 68 percent of the teaching corps. By 1897 "articulation teachers became the majority among all instructors of deaf students, including superintendents and principals" (American Association 1899, 75). The percentage of students taught speech rose from 27 to 65 percent from 1884 to 1900; those taught by oral methods alone from 20 to 40 percent (Wing, "Statistics," 1902). By 1905, 95 percent of American schools for the deaf were designated as oral schools (Crouter 1907).

The increasing presence of women was explicitly related to the advent of the oral modes of instruction. Because of the oral methodology she adopted, and in response to the young age of her pupils, Harriet Rogers chose to employ only women teachers at the Clarke Institution, a policy wholly or partly adopted by other oral facilities. In fact, in many oral schools it appeared to be unwritten policy to hire only women. When, for example, Harriet Rogers retired from the principalship of the Clarke School, the position was offered to Caroline Yale, the associate principal. Yale wrote that "she urged upon the board the possible wisdom of appointing a man to the vacant principalship," a suggestion rejected by the trustees who "felt strongly that it was wiser to continue the policy of the school without change" (Yale 1931, 163).

School statistics from 1900 spell out the division. In that year the *Association Review* reported fifty-nine residential institutions and fifty-five day schools. Of the former, fifty-three (almost 90 percent) were led by men;

forty-eight day schools (87 percent) were headed by women (Wing, "Statistics," 1902). As more precise examples, in 1873 the Jacksonville, Mississippi, institution was, except for the directors of "mechanical labor," all women. The Horace Mann School employed only women. Women filled the highest administrative positions. In 1884 such prestigious oral schools as the Chicago Voice and Hearing School, the Portland Day School, the Rhode Island School for the Deaf, and the oral branch of the Pennsylvania Institution for the Deaf and Dumb were all under the leadership of women. In the same year, manual institutions such as the New York Institution for the Deaf and Dumb, the American Asylum, and the Halifax Institution for the Deaf and Dumb were not only administered by men but were staffed predominantly by males.

Creating the Oral Paradigms

From the time of the founding of the Clarke School in 1867 until about 1905, the oral and manual factions assumed irreconcilable stances and engaged in a bitter ideological dispute. Educators were forced to confront their ideas critically and to rationalize the advantages of their preferred system of communication.

Manual teachers decried the oral reform and criticized the women who ventured to dispute the traditional pedagogical practices of experienced male teachers. Women, both inadequately educated and improperly socialized, were not only viewed as carriers of an unfortunate professional ideal but also as threats to the gender order.

The flavor of the dissention is conveyed by the carps and criticisms that flooded the contemporary literature. The oral faction, contemptuous of the restrictive social intercourse and intellectual development allowed by that mode, directed "a continued avalanche of sneers and jeers at the so-called old-fogyism of the manual methods" (Wright 1915, 219).

From their corner, the manualists contended that "the logic of facts was entirely against the system of articulation" (Hubbard 1876, 179). For example, they "were disposed to look upon Miss Rogers' attempt to teach congenitally deaf children to speak and read lips as an absurdity, *perhaps not surprising in a woman*, but certainly unworthy of serious consideration" (Moore 1934, 193; italics mine). Manual advocates held that only residential schools could comprehensively address all needs and character-ized day schools as "cruel" and "barren of good results" (Wing 1886, 22).

Women ran afoul of men who disapproved "of the preponderance of female teachers" (Ontario, Department of Education 1904, 37); they contended that women undermined male teachers' most important pro-fessional quest and clearly identified connections between femininity and failure. "I do not wish to be understood as condemning the employment of women in schools for the deaf," said Gallaudet in 1892, but "in no corps of instructors should women be in the majority" (6). A contempo-rary argued that "one good man teacher is worth more in preparing these boys for their life work than ten or a dozen women teachers" (Howard 1902, 278–80).

Progress was linked to male superiority and patriarchal processes over female independence. The institutions functioned overtly as a special form of household where women were encouraged to act out traditional domestic, nonassertive roles. One male principal visualized the ideal insti-tution for the deaf as having "each class . . . under the charge of a zealous and faithful female instructor, who would teach . . . written language . . . and spoken language," but "the institution should have a male principal and vice principal, men of liberal education, and accomplished sign-makers" who would "lecture daily to the pupils in the language of signs" (Pettergill 1872, 32–33).

The large numbers of women teachers generated a persistent discourse of moral danger. If "the arduous nature of the work" and "the strain on the nervous system" could not induce frail women to seek more compati-ble occupations, then the pernicious effects of pampering, especially on boys, was cited (International 1907, 120). Because there existed an "es-sential difference between the mind of a man and the mind of a woman," the oral schools would "simply develop the female mind in the male body" (Cooke 1902, 279–80).

Women were daily exposed to a male ethic that allowed success, status, and leadership in all areas to men, while they were denied the right to open competition by laws and mores that relegated women to an inferior social position. It is not surprising that in face of obdurate opposition to their presence and their methodology, women set about forming their own parallel profession.

Men made it clear that manualism was their domain. Women, distrusting manualism, distrusted masculinity, which created a need for feminine schools and for female staff. From the outset, the oral schools were female oriented and matriarchal in tone. Institutional aspects were deemphasized and replaced by modes of familial ambience appropriately analogous to middle-class family life (see Numbers 1974).

Curriculum and pedagogy were expressions of changing views of deaf people and their role in society. Decrying the mediocre intellectual products of the manual schools, oral teachers placed an unprecedented emphasis on academic claims, with intellectual development superseding the inculcation of moral values. Reforms in curriculum led to the imposition of rigorous standards and greatly heightened expectations of the intellectual capacities of deaf children. In 1898, for example, Carolyn Yale reported that of the past twenty-five graduates of the Clarke School, nineteen successfully pursued courses in regular high schools and institutions of higher learning (Numbers 1974).

Despite Yale's enthusiasm, it must be remembered that the students in most oral schools were select, not heterogeneous. For example, when Gardiner Greene Hubbard addressed the Massachusetts Special Joint Committee on Oral Schools in 1867, he observed that "if a child were of poor parents, I should not attempt articulation," suggesting that indigent pupils be sent to the American Asylum at Hartford (cited in Moores 1978, 56).

Innovative curriculum and pedagogy within novel instructional milieus were not enough. Oral teachers further held that the course of pure oralism could be more effective in independent organizations and set about creating a parallel profession to that of manual workers.

Denied access to the National Deaf Mute College, academic expertise, and opportunities for status in the manual institutions, women instructors had only one resource to which to turn—a separate training system. For the oral faction, the training of teachers became a pivotal process that validated a sense of separateness from both manualists and common school teachers and transmitted expertise to a new generation of committed women.

The first formal program held in schools for the deaf and led by master teachers emerged in 1889 at the Clarke School when Carolyn Yale established a normal training class "in order more adequately to equip the teachers of her own school" (Moore 1934, 194). In 1892 the Clarke School trained teachers for other schools. Training followed at the North Carolina School for the Deaf in 1894 and the Central Institute for the Deaf in 1914. Through an apprentice-type training unrelated to the university, teachers for oral schools gained professional qualifications and certification.

Based on teachers' own beliefs and the apparent belief of others that their work was particularly challenging, teachers of the deaf have long claimed that "teaching the deaf child is the most difficult job in the whole field of education" (Lane 1952, 497). Personnel required indispensable qualifications above those of general teachers. Training provided a practical knowledge of the oral methods and practice geared to a specific program and situation. It emphasized the importance of a specific body of knowledge for their profession and developed a unique technical expertise, all with a separate lexicon.

Unique attributes attached to potential teachers and expectations regarding their superior teaching skills and personal characters were set high. Trainees, often from the common schools, were carefully selected. When the Horace Mann School, for example, recruited young women, preferred candidates were "gentle, sympathetic, patient, firm, self-sacrificing, and devoted to their work." They had to possess good sense, tact, and skill and "know the principles of education and the best methods of teaching" (Osgood 1999, 93).

As oral teachers established their professional legitimacy, they developed an infatuation with professional status. Treading the paths of other occupational groups seeking to transform work into profession, they developed a professional mien manifested by participation in associations, conferences, and journals.

Journals and conventions served to foster the oralists' conception of themselves as a group separate from the manualists; associations promoted the development of members as a social group with a distinctive style and distinctive values. For example, the American Association to Promote the Teaching of Speech to the Deaf (AASTPD), established in 1891 for the dissemination of the oral creed, was an effective forum. The AAPTSD allowed public advocacy of pedagogical philosophy and enabled the oral teachers to see themselves as a special group of experts with their own professional ideals and values. This was similarly true with the Society for Progressive Oral Advocates begun by Max Goldstein in St. Louis in 1917.

Oral teachers assumed public roles not previously thought consonant with their gender. Yale, for example, earned honorary degrees from Wesleyan and from Mount Holyoke, her alma mater. Sarah Fuller participated in the formation on the AAPTSD. Women were seen as the holders of extraordinary expertise and were widely sought. For example, the principal of the California Institution for the Deaf and Dumb offered a teacher from the Clarke Institution $1,200 in gold to introduce the oral methods into that state (Numbers 1974).

The distinctive cohorts forged with the unique professionalism of oralism together with the structures in which teachers' lives were embedded beg a question. In a period when marriage was universally regarded as the destiny of all natural women, and many young women saw teaching as a transition between girlhood and motherhood, did oral women teachers follow traditional paths? Higher social esteem was accorded to married women, and economic and social reasons meant that women needed marriage more than did men. Nevertheless, oral teachers were protected by entirely women's institutions and a mantle of professionalism.

To isolate a historical question is far easier than to examine it empirically. In this case, interpretation of the world of female teachers presents formidable problems of evidence: figures are not available on marriage patterns. Some data derive from the yearly details of schools for the deaf found in the contemporary literature. In 1903, for example, the Association Review listed the 135 programs in the United States and Canada, the percentage of pupils taught speech, and the names of most, but not all, school principals. The listing gives married women a title; the full names of those who appear to be single. If this interpretation is valid, of the women who led these 62 schools, fifty-one (82 percent) were single; seven (11 percent) were nuns; and four (almost 7 percent) were married women (Wing, "Statistics," 1902).

INTO THE TWENTIETH CENTURY

For female teachers of the deaf, identities were forged amid a bitter ideological battle. Because of their perceived expertise in oral methods, their exclusion from specific university training, the consequent denial of status to them in the manual schools, and the training offered by oral facilities, women staffed, almost exclusively, the oral schools in the final three decades of the nineteenth century. The advent of oralism polarized the masculine and the feminine and their spheres of influence.

As the manual institutions failed to defend their existence successfully against the promises of oralism, the philosophy snowballed and was adopted by parents, educators, and other stakeholders. By about 1910, it became the dominant mode. However, separated from the novel settings envisaged initially, it became, while still the province of women, merely another pedagogical technique rather than the total philosophy practiced by Yale, Rogers, and others in the final three decades of the nineteenth century.

Once oralism was almost universally accepted and men assumed leadership, the frankly militant quest of women faded, and, in this sense, the gender divide disappeared. The two parallel professional strands merged; for example, interest in oral associations such as the AAPTSD waned dramatically (see Goldstein 1876). Literature from the early decades of the twentieth century departs from the factionalism and criticisms of women so pronounced only a few decades before. Teacher recruitment, teacher training, and teacher salaries became a dominant theme.

Teacher training, now entirely in oral pedagogy, defined and refined the nature and legitimacy of the work as well as promoting a sense of separateness and professionalism among practitioners. At the same time, the clientele and types of programs expanded. By 1910, segregated classes within regular schools became a feature of most urban school systems; by the 1920s, two thirds of large cities in the United States and Canada had special classes. Institutions passed into the aegis of departments of education. For hearing-impaired students, the invention of the hearing aid in the 1920s stimulated general or special class placement.

With the burgeoning special schools and classes, the professional paradigms that guided special education shifted and expanded, and the stress on structure spilled over into pleas for expanded professional expertise. As it became important to train teachers in approved methods and to provide them with a sense of vocational identity and spirit, the professionalization and sophistication of teacher training developed steadily. Training teachers of special education for the general schools was initiated at the Michigan State Normal College in 1924 (Lee 1936). By 1930, programs for training special educators in several areas of disability had become widespread.

Deaf education, always separate and very specialized, responded slowly. While the pressure for graduates from accredited training schools began in the first decades of the twentieth century, no clearly conceived pattern of teacher training emerged.

Training was almost exclusively in teacher-training departments of schools for the deaf until the 1940s (Lane 1952). Most programs were an apprentice-type model or in-house plus normal school training. The teachers in training observed and worked with master teachers and at the same time performed a service to the school by aiding the teacher in the classroom and the houseparent in the dormitory (Withdrow 1967). A small number of programs was offered in colleges and universities by 1920, although there was no uniformity in method, purpose, or standards. Programs varied from a few months to two years.

Programs required their participants to undergo training above and beyond that asked of teachers in the standard streams and to bring additional qualifications. Teachers needed "natural qualifications" such as "an attractive personal appearance, a cheerful disposition, good health, and an active, energetic temperament." "Acquired advantages" included a good education and a cultivated mind (Crouter 1917, 293–95).

Programs hoped to acquire the services of college graduates; more often, they recruited from high schools. Numbers (1927) chided that most could not teach arithmetic to the upper grades: "Algebra is entirely out of the question" (343). Moreover, he said, perhaps tongue in cheek, "Oftentimes girls just out of high school don't know how to discipline themselves. Springtime, a moonlight night, and a 1927-model sport roadster, with the accent on the 'sport'—and most normal students forget the technical difference between a consonant and a vowel" (345).

If training was problematic, recruiting enough teachers was a central theme. Lane (1946) pointed out that "unemployment has never been a worry of well-trained and teachers of the deaf" (704); at no time was there a surplus of trained teachers (Craig 1946).

Salaries offered no great inducement. For example, at the Missouri School for the Deaf in 1929 men earned $2,000; women $1,500. Men received one third more than women, although some of the women were doing "incomparably better work than the men" (The salary 1929, 262). Placing salaries on a par was a constant cry of principals. Moreover the pattern of requirements and salaries differed for teachers in residential schools and day schools, and in-house programs lost graduates to the higher-paying school systems.

POSTSCRIPT

During the nineteenth century, women's work in the classroom became deeply entrenched in both general and special education. Much has been made of the two main factors accounting for women's numerical dominance in teaching. One is the ideology of women's sphere and the rhetoric of women's natural mission as teachers. Second was the economic necessity that determined the entry of women into all areas of the teaching profession in the early decades of the nineteenth century.

On the tiny stage of deaf education, the major players were further divided into opposing factions based on lines of sex by virtue of the major theme in the education of deaf people—the controversy concerning the most appropriate communication mode.

Women teachers in the oral schools formed a community of articulate and self-conscious educational innovators, being the carriers of a new professional ideal, dedicated to reforming their profession and thereby drastically altering the parameters of the education of the deaf. Holding a vigorous optimistic outlook, women disseminated their ideas widely, challenging the trenchant conservatism of the manualists not only in relation to pedagogy but also concerning the value and content of the education of the deaf. Every aspect of schooling, from administration to pedagogy, and from finance to the sex of the teachers, was examined and transformed by the oralists; all reforms explicitly related to the explosion of the myth that deaf children could only learn the elements of language manually.

So successful was the campaign of the women teachers to elevate oralism to the status of the dominant ideology that by the beginning of the twentieth century it constituted the preferred mode for educators in the majority of North American institutions for the deaf. Sign language was relegated to the status of a ghetto slang, its use forbidden in the schools.

Women's work in schools for the deaf was universally accepted in the early twentieth century. Issues around separate spheres of influence faded once oralism dominated. All practiced oralism, and a bias along methodological lines was not apparent. Pragmatic concerns of training, recruitment, and retention riveted the attention of the field.

WORKS CITED

American Annals of the Deaf and Dumb. 1852.

American Association to Promote the Teaching of Speech to the Deaf. 1899. Proceedings (except papers and lectures) of the Sixth Summer Meeting of the AAPTSD, held at Clarke School for the Deaf, Northampton, Mass., June 22–28, 1899. *Association Review* 1: 53–106, 162–76.

Bell, A. G., and Gillett, J. L. 1884. *Deaf classes in connection with the work in public schools.* Washington, D.C.: Gibson Brothers.

Berkeley, K. C. 1984. The ladies want to bring about reform in the public schools: Public education and women's rights in the post–Civil War south. *History of Education Quarterly*: 24, 45–58.

Bush, M. G. 1942. The handicapped child helps all children in Wisconsin. *Exceptional Children* 9: 153–55.

Clifford, G. J. 1991. Daughters into teachers: Educational and demographic influences on the transformation of teaching into "women's work" in America. In *Women who taught: Perspectives on the history of women and teaching,* ed. A. Prentice and M. Theobald, 115–35. Toronto: University of Toronto Press.

Cooke. 1902.

Craig, S. B. 1946. Recruitment of teachers. *Volta Review* 48: 701–704.

Crouter, A. L. E. 1907. The organization and methods of the Pennsylvania Institution for the Deaf and Dumb. In *Proceedings of the International Conference on the Education of the Deaf held in the Training College buildings, Edinburgh, on 29th, 30th, and 31st July and 1st and 2nd August, 1907,* 125–55. Edinburgh: Darien Press.

Crouter, A. L. 1917. The training of teachers of the deaf. *American Annals of the Deaf,* 62: 293–304.

De Land, F. 1906. The real romance of the telephone, or why deaf children in America need no longer be dumb. *Association Review* 8: 1–27, 120–35, 205–222, 329–44, 406–427.

Gallaudet, Edward Miner. 1892. Our profession. *American Annals of the Deaf,* 37: 1–9.

Goldstein, M. 1876. Excerpts from the society of Progressive Oral Advocates: Its origin and purpose—1917. *Volta Review* 78: 140–44.

Howard, J. 1902. Men and women teachers. *American Annals of the Deaf* 47: 278–81.

Howe, S. G. 1874. The co-education of the deaf and the blind. *American Annals of the Deaf and Dumb* 19: 162.

Hubbard, G. G. 1876. The origin of the Clarke Institution. *American Annals of the Deaf and Dumb* 21: 178–83.

Lane, H. 1946. Recruitment of teachers of the deaf. *Volta Review* 48: 704–705.

Lane, H. S. 1952. Teacher recruitment and training: A summer meeting panel discussion, June 18, 1952. *Volta Review* 54, no. 49: 500, 512–13.

Lee, J. L. 1936. Problems in organization of teacher training in special education. *Journal of Exceptional Children* 3: 142–43.

Moore, L. M. 1934. Caroline A. Yale—pioneer and builder. *American Annals of the Deaf* 79: 189–96.

Moores, D. 1978. *Educating the deaf: Psychology, principles and practices.* Boston: Houghton Mifflin.

Numbers, F. C. 1927. Advantages and disadvantages of conducting a normal training class in connection with school work. *American Annals of the Deaf* 72: 341–49.

Numbers, M. 1974. *My words fell on deaf ears.* Washington, D.C.: Alexander Graham Bell Association for the Deaf.

Ontario, Department of Education. 1904. *Annual report.* Toronto: Government Printer.

Osgood, Robert L. 1999. Becoming a special educator: Specialized professional training for teachers of children with disabilities in Boston, 1870–1930. *Teachers College Record* 161: 82–105.

Palen, I. 1923. Ears that hear not. *Social Welfare* 5.

Pettengill, E. D. 1872. The instruction of the deaf and dumb. *American Annals of the Deaf* 17: 21–33.

The salary question. 1929. *American Annals of the Deaf* 74: 260–72.

Seguin, E. 1876. Education of the deaf and mute. In *Commissioners of the United States, report to the International Exhibition held in Vienna, 1873*, vol. 2. Washington, D.C.: Government Printing Office.

Seminary for female teachers. 1831. *American Annals of Education* 1: 341–45.

Taylor, H. 1900. The ichthyosaurus, the cave bear and the male teacher. *Association Review* 2: 361–66.

A teacher in a small school. 1902. Is the small school a boon to the deaf? *American Annals of the Deaf* 47: 455–63.

Wheeler, F. 1920. Growth of American schools for the deaf. *American Annals of the Deaf* 65: 367–78.

Wing. 1886. The associative feature in the education of the deaf. *American Annals of the Deaf and Dumb* 31: 22–35.

Wing, G. 1902. Statistics of speech teaching in American schools for the deaf. *Association Review* 2: 298–315.

Withrow, F. B. 1967. Public Law 87-276: Its effects on the supply of trained teachers of the deaf. *Volta Review*: 656–63.

Wright, A. 1915. The manual and oral combination. *American Annals of the Deaf* 60: 219.

Yale, C. 1931. *Years of building: Memoirs of a pioneer in a special field of education.* New York: Dial Press.

"Like Ordinary Hearing Children"
Mothers Raising Offspring according to Oralist Dictates

Emily K. Abel

Uring the early twentieth century, a broad campaign sought to transform maternal practice in the United States. Advice manuals proliferated. Mass-circulation magazines such as *Good Housekeeping* and the *Ladies Home Journal* were filled with recommendations about feeding and disciplining infants and children. National women's organizations, such as the National Congress of Mothers (later the Parent-Teacher Association), the Child Study Association of America, and the American Association of University Women, helped to make maternal education an issue of national concern. Social workers and public health nurses spread the new information to poor mothers in tenements, settlement houses, milk stations, and clinics. Home-demonstration agents carried it to rural communities. Secondary school and college teachers instructed young women in home economics classes. Although advice literature for mothers had long been available, it had never before reached such a broad segment of the population or been presented in such a standardized format.[1]

Advice givers often described themselves as promoting "scientific motherhood," despite the absence of studies to support many of their recommendations.[2] Assuming that uniform standards were applicable to

This essay is a revised version of chapter 9 of Emily K. Abel, *Hearts of Wisdom: American Women Caring for Kin, 1850–1940* (Cambridge, Mass.: Harvard University Press, 2000), 239–50.

all children, experts denigrated mothers' knowledge about individual offspring as well as the intimacy that might form the basis for such knowledge. John Broadus Watson, whose theories underlay the widely disseminated pamphlets of the federal Children's Bureau, titled a chapter of his book "The Dangers of Too Much Mother Love."[3] Mothers were routinely reproved for being "doting," "over-solicitous," and "blindly fond."[4] Because maternal affection resulted in irrational actions, experts claimed, it caused mothers to inflict various types of harm. Those who refrained from curbing infants' "strong and dangerous impulses" produced little tyrants.[5] Rocking, cuddling, playing with, or singing to infants overstimulated them.[6]

Mothers of children with long-term health problems were encouraged to surrender those offspring to institutions. Tubercular children, for example, were viewed as sources of infection that had to be segregated from both the family and the rest of society. Mothers who protested were reproached for overindulgence.[7] The principal recommendation for "feeble-minded" children was permanent institutional placement.[8] When an Ohio mother wrote to the Children's Bureau in 1939 that she hesitated to put her eleven-year-old "Mongolian type" boy in an institution, Agnes K. Hanna, the director of the Bureau's social service division, responded:

> Although we appreciate how difficult it is for you to reconcile yourself to do so, we believe that since the recommendation has been made by competent doctors, that it would be best to place your son in an institution while he is young enough to make a happy adjustment easily. After the first strangeness wears off, he would be happy in the companionship of other boys of his age and capacity, would be taught to be as useful as possible, and he would not be made unhappy by trying to compete with children better equipped than he is.[9]

Professionals often contrasted the reasonableness of institutionalization with the emotionality of maternal resistance. Asked to investigate a two-year-old girl whose mother had consulted the Children's Bureau, a Florida doctor wrote that if the parents attempt to care for her at home, "it will be at the expense of what the Other Members of the family, particularly the Children, should enjoy. In my opinion there is no justifiable reason for giving this attention to a child who absolutely can not appreciate what is being done for Her." The doctor acknowledged that "of course a mother feels much differently towards her own child than someone who is removed from the environment would feel." But he was confident that professional expertise would prevail. "I believe the mother can be brought to see the problem from our standpoint."[10]

Early-twentieth-century mothers of deaf children escaped much of the hostility directed toward mothers of "feebleminded" children. The role entrusted to them was also different. Rather than permanently exiling their offspring to institutions, mothers of deaf children were supposed to prepare them for integration into the broader society. Nevertheless, these women too operated within a set of assumptions that disparaged their attachment to handicapped children and diminished the children's essential worth.

Most nineteenth-century educators of deaf children had been "manualists," emphasizing instruction in sign language and establishing residential schools that fostered the creation of a distinct deaf community. At the end of the century, however, "oralism" became the dominant discourse. Like charity workers and public health nurses encountering immigrants and people of color, oralists preached the virtues of assimilation. Those who founded residential schools taught lipreading and speech exclusively and discouraged the formation of separate deaf cultures. Some advocated boarding school placement only when appropriate day schools were unavailable.[11]

Historian Douglas C. Baynton links the triumph of oralism to the increasing importance of the concept of normality. "Oralists argued that the best principles of work with other children are best also for the deaf, that they were 'trying to make our children like ordinary hearing children,' and would therefore try anything that came 'nearer to making them like hearing people.'"[12] Appearance was almost as important as performance. Even when "normal" functioning was impossible, deaf people were expected to imitate the hearing and thus appear less obviously different.

Here too we are examining a practice considered scientific in the late nineteenth and early twentieth centuries but now widely discredited. Oralist reformers were often educators rather than physicians, but they spoke with the absolute conviction and authority of medical science. Recent

research suggests that the suppression of sign language disastrously affected several generations of deaf people. Although deaf children often
learned to sign eventually, the denial of language during their formative
years seriously retarded their ability to learn.[13] Oliver Sacks cites a 1972
study that concluded that the average deaf eighteen-year-old high school
graduate could read only at the fourth grade level.[14] Today many educators of deaf people provide instruction in the use of sign language along
with lipreading and speech.[15]

Growing numbers of deaf people now regard themselves as members
of a distinct linguistic and cultural minority, but in this essay I consider
deaf children a disabled group because both the experts and mothers I
examine viewed them as such.[16] The essay draws from articles appearing
in the *Volta Review* in the 1930s, as well as from mothers' letters published
by the journal. The *Volta Review* was established in 1899 as the *Association
Review* of the American Association to Promote the Teaching of Speech
to the Deaf, the leading oralist organization.[17] The association's first president was the inventor Alexander Graham Bell, who had deaf family members and advocated integrating deaf people into society to prevent the
"formation of a deaf variety of the human race."[18] In 1910 the name of
the association was changed to the Volta Bureau and the name of the
journal to the *Volta Review*.[19] The journal published numerous articles by
teachers and other experts offering advice for mothers of deaf children. In
the early 1930s, the bureau established correspondence clubs for mothers.
Club members communicated with one another by means of a "roundabout letter," portions of which appeared in the journal each month.
Women who felt deeply alone raising deaf children in a hearing world
looked to the clubs for suggestions, inspiration, and support.

Experts writing in the *Volta Review* shared the dominant cultural belief
that mothers could assume virtually unlimited responsibilities for their
children. "All parenthood means sacrifice," an article proclaimed, "but
the parents of deaf children are called upon far more than the normal
amount because of the extraordinary means that must be used in overcoming the handicap of a missing major sense."[20] Another article noted
that mothers had to take the lead because fathers "may become discouraged, some of them even a bit estranged, from the children who require
so much and respond so slowly."[21]

A central obligation of mothers was teaching their children to speak and read lips. Although schools for the deaf undertook this work, most accepted students beginning at the age of six or seven, long after training was supposed to commence; oralist doctrine held that even infants could, and should, be given special sensory training.[22] Mothers of day school students were supposed to supplement classroom instruction at home in the afternoons and evenings. Those whose children attended residential schools needed to provide extra training during vacations and holidays to prevent laxness and carelessness.

During the intervals between formal lessons, mothers were expected to exert constant vigilance over their children, preventing them from acquiring any of the "telltale" habits of the deaf, such as gesturing or pantomiming. The emphasis on social acceptability also meant that mothers were admonished to pay particular attention to discipline. Deaf children were believed to be especially prone to temper tantrums. One of the hallmarks of the good mother was the ability to control such undesirable displays of frustration and rage.

Mothers also were exhorted to control their own emotions. Baynton argues that late-nineteenth-century oralist leaders tended to sentimentalize the mother-child relationship, which their methods were intended to foster. Rather than surrendering children to the alien culture of deaf schools, mothers could keep their offspring home, teaching them "the satisfying, comforting language of kith and kin."[23] We have seen, however, that mother love lost favor among childcare experts during the 1920s and 1930s. Maternal affection was assumed to be especially dangerous for deaf children. Indulgent mothers responded to gestures, ignored misbehavior, allowed children to play rather than study, and, in general, failed to prepare them for the hostile world awaiting them.

It was especially important for mothers to be wise and intelligent as school age approached. Late-nineteenth-century oralists had envisioned replacing residential schools for the deaf with day schools. Largely as a result of the efforts of oralist leaders, many large public school systems established special schools for the deaf in the late nineteenth and early twentieth centuries. Boarding schools, however, remained the only option for the great majority of deaf students living in small towns and rural areas.[24] Ironically, many oralists now advocated sending deaf children to separate schools in the name of integration. Unlike the earlier boarding schools that oralists had long opposed, these new institutions taught speech and lipreading as the only form of communication, and most prohibited students from signing even outside the classroom. The real tragedy, according to oralist experts of the 1930s, was not the child banished to an impersonal and foreign institution but rather the one "who is kept at home because his parent could not bear to part with him."[25]

Article after article reminded women of the "cheery courage," "invincible spirit," and "endless patience" expected of them. In his study of polio patients and their families in the 1950s, Fred Davis writes that "the paralytic polio treatment procedure is of the quintessence of the Protestant ideology of achievement in America—namely, slow, patient, and regularly applied effort in pursuit of a long-range goal."[26] Like the physical therapy regime imposed on recovering polio sufferers, the job of teaching deaf children to communicate orally in the 1930s was exceedingly arduous, painstaking, and frustrating, involving endless repetition and often producing imperceptible results. One observer compared the effort by profoundly deaf children to master oral communication to that of English speakers attempting to learn Japanese in soundproof glass enclosures.[27] Nevertheless, the *Volta Review* assumed that all mothers could prevail, given sufficient determination, willpower, and optimism.

Extenuating circumstances were rarely noted in *Volta Review* accounts. Inspirational stories about students' achievements typically failed to mention the level and onset of the hearing loss, although both greatly affect the ability to master speech. At a time when conditions in state schools for the deaf were deteriorating, as the Depression forced state legislatures to cut budgets, *Volta Review* authors minimized the differences between public and private schools. The experts also occasionally implied that more women could afford private school tuitions if they were more creative, thrifty, or self-sacrificing. Limited income, like deafness, was simply an obstacle any suitably motivated individual could successfully overcome.

Although the mothers' roundabout letters provide a window into the way women negotiated the messages directed at them, we should remember that they represent a biased sample. The *Volta Review* correspondence club members were overwhelmingly white and middle class. Oralists claimed that their model was culturally neutral, but it has traditionally been associated with social privilege; indeed, one of the attractions of oralism was its promise to keep children apart from the stigmatized deaf community.[28] The children displayed in photographs accompanying the letters typically were impeccably dressed and posed in large yards or affluent houses. Even in the depths of the Depression, most letter writers remained out of the workforce. Many were able to afford private school tuitions or hire special tutors. None identified herself as deaf. We also must be cautious about generalizing from these letters because just a few of the mothers' contributions were published, and rather than including each contribution in its entirety, the editors selected certain portions.[29]

Not surprisingly, the mothers' writings echoed themes found in the journal articles. Many women portrayed themselves in heroic terms, harnessing extraordinary willpower and determination to the task of teaching their children to act like the hearing. Several employed the language of war. A West Virginia mother wrote, "After a period of heartache and despondency we brushed away the tears and bravely began the battle of preparing her for life."[30]

The letter writers also asserted that they cheerfully sacrificed friendships, time alone, and even other household responsibilities to devote themselves to their children. A Texas woman explained how she made time for her son's lessons: "From the very beginning Charles and I have kept regular hours, and have allowed nothing to interfere. My friends have cooperated beautifully. They never telephone me in the mornings, and after the first month or so stopped inviting me to luncheons."[31] When one mother noted that she had just begun transporting her son to day school, another responded,

> I am glad you are getting Richard off to school and that you don't mind the hour's drive. It will take two hours of your day five times a week, but it will be the best ten hours you ever spent. I know because I spend an hour traveling each day to get Billy, and an hour traveling home with him. But I love it, because I know I am helping him in the best way I can. When I call for him and he proudly produces a paper out of the inside pocket of his first suit, I feel that life is grand.[32]

No difficulty was insurmountable. Because appropriate schooling was unavailable locally, two women moved, one to a town with a special public school for the deaf, another to Northampton, Massachusetts, the location of the Clarke School, a well-known private institution.[33] Although one woman feared she would be unable to afford private tuition, she "did manage . . . by undertaking great economies at home."[34] After a flood forced a Harrisburg, Pennsylvania, woman to flee her home, she reported, "Things have been so topsy-turvy for awhile that I have done little else but clean, and get furniture to rights. Yet I've managed somehow to keep on talking to Nancy as much as ever."[35] External hardships occasionally became blessings in disguise. A woman who originally resented having to do her own housework in addition to training her two deaf sons gradually realized that her onerous workload "teaches the children to be helpful, gives me no time to spoil them and affords many opportunities to teach the homely—and homelike—things of life."[36]

The progress women witnessed confirmed their faith in the virtues of hard work. The following quotations are typical: "We can see much improvement in Frank this year, especially in his desire to talk. When we have a guest, he comes and asks the names."[37] "Lately I have noticed [Richard] uses any number of colloquialisms, which make his speech more natural."[38] "We feel that Priscilla is gaining in her ability to read our lips. It is seldom that she fails to get our meaning about things when we try to tell her."[39] "I am just now beginning to appreciate fully the miracle of oral training and we are all getting so much pleasure out of talking to Barbara and asking her about things, just enjoying how much she has learned."[40]

As spoken language improved, children became more tractable. A woman living in Mexico reported, "In the past we had quite a lot of temper tantrums and crying to combat and we are glad that, with her increased power of making us understand and our power to make her understand us, she seems to be an entirely changed child. Her disposition has improved so much, and she is such a happy, lovable child now."[41]

Mothers were proud when their children could pass as hearing. A California mother wrote, "I am sometimes amused at the look of utter bewilderment on the faces of sympathetic strangers and acquaintances (whom

I've told, "I have a little deaf girl") when she barges in with that give-no-quarter-and-expect-none air, and all full of smiles and interest. She usually shakes hands and then drags out candy . . . and passes it—sometimes specifying 'One' if the supply is low!"[42] Another mother wrote, "I take my child everywhere I go, parties and just everywhere. . . . You cannot tell in any way by his actions that he is deaf. He never seems to be puzzled by not understanding what I say."[43] Other women delighted in the friendships their children developed with hearing children. "It is the most wonderful thing in the world to me to learn that children of all ages really like my little deaf boys and want to be with them," wrote an Iowa woman.[44]

Women also took pride in their own sense of mastery. Many letters writers portrayed themselves as accomplished individuals who had learned a set of technical skills and now had valuable experiences and specialized knowledge to share. Women filled their letters with suggestions for others. "I should like to tell you of a little experiment that is working out beautifully for all of us," wrote a mother who made a doll to take speech exercises with her five-year-old son and make him more comfortable with his lessons.[45] Other women described strategies they had perfected for enforcing discipline, engaging babies' attention, and communicating with residential school students who were too young to read letters from home.

Nevertheless, compliance with oralist dictates was often imperfect, even among members of the *Volta Review* correspondence clubs. Some women lacked the material advantages the journal took for granted. "I know I do not devote enough time to Margie," one mother wrote, "but in addition to all the usual work of a housewife I run a filling station, take care of a large yard and do a lot of my own sewing. We live in back of the station and about the time Margie and I get a lesson started someone is sure to stop and want gasoline, so we are usually interrupted."[46] Another wrote, "I believe I am much behind you other mothers with my teaching. I did not start until Eddie was almost 4 years old. You might ask 'Where were you the rest of the time?' Well, you see, I have eleven other children besides Eddie—one younger—so I had no time."[47] Whereas one letter writer extolled the benefits of driving children to school, another noted that she lacked access to a car. The credo that all difficulties could be overcome must have had a hollow ring to many women.

A few letter writers admitted that they departed from key oralist recommendations. "I have a confession to make," a North Carolina mother wrote. "I do use quite a few signs."[48] Another woman unabashedly wrote, "My boys all speak well, and they also use the sign language and the manual alphabet. I think this opens up a world they could never enter by lip reading alone."[49]

Opposition to boarding school placement was common. A mother who lived outside the catchment area of the closest public day school for the deaf wrote, "Peter is a splendid boy, but has his peculiarities. At table he never eats very much, but I try to find things he likes. Another thing, he occasionally has involuntaries [bed wetting] at night, and he would have them oftener if I did not get up with him every night. These are just two of the many things I do for him, and who would understand him and do such things for him if I send him away?"[50] After other mothers tried to extinguish her fears, she decided she was "mistaken" and made plans to visit the state residential school. Nevertheless, she remained ambivalent:

> If I could be sure that in an hour or so he would cease crying, and not carry on until he is exhausted, if I were sure that his pillow would not be soaked with uncontrollable weeping, I could stand it. It is only for the dear child that I feel. I wonder if leaving a deaf child so completely alone and miserable doesn't cause a severe nervous shock, even if it doesn't destroy his confidence in mother, whom he always trusted, and who has never before failed him? I went for two years to a boarding school far from my home, and although I was sixteen I was so homesick I was ill.[51]

A New Jersey mother wrote,

> I visited a residential school and almost decided to send my little girl there as a resident from Mondays through Fridays. But when I came home I had such terrible dreams about her lying in one of those little white beds calling and calling for me, and I couldn't go through with it. I know she probably would not take it nearly so hard as I, but I still can't bring myself around to sending her away from home. She is very sensitive, and to send her off to where

she knows no one and has no one to love and comfort her, especially at night, would have an effect on her personality and character for life. It seems to me it would be like sending one of us to jail.

Although she realized that schools conferred important benefits, she concluded that "a little girl needs the love and association of her parents."[52] Oralist discourse implied that women's empathic knowledge was irrelevant because children were predictable and malleable and could be relied on to respond to standardized training. These mothers, however, continued to trust their own understandings of the characteristics and needs of their offspring.

Some fears transcended children's individual personalities. Reports of cruelty at state schools frightened mothers who could not afford private tuitions. Although women expressed confidence in the private schools they selected, these facilities often accepted students as young as three years old, when children were still closely bound to their mothers and had no way of comprehending their banishment. Moreover, private boarding schools frequently were located hundreds of miles from home.

After children departed, many women continued to express ambivalence, interlacing descriptions of the stunning grief that assailed them with assertions of the advantages of residential schooling. One mother wrote,

> I have just been through the trying circumstances of leaving my little three year old daughter, Joyce, in school. We placed her in Central Institute, St. Louis. It was a three days' drive from our home to St. Louis. . . . She cried a great deal and it was all I could do to restrain myself; but I did not let her see the agony it cost me. . . . We have heard from the school every week, since our return home, and the reports from her teacher . . . have been most encouraging. I miss her more every day. Joyce seems essential to my life. Even her pony comes and hangs his head over the fence, and her dog sits before the door and whines. Her little sister, Helen Ruth, runs all over the house crying, "Oyce, Oyce!" You see, it isn't easy to have her gone, but we feel we are doing the best that can be done for her.[53]

Four months later she wrote, "My deepest fear is that I may have lost something I'll never regain."[54]

Another mother justified her decision to send her young son away to school thus: "He is so strong willed that I feel a residential school is the place for him until he learns there are certain rules which must be obeyed. He is an only child, so the school offers the additional advantage of the companionship of the other children." Nevertheless, leaving him "was one of the hardest things I have ever had to do. There were no tears until we were safely out of sight, but then there was 'a regular flood.' "[55] A New York woman recalled that her son's first years as a weekly boarder at the Lexington School were

> terribly hard for both of us. He cried every Sunday when it came time to take him back to school, and when he used to say, "I don't want to learn how to talk or write, I want to stay home with Mama," it just broke my heart, I had to grit my teeth to see that he arrived at school on Sunday evening. I realized that he had his own way to make in the world, and I wanted to do everything in my power to help make him a good citizen. I used to keep the door of his room closed all week while he was away, for it seemed to me sometimes as if he had died; but I have got over that foolish idea.[56]

Some mothers never reconciled themselves to the loss. At the end of a school holiday, one mother wrote that her daughter "seems to like school better every year. For a week, she kept counting the days, and when we took her back to school she was the first one out of the car and ready to go in. Naturally, this makes us happy at the thought of leaving her where she is so contented and satisfied; but it also gives me a pang to think that she is growing away from us. As she grows older, I fear she will feel that school is really her home."[57]

Departures remained wrenching. "Eddie will soon be home for Christmas," wrote one mother. "I am already dreading the parting that will come after the brief holiday."[58] Another woman confessed, "Some of you speak of having trouble with discipline, and the relief it is to have the children back in school, while I am a regular baby about parting with mine."[59]

The letter writers also displayed a broader range of emotions about the pace of learning at home than the *Volta Review* deemed appropriate. Despite considerable pressure to portray themselves as relentlessly optimistic, some women acknowledged discouragement. "Thank you for your kind remarks about my efforts," one mother wrote to another. "I needed a boost, for, in spite of indications to the contrary I don't always feel like Pollyanna."[60] A Nebraska woman wrote, "My little deaf son's education sometimes seems to me like a long steep hill that is hard to climb and I wonder if we shall ever reach the top."[61] Although the mother added that "it certainly is a consolation to have someone in our group who has almost reached the top," reports of other children's accomplishments sometimes lowered morale. Responding to a request for more information about her daughter, a North Carolina mother wrote, "Frankly, I am ashamed of her progress compared with other children I have read about."[62] A Kansas woman wrote in a similar vein, "Mrs. C. has made such splendid progress with Freddie I am ashamed of my efforts."[63]

In her classic study of women's deference to modern ideals of female physical beauty, Sandra Lee Bartky writes, "Since the standards . . . are impossible fully to realize, requiring as they do a virtual transcendence of nature, a woman may live much of her life with a pervasive feeling of deficiency."[64] Oralism was based on a similar myth of control over nature. The intense training process prescribed by oralists provided one type of communication skill to many moderately deaf, and some severely deaf, children, but virtually none could converse at the level of hearing counterparts. The language development of profoundly deaf children was seriously stunted.

Assuming that maternal responsibility was virtually unbounded, many women blamed themselves when their children failed to fulfill expectations. "I am always under a nervous strain when I take [Kenneth] to and from school," wrote one mother. "I try to get him to stop and look when we cross streets, but he will dash out quickly. I can see more and more the many mistakes I've made. I see that I haven't been as firm with him as I should have been. I've been over anxious about him, and haven't let him feel any responsibility."[65] A Kansas woman, whose son showed little interest in educational games, wrote, "I know it is my mistake somehow, and I need to learn as much as Billy Lee does."[66] A Pennsylvania mother wrote that her daughter's "lip reading isn't progressing as fast as I'd like, but it will come along, I know, after more effort on my part."[67] The many women who expressed a wish for greater patience similarly implied that the problem lay within themselves, rather than with the methods they struggled to apply. Disappointment engendered redoubled commitment, often leading, we may surmise, to deeper discouragement.

Conclusion

Like their offspring, the mothers of deaf children could gain approval from oralist experts and acceptance from the broader society only by conforming to an ideal. Regardless of circumstances, children's personal traits, or the severity of their hearing loss, all women were expected to display optimism, determination, detachment, and self-control. The *Volta Review* pressured mothers to comply with oralist dictates but also provided a forum for chronicling the more complicated realities of their lives. Some correspondence club members expressed joy as their children's speech clarified, temper tantrums disappeared, and friendships with hearing children flourished. The tone of the letters, however, was not uniformly triumphant. Even mothers who adhered closely to the views sanctioned by the journal wrestled with frustration, shame, sorrow, and despair.

Notes

1. See Julia Grant, *Raising Baby by the Book: The Education of American Mothers* (New Haven: Yale University Press, 1998).

2. See Rima Apple, *Mothers and Medicine: A Social History of Infant Feeding, 1890–1950* (Madison: University of Wisconsin Press, 1987).

3. Cited in Grant, *By the Book*, 45.

4. Cited in Jacqueline Litt, "Pediatrics and the Development of Middle-Class Motherhood," *Research in the Sociology of Health Care* 10 (1993): 161–73.

5. Grant, *By the Book*, 45.

6. Julia Wrigley, "Do Young Children Need Intellectual Stimulation? Experts' Advice to Parents, 1900–1985," *History of Education Quarterly* 29, no. 1 (Spring 1989): 57.

7. See Emily K. Abel, *Hearts of Wisdom: American Women Caring for Kin, 1850–1940* (Cambridge, Mass.: Harvard University Press, 2000), 150–76.

8. See Joan Gittens, *Poor Relations: The Children of the State in Illinois, 1818–1990* (Urbana: University of Illinois Press, 1994); James W. Trent Jr., *Inventing the Feeble Mind: A History of Mental Retardation in the United States* (Berkeley: University of California Press, 1994).

9. Agnes K. Hanna to Mrs. L. J. G., Ohio, Dec. 22, 1939, file 7-6-1-3, Records of the Children's Bureau, RG 102, central files, National Archives, Washington, D.C.

10. P. L. Dodge to Archer Smith, June 29, 1933, file 7-6-1-2 (attached to letter of Mrs. A. K. to Children's Bureau, Florida, Feb. 11, 1933), Records of the Children's Bureau, Washington, D.C.

11. For an excellent historical analysis of the oralist campaign, see Douglas C. Baynton, *Forbidden Signs: American Culture and the Campaign against Sign Language* (Chicago: University of Chicago Press, 1996).

12. Ibid., 145.

13. See ibid., p. 5; Oliver Sacks, *Seeing Voices: A Journey into the World of the Deaf* (New York: Harper Perennial, 1990), 28, 142.

14. Sacks, *Seeing Voices*, 28.

15. Baynton, *Forbidden Signs*, 5.

16. See Harlan Lane, *The Mask of Benevolence: Disabling the Deaf Community* (New York: Alfred A. Knopf, 1992); Carol Padden and Tom Humphries, *Deaf in America: Voices from a Culture* (Cambridge, Mass.: Harvard University Press, 1988); Sacks, *Seeing Voices*.

17. Baynton, *Forbidden Signs*, 25.

18. Quoted in Baynton, *Forbidden Signs*, 6.

19. Baynton, *Forbidden Signs*, 102.

20. *Volta Review* (hereafter cited as VR), October 1935, 594.

21. VR, January 1934, 60.

22. John Dutton Wright, *The Little Deaf Child: A Book for Parents* (New York: Wright Oral School, 1928). The Volta Bureau encouraged all mothers of deaf children to read this book.

23. Quoted in Baynton, *Forbidden Signs*, 67.

24. Baynton, *Forbidden Signs*, 66–67; Gittens, *Poor Relations*, 201.

25. VR, January 1937, 18.

26. Quoted in Daniel J. Wilson, "Covenants of Work and Grace: Themes of Recovery and Redemption in Polio Narratives," *Literature and Medicine* 13, no. 1 (Spring 1994): 29.

27. Cited in Baynton, *Forbidden Signs*, 5.

28. See Leah Hager Cohen, *Train Go Sorry: Inside a Deaf World* (Boston: Houghton Mifflin, 1994), 118; Padden and Humphries, *Deaf in America*, 51–52.

29. See VR, March 1935, 143.

30. VR, April 1939, 217.

31. VR, Feb. 1939, 88.

32. VR, April 1939, 215.

33. VR, Feb. 1939, 84; VR, April 1939, 215.

34. VR, Jan. 1937, 22.

35. VR, Sept. 1936, 515.

36. VR, Feb. 1934, 93.

37. VR, April 1936, 209.

38. VR, May 1936, 280.

39. VR, July 1936, 402.

40. VR, Aug. 1936, 519.

41. VR, Sept. 1936, 518–19.

42. VR, June 1937, 345.

43. Ibid., 346.

44. VR, March 1935, 143.

45. VR, June 1938, 337.

46. VR, Aug. 1936, 456

47. VR, May 1936, 282.

48. VR, Dec. 1936, 708.

49. VR, July 1936, 436.

50. VR, Jan. 1937, 19.

51. VR, April 1937, 217.

52. VR, Nov. 1939, 650.

53. VR, Jan. 1937, 18.

54. VR, May 1937, 282.

55. VR, March 1935, 143.

56. VR, Dec. 1938, 697.

57. VR, Dec. 1939, 698.

58. VR, Jan. 1939, 21.

59. VR, March 1936, 146.

60. VR, Aug. 1936, 452.

61. VR, March 1935, 197.

62. VR, Oct. 1939, 602.

63. Ibid.
64. Sandra Lee Bartky, "Foucault, Femininity, and the Modernization of Patriarchal Power," in *Feminism and Foucault: Reflections on Resistance*, ed. Irene Diamond and Lee Quinby (Boston: Northeastern University Press, 1988), 81–88.
65. VR, Feb. 1939, 84.
66. VR, Oct. 1939, 603.
67. VR, May 1936, 281.

Merging Two Worlds

Gina A. Oliva and Linda Risser Lytle

O n a sunny day in May 2002, Summer Crider was first in line as she marched toward the stage with her graduating class. That she was the valedictorian at Florida School for the Deaf and Blind (FSDB) (instead of her local high school) was no small wonder, considering that she had received one of the first cochlear implants in the state of Florida at age six. She attended public schools, mostly as a "solitaire," from preschool through the ninth grade.[1] Summer herself, with the support of her family, made the decision to attend FSDB for her high school years. After attending a summer program for teenagers at Gallaudet University, she had a taste of life with a "critical mass" of D/deaf peers.[2] There was no going back to the mainstream school for her.

In the space of a short paragraph, we have learned of many choices Summer and her parents made, which resulted in the person she is today. First and foremost, we have learned she was highly successful in her academic career. Class valedictorians are first in line. We also learned that Summer's deafness presented a dilemma to her parents, and they chose to deal with it actively and creatively. On the one hand, they provided her with what was considered a controversial surgical procedure at the time—a cochlear implant. On the other hand, they allowed her to attend a summer program at a university for D/deaf students.

We have also learned that Summer spent many of her school years as the only deaf child in her school. However, once she experienced socialization with D/deaf peers, she chose to attend a residential school, and her parents were able to support this. We learned indirectly that Summer's knowledge of sign language began to blossom at a summer program at

Gallaudet. All of these choices, as well as others we have yet to discover, defined the process of Summer's path toward identity as a Deaf woman. The decisions Summer and her parents faced are not unlike those faced by many families of deaf children in today's world. Summer's story may help others to know more about these paths and thus help them in this process.

Erik Erikson (1963, 1968) defines identity versus role confusion as the fifth of eight developmental stages he conceptualized in his pioneering work on human development. Taking place roughly between the ages of twelve to twenty-two, this stage incorporates childhood identity, self-esteem, competence, identification with parents, personal abilities, skills and knowledge, and a concept Erikson calls the ego ideal. The ego ideal is the self one envisions becoming in the future. It includes both one's identification with parents and one's hopes and dreams for the future. Another important part of Erikson's model of identity development is psychosocial mutuality. This central concept of his theory is that an individual could achieve a stable self-concept, but as long as this was unacknowledged by the community, the process of identity would be incomplete. In other words, both the individual and the community must have the same basic definition of the individual, or there will be conflict and confusion. Psychosocial mutuality, as we describe through Summer's story, is uniquely important to the development of identity in D/deaf individuals. A predicament is inherent when a deaf or hard of hearing child is the only such child in her family and/or school.

Several researchers have attempted operational definitions of Erikson's theory. One of the best known was developed by James Marcia (1966). Marcia believed that individuals experiment with various childhood identities until they reach a point where they are able to make some kind of choice or commitment. These commitments about what to believe about various issues (beliefs), how to behave in various situations (moral behavior), and what to become (occupation, other roles) form the basis of identity.

Marcia believed that areas of personal significance, such as occupation, religion, and politics, could be used to study the identity development process. Later researchers, studying the identity process of women and realizing that Marcia's construct was insufficient, added content areas emphasizing relationships, specifically that of sex-role attitudes and sexual behavior (Rogow, Marcia, and Slugoski 1983). Using four of these areas (occupation, religion, sex-role attitudes, and sexual behavior), Lytle (1987) found that D/deaf women and hearing women follow similar processes when developing their identity. However, D/deaf women also had to resolve their beliefs and attitudes about their hearing loss, including dealing with inconsistencies or barriers to psychosocial mutuality.

Because identity development starts in the home environment, it is important to mention Summer's early life, including information about her parents and how they dealt with the diagnosis of deafness in their oldest child. Summer's parents are well educated (Mom has a PhD and Dad has done work toward a master's degree), committed to environmentalist causes, and experienced with using multimedia to promote their causes. This family has strong beliefs and values. Summer's mother, Linda, describes herself as a "researcher," among other things, and it was this characteristic that became prominent when Summer survived the spinal meningitis that left her deaf at age three.[3] Naturally, Linda and Summer's father Dale were both saddened by Summer's hearing loss, but Linda from the start had great expectations for Summer. Summer's father, on the other hand, coming from a background where deafness and other disabilities were viewed with considerable pity and regret, had a much harder time accepting Summer's deafness. Although father and daughter today have a strong bond nurtured in part by their ability to communicate through the Internet, irreconcilable differences magnified by the stress of Summer's deafness caused the parents to part ways when Summer and her sister and brother were still young.

Summer was fortunate that her parents became aware of and open to both the latest technology *and* the Deaf community when she was in her early years. Her mother is the kind of woman who is always trying new things. In 1989, after much testing, reading, talking, and listening on the subject of cochlear implants, Linda Crider decided that her six-year-old daughter would be one of the first children in the state of Florida to receive a cochlear implant. One year later, a colleague introduced Linda to one of the authors of this chapter, and that began the family's involvement with D/deaf adults. Linda Crider, a hearing person with little previous contact with D/deaf individuals, sensed that her daughter would need such association regardless of technological advances. She knew intuitively that Summer would still be deaf, even with her cochlear implant.

Summer's introduction to D/deaf adults and peers ensured that she would have a community of others who saw her as intact rather than impaired. It also ensured that her developing sense of competence and esteem could be measured by experiences with D/deaf children and D/deaf adults whom she and her mother liked, respected, and admired. Summer's involvement with other D/deaf and hard of hearing individuals ensured the healthy development of psychosocial mutuality. By the time she was in high school, she had significant people in her life who were able to mirror her emerging sense of identity.

Even the best prepared and supported D/deaf and hard of hearing children experience their share of frustration and pain within the educational system. Summer's first school placement was in a public school "hearing impaired program." Here is what Summer's mother had to say about Summer's beginning educational journey:

> Basically, they [the first public school Summer entered] were *not* supportive of the implant. Their "hearing impaired" program involved an excellent "self-contained" program, and when I asked to have her "mainstreamed" for several academic classes, they were less than prepared. I would find her sitting in the back of the mainstream classroom with her back to the teacher, facing an interpreter, at a separate table from the rest of the hearing kids. Obviously they didn't "get it." I tried getting them set up with consultants to understand better the mainstreaming concept, but they resisted. I think things have changed since then . . . hopefully. That was around 1991–1992. At [the small private school], she was happy but lost ground because of their philosophy—no textbooks and everything is done orally. At this time, I personally hired [Summer's first interpreter] (the school could ill afford to pay for interpreter. . . . They were a small struggling private school). Two years later, she was accepted into [Summer's second public school]. She had no interpreters in the fourth to seventh grade, but excellent teachers who reorganized their teaching techniques to include her needs . . . overheads for much of the teacher's information . . . handouts, reading, individual one on one.

This worked very well—Summer grew a lot during those years—
even though looking back now, Summer will tell you she still
missed the class discussions. . . . But I knew once she started high
school with lectures and many different teachers, she would be
lost. So that is when I insisted on a sign language *or* oral
interpreter. . . . No one knowing anything about the second category. I settled for a sign language interpreter and then spent
months tracking them down—three consecutive years looking for,
hiring, and dismissing interpreters for Summer. Some were good,
some not so good, and the school, while reluctant, was willing to
pay. One of these interpreters was really special and Summer really
loved her. Summer commented that she was very good as a social
interpreter—that was important for her. She was the one who
taught Summer ASL and helped her to accept her Deafness in a
hearing world.[4]

Summer entered school in 1988, after the Education for All Handicapped Children Act had been in effect for almost fifteen years. Nevertheless, her mother clearly found it necessary to function as a nearly constant
advocate, fighting the school system over something virtually every single
year. Linda had high expectations for her daughter and was not about to
let the school system make success an impossibility for her child.

The expectation of high achievement by parents is important. In find-
ings from the Rimm report, a study of important childhood experiences
of successful women (Rimm 1999), 70 percent of the successful women
respondents believed that both of their parents had high expectations for
them. They were expected to be competent, and they were valued for it.
This sense of personal competence is critically important in the development of identity. Summer's mother had high expectations, and these expectations most likely influenced Summer's academic achievement in the
mainstream program in spite of the obstacles she faced.

With middle school came important changes, and many of the social
skills Summer had developed in elementary school became ineffective.
Various researchers (Orenstein 1994; Pipher 1994) have found middle
school to be a period of drastic reduction in girls' self-esteem. This period
of time for a solitary deaf girl is destructive in ways most cannot even
imagine. Summer described her middle school years of being the only

deaf child in her school as "times of depression, self-pity and just awful." The limited finger-spelling abilities of her peers were no longer adequate. What is more, Summer felt that her implant made her "look like a nerd" so she gradually, with stealth and care, stopped wearing it.

> I had this group in fourth to sixth grade. . . . we were tight, but then new popular groups developed, and some left on their own ways, leaving me alone. Puberty started, and I was very self-conscious about myself. My interpreter started getting on my nerves because she was involved in my social life. Nobody wants a forty-year-old woman sitting and interpreting their gossip and middle school talks! I started thinking nobody wants to be my friend because I'm different, I'm deaf.[5]

Summer relates further that in the middle of her depression, while wallowing in self-pity, her speech teacher confronted her one day, saying in essence, if you want a friend, you need to be one! Summer used this confrontation to turn herself around—when a new girl moved into the school two weeks later, Summer was ready. She ripped out a page of her notebook and started writing to the new girl, and a friendship blossomed. Summer calls this her "wish-granted best friend."[6] This may have been the first time Summer made an active choice that moved her from crisis and resulted in positive change in her identity.

Summer's experiences with peers while being mainstreamed were not unusual. At least two studies have carefully examined how hearing peers communicate with a solitaire in their midst. The picture presented is disturbing. Ramsey (1997) spent a full year observing three mainstreamed seven-year-old deaf boys. She noticed that hearing classmates used a limited sign language vocabulary with the deaf boys in limited ways. The following are examples of such interactions, which Ramsey labeled "directives and hints":

> The children were doing seatwork and [the teachers] were roaming around the room. Janna [hearing] poked Paul [deaf] and showed him the spider-shaped ring she was wearing. Although Mrs. Rogers did not see Janna get Paul's attention, she did notice that Paul suspended work on his math paper to admire Janna's ring. She

called out "Janna, please touch Paul." (This was a method she had developed for enlisting the hearing children's help in physically managing the deaf children's attention.) Janna poked Paul and brusquely signed PAY ATTENTION, a much more explicit directive than Mrs. Rogers' tone of voice indicated. (70)

The hearing classmates would also use their limited sign vocabulary to make evaluative comments, such as "GOOD," to a deaf classmate. Thus, interactions between these deaf children and their hearing classmates were limited to questions and answers about school work or expectations. Ramsey concludes:

> For the purposes of learning and development, the interaction among deaf and hearing children in the mainstreaming classroom . . . was highly constrained and not developmentally helpful. . . . few parents of hearing children would judge sufficient for their own children the personal contact and peer interaction that was available in the mainstream for deaf second graders at Aspen School. (74)

Keating and Mirus (2003) also observed deaf children in public schools, focusing on differences among hearing-hearing interactions, deaf-hearing interactions, and deaf-deaf interactions. Their report includes the following statement about lunchroom conversations:

> While conversational interactions between hearing children most often involve more than two children, deaf-hearing and deaf-deaf interactions were most often dyadic. We observed that dyadic interactions among hearing children are relatively short, and often build quickly to a multiparty interaction involving as many as six children. However, if a third (hearing) student joins a dyadic deaf-hearing interaction, the deaf participant often drops out as the interaction becomes less visually oriented. (123)

In spite of the unfortunate phenomena that these scholars have brought to light, we also know that at least the more successful deaf and hard of hearing children in neighborhood elementary schools tend to have a friend or two who fills their need for a playmate (Oliva 2004). Having a single playmate with whom to engage in active childhood things seems to help solitary children weather the elementary years. When children reach the middle school years, however, more and more informal activities involve conversation rather than physical activity and take place with *groups* of peers. Adolescents thrive on group membership, and the deaf or hard of hearing youngster becomes more and more isolated as the preteenage years proceed. Linda commented, "Summer would come home from school exhausted from the stress of trying to follow conversations and from the pervasive feeling of being left out."[7]

As painful as the preteen years must have been for Summer, she was learning important lessons in resiliency. Erikson (1963, 1968) in his theory of development describes ages six to eleven as stage 3, the development of industry and competence versus inferiority. Rimm (1999) found that "isolation from peers" was mentioned as the most frequent negative childhood experience of the successful women studied. Rimm concludes that valuing independence from peers is important for developing the strong sense of competence and resiliency that characterized these women. Isolation, although a source of great pain, also has the potential to stimulate great growth. It was during middle school that Summer became interested in social activism. She decided to go to Washington, D.C., to attend an animal rights convention. The theme at this convention was "Be a voice for the voiceless." Summer was "trying on" a role. We see, as we look at Summer as a college student, that this role has remained constant, although not focused on animals per se. We can surmise that Summer as a young girl could relate to the "voiceless" because of her (literal and figurative) voicelessness in a strong and vocal family. Without the experience of social isolation, particularly in school, Summer may have not felt the need to act on her political inclinations at such a young age.

What we know from scholars such as Erikson and Rimm about child and adolescent development suggests to us that the solitary and almost-solitary deaf and hard of hearing child's self-esteem and emerging sense of identity takes a beating during puberty. Summer may have been able to salvage some sense of competence from academic achievement, but as she entered middle school and social life started to revolve around relationships rather than games, things started to change for her. Feminist models of identity development such as Gilligan's (1982) suggest that developing connections with others through friendships are important to the development of female identity. What chance did Summer have of forging deep and nurturing school-based relationships when so few of her peers and teachers could communicate with her directly? How could she develop a strong identity when only a few of those around her could finger spell or muster a few signs?

As good fortune would have it, and perhaps also because she had been raised by obviously open-minded parents, Summer had an experience during the summer after ninth grade that changed her impoverished social world. She enrolled in the Young Scholars Program (YSP) at Gallaudet University. This program provides D/deaf and hard of hearing high school students with academically challenging and socially rewarding college-like experiences. For those who, like Summer, have been mainstreamed as solitaires, the YSP is often the first opportunity to spend time with other ambitious D/deaf youth. "YSP was the first time I got the full rich taste of real camp fun, making real friends (still in touch with many of them to this day), and the taste of opportunities without any barriers . . . so many laughs, so many intellectual debates and now have so many memories—I could not stop thinking of them when I returned to school."[8]

Upon beginning the fall semester back in her tenth grade public school classroom, she was struck with how different the two environments were. After that very first day, she walked up to her Mom and declared, "I want to transfer to FSDB. I want to have what I am missing . . . a social life."[9]

Why was Summer able to ask her parents to let her attend the Young Scholars program? More precisely, why was she able to attend that summer institute and allow herself to experience it so fully? Surely part of the answer is that Summer had already been exposed to Deaf culture through her mother's D/deaf friends. Her mother had maintained contact with a Deaf family; the two spent time with this family once or twice a year from the time Summer received her implant. She was perhaps open to the experience of the Deaf community without even realizing it.

Glickman (1986) describes the sense of being caught between the hearing world (which views deafness as a loss) and the Deaf world (where deafness is an asset) as being culturally marginal. It seems that Summer, exposed to her first experience with "opportunities without barriers," chose at that moment in time to move from being marginal to full acceptance of deafness and furthermore allowed herself to desire full acceptance into the community. A defining moment for Summer during YSP was to hear her D/deaf peers describe her as "really friendly, outgoing, and always bursting with ideas." These were very different adjectives from those to which she was accustomed. No longer was she in a community that defined her as a shy, self-conscious, nerdy girl.

Summer describes YSP as a high point in her life. Looking back on that year, she says, "From there on, my life changed—I had much more access to a variety of experiences and I grew up so fast after that year."[10] Many of these new experiences took place at FSDB. Summer arrived in the middle of her sophomore year and immediately began to join as many activities as possible—student council, track, swim team, soccer team, outdoors club, various dance groups, acting clubs, and the Junior NAD (National Association of the Deaf). In Junior NAD, she learned that she had leadership skills and "wasn't limited to anything." Learning that others saw her as a leader became a pivotal point for Summer because it validated her own feelings that she was doing something important and doing it well. For Summer, Junior NAD stands out as important because her "self-love as a Deaf person sort of started there."[11]

In all of these positive experiences, Summer discovered that she and her chosen community (FSDB) could both readily agree on defining her as an effective leader. In her senior year, her peers voted her homecoming queen, and although this honor was a bit politically uncomfortable for her, coming as she did from a strong social activist upbringing, it also was further proof that her peers accepted her as one of them. The years at FSDB were evidently full of that much-needed psychosocial mutuality.

In May 2002 Summer gave the valedictory address at FSDB. The Florida school had an entire weekend of festivities, including entertainment by the graduating seniors. Saturday morning there was a brunch, then graduation, and then dinner. At the actual commencement, Summer gave the valediction. Tears were in many eyes when she held up the universally known "I love you" sign and gave her analysis of what the sign really means.

We will all, sooner or later, realize what our "famous Deaf sign" really means. This [the I LOVE YOU sign] is the greatest hello and the greatest "see-you-later." I refuse to say goodbye because I believe we are going to bump into each other. This sign doesn't mean "I love you, good-bye"; this sign is the greatest "see you later," because I know I will see all of you again in the future somewhere.[12]

This touching commentary was delivered by a young woman who just three years earlier was limited to finger spelling conversations with a handful of classmates. It is clear that she has made friendships and connections that she expects to last throughout her lifetime. Summer, in three short years at FSDB, recognized and claimed the wide and supportive Deaf community as her own. Her classmates publicly recognized her as a bona fide member of their community, which they demonstrated when they voted her homecoming queen. Summer's sense of self and her community's sense of her matched. This is was yet another clear statement of psychosocial mutuality, promoting the solidification of Summer's identity.

With high school drawing to an end, Summer had to ask, what next? One particular friend, a young man who was salutatorian in Summer's graduating class, encouraged her to ignore messages she was getting about staying close to home and to instead join him at Gallaudet University. They agreed they wanted the same thing—"to be able to live as university students without communicative barriers."[13]

Gallaudet's barrier-free communication environment has helped Summer continue to develop both emotionally and intellectually. One thing she loves about Gallaudet is the international flavor, both in students and in opportunities to study abroad. She has just returned from a five-month-long study-abroad program in Costa Rica. She has chosen a self-directed major in "psychology and the expressive arts" and dreams of being able to help others find ways to communicate their thoughts, feelings, and experiences, even when they may not have words. Summer's choice of career goals reflects much about her own experiences growing up as well as gives her an area where she can improve the world.

Summer's identity continues to evolve in her undergraduate years as she finds parts of herself through her relationships with the men she dates.

She admits that she used to dream of marrying a hearing man and has enough insight to know this was mostly a reflection of her own inferiority about being deaf. In discussing what she learned from dating D/deaf men, she states:

> I realized I wanted someone who was "half-Deaf" and was able to give me Deaf children. Our hearing status (me with my implant and him being hard of hearing) gave us many opportunities to use different modes of communication—I would talk to him, sign to him, listen to music with him, learn words and lyrics together. I was elated to find someone who was "in both worlds" as I am. This made me realize what I wanted in a husband.[14]

In addition to dating Deaf men, Summer has dated both deaf and hearing men who have Deaf parents, a group of people known in the community as CODAs (children of Deaf adults). Relationships with CODAs raise dependency issues for Summer. This has resulted in a determination to not depend on her hearing boyfriend to constantly serve as her interpreter. She makes her phone calls through the relay and orders for herself in restaurants.

Relationships with D/deaf men and with CODAs give her even more to think about in terms of her future family. These relationships expose her to the possibility of having a family where signing rather than speaking is normal for *every* member. Even so, at this point, Summer is able to say that the hearing status of her future spouse is not an issue because she has chosen to be part of the Deaf community and she expects her family to be part of it as well. Although Summer is ready to adjust and accommodate to others, she clearly expects this to be a two-way street, with her family making accommodations for her as well. Summer has a clear picture of the future she wants for herself:

> I envision myself being a wonderful mother who frequently takes her kids around the world, exposing them to different beautiful things. I also dream of adopting deaf children from other countries. As a professional, I already have my career goals set up for me—being a creative artist. I have passion to explore the world and to learn the lessons other countries and cultures will teach

me. I hope to merge all my careers, family, and dreams together. Whoever I marry, what kind of kids I will have, and where I live would all be based on my happiness—and I am pretty sure I am a good judge of my happiness.[15]

As does any D/deaf individual from a hearing family, Summer deals with communication issues daily. As she grows and has new experiences (such as spending a semester in Costa Rica or having a boyfriend from a Deaf family), new issues arise and old issues change and need to be addressed. These new experiences prompted her to express her feelings about communication within her family.

> My family members, when it comes to communicating with me individually, do just great. They always have their hands up in the air; they each have a weird combination of very "SEE" signs, the Rochester method (endless finger spelling), home signs, ASL, and voice. If they were communicating within the Deaf community/ with other Deaf people, I would rate them "understandable." I think the most important thing is that they chose to teach me sign language when I became deaf and they accept sign language as my language. It is, however, hard when they talk to each other in my presence, they usually don't sign. Last night, we had this intense discussion about my feelings that the family should learn to sign to each other in my presence so that I have access to information—I just had enough of being left out of these conversations. I think all my experience with Gallaudet, Deaf community in general, and the Costa Rican Deaf culture has made me really analyze my family situation. It is my responsibility to teach them, make them aware. I am glad I brought it up to my family and even more grateful that my family understood and agreed to try and change for me. Hopefully in the future I will see everyone sign at the dinner table and I won't have to worry about whether I should bring my Deaf friends or Deaf family to spend time with my family.[16]

Summer's mother is a particularly important person in this narrative, and Summer sees her as the most influential person in her life. She says she sees herself becoming more like her mother each day, and she actually says this with a smile. They are very close, conversing regularly through e-mail and instant messaging when they are apart. Although Summer finds other women to admire, her mother is still her primary role model. Summer is unabashedly proud of her mother, saying, "Sure, there are other women in my life that are important to me. But many of them resemble my mother."[17] She looks up to women who have struggled with various issues and who are hard working, self-assured, and good mothers able to offer lots of love.

Summer is pretty much describing herself when she describes her mother. Both Summer and her mother have had strong drives for independence. Both are also able to put their thoughts and dreams into action, and both are able to somehow combine the creative with the intellectual. They are strongly goal-directed individuals. Linda was able to raise three children by herself and is now building a cabin in Alaska. Summer, as we just learned, asked for a school transfer while in tenth grade and in college chose to spend five months in a new country. They, and Summer's father as well, share a strong social and environmental consciousness. The relationship Summer has had with her mother has evolved over the years, and the connection between the two has strengthened as the years go by. It is a connection they both can count on, in spite of Summer's Deafness and Linda's hearingness. Summer seems secure enough in her own identity that she is not overwhelmed by her mother's.

In talking about Summer, we have touched on various themes relevant to the identity process. Summer was perhaps unusual in the fact that many of her crisis points occurred for her in early adolescence. Dealing with deafness in a mainstreamed program may well have been the impetus for such crisis and commitment to change. Learning she had the power to affect positive changes for herself most likely prompted further changes. Deafness and communication issues are a dominant thread throughout this story as Summer weaves together the various parts of her identity.

Josselson (1987, 2002) believes that identity in women is far more about the kind of person one will become than it is about occupational choice or ideological beliefs. The emphasis on interpersonal relationships and on connections seems a uniquely feminine aspect of identity development. For Summer, this certainly seems true. We see her mother as her primary source of love and approval and, although we learned less about her father and siblings in this treatise, their love and support seem vital as well. D/deaf friends, hearing friends, teachers, interpreters, and boyfriends all are important. In all of her choices for fields of study, activities, and career, Summer has chosen ways to help others and to improve the world by relating to others in ways that are mutually satisfying. Because interpersonal competence is so vital to successful identity development for women, it is important to ask what would have happened to Summer if she had not had that "aha!" moment with her speech therapist nor had the opportunity to attend YSP. These were both formative experiences for Summer, without which she would probably be a different person.

As an adventurer, researcher, and pioneer, it should be no surprise that Linda produced a documentary, *Summer's Song*, about the process of deciding to get Summer an implant. It should be further no surprise that Summer herself made the sequel, *Summer's Story*, during her senior year of high school. Both are driven by altruism to educate people who could benefit from knowledge that may still be elusive today.

Narratives and life stories are becoming increasingly important as ways to understand people and are appearing more frequently in the field of psychology. This chapter offers a unique way to understand the identity process of D/deaf women—in reading the story of Summer, we learn much about communication and connection as vital parts of female identity.

Studying the lives of individual D/deaf women through subjective telling and interpretation adds an element to psychological research that is rich and revealing and can inform further research.

NOTES

1. Oliva (2004) coined the term *solitaire* to indicate a D/deaf or hard of hearing child who is essentially the only such child, or one of a small handful of such children, in her school.

2. We use D/deaf to be inclusive: The capitalized *Deaf* has been used to refer to individuals who consider themselves culturally Deaf whereas the lowercase *deaf* refers to the absence of hearing. *D/deaf* is used to include both groups.

3. Linda and Summer Crider, interview by Gina Oliva and Linda Lytle, December 2004.

4. Oliva 2004, 172–73.
5. Linda and Summer Crider, interview.
6. Linda and Summer Crider, interview.
7. Linda and Summer Crider, interview.
8. Linda and Summer Crider, interview.
9. Linda and Summer Crider, interview.
10. Linda and Summer Crider, interview.
11. Linda and Summer Crider, interview.
12. Summer gives credit to one of the YSP counselors, a Deaf man named Francis Cooney, who explained to the participants at the "good-bye circle" that in the Deaf community there is effectively no good-bye; the sign for "good-bye" really means "see you later." She attributes Cooney with teaching her this important part of Deaf culture.
13. Linda and Summer Crider, interview.
14. Linda and Summer Crider, interview.
15. Linda and Summer Crider, interview.
16. Linda and Summer Crider, interview.
17. Linda and Summer Crider, interview.

Works Cited

Erikson, E. 1963. *Childhood and society.* 2nd ed. New York: Norton Press.
———. *Identity: Youth and crisis.* New York: Norton Press.
Gilligan, C. 1982. *In a different voice: Psychological theory and women's development.* Cambridge, Mass.: Harvard University Press.
Glickman, N. 1986. Cultural identity, deafness, and mental health. *Journal of Rehabilitation of the Deaf* 20: 1–10.
Josselson, R. 1987. *Finding herself: Pathways to identity development in women.* San Francisco: Jossey-Bass.
Josselson, R. 2002. *The space between us: Exploring the dimensions of human relationships.* San Francisco: Jossey-Bass.
Keating, E., and G. Mirus. 2003. Examining interactions across language modalities: Deaf children and hearing peers at school. *Anthropology and Education Quarterly* 34, no. 2: 115–135.
Lytle, L. 1987. Identity formation and developmental antecedents in deaf college women. PhD diss., Catholic University of America.
Marcia, J. 1966. Development and validation of ego-identity status. *Journal of Personality and Social Psychology* 34: 551–58.

Oliva, G. A. 2004. *Alone in the mainstream: A Deaf woman remembers public school* Washington, D.C.: Gallaudet University Press.

Orenstein, P. 1994. *School girls: Young women, self-esteem, and the confidence gap.* New York: Doubleday.

Pipher, M. 1994. *Rescuing Ophelia: Saving the selves of adolescent girls.* New York: Ballantine Books.

Ramsey, C. 1997. *Deaf children in public schools: Placement, content, and consequences.* Washington, D.C.: Gallaudet University Press.

Rimm, S. 1999. *See Jane win: The Rimm report on how 1,000 girls became successful women.* New York: Three Rivers Press.

Rogow, A. M., J. E. Marcia, and B. R. Slugoski. 1983. The relative importance of identity status interview components. *Journal of Youth and Adolescence* 12: 387–399.

Part Three

Reading Deaf Women

Editors' Introduction

The broad theme of this section is the body as a vehicle for cultural manifestation. The essays here explore various corporal characteristics in the expression of Deaf and gendered identity. Brueggemann illustrates the creative, authoritative space offered by deafness for two women during what was an otherwise particularly disadvantaged age for deaf people (the turn of the twentieth century). Forced away from teaching because of their hearing losses, the Allen sisters' deafness actually became the shaping force that allowed them to maintain—via the double vision of their shared photographic art—a self-sufficient, authorized, and meaningful space in the hearing world. Harmon's work, like Brueggemann's, traverses the boundaries between Deaf and hearing worlds, describing negotiated space and the challenge of language barriers. This first-person account offers an exploration of cultural identity that blends the public-private, Deaf-hearing, and religious-secular worlds.

In contrast, Kelly focuses on Deaf women and language issues. Her essay explores how five Deaf female ASL teachers define terms such as "gender," "feminism," "sex," and "patriarchy" in ASL and English. The results of her study suggest the need to raise "female consciousness" among Deaf women and the significance of incorporating feminist terms into ASL teaching. The ethnographies by Harmon and Kelly both provide first-hand observations on (Deaf/gendered) identity and (Deaf/gendered) language.

Employing feminist and film theory, Nelson assesses language and the body from a perspective outside the Deaf community by examining two Hollywood depictions of deaf or mute women. Her critique of "muteness envy," further extended in her argument to "linguistic envy," reveals powerful links between idealized silence and sexual control. Films such as

The Piano and *Children of a Lesser God*, she argues, "are ultimately about the colonial struggle over the envy of language, art, body, voice, and self, as played out on a gendered stage." Burch complements and complicates Nelson's line of thought here by assessing the rise and continued popularity of American Deaf beauty contests throughout the twentieth century. These competitions primarily emphasized the physicality of women while denying or downplaying their Deaf cultural identity. At the same time, such pageants challenge prevalent notions of "the perfect body" exhibited by mainstream beauty contests. Taken together, the five essays in this section critique literal bodies and "voices" of deaf women, questioning definitions of beauty, success, normalcy, cultural Deafness, and hearing.

"Reading," as a highly visual activity, has additional meaning in the Deaf world, and the chapters in this section demonstrate new interpretations for their fields (history, ethnography, rhetoric, and American studies) by rereading women's bodies with a Deaf cultural lens. Through such rereading, a relationship with the audience (the ones who are "reading") plays an important role. How "Deaf" and "female" becomes read in each of these five essays—and the audience/reader's active role in that reading and shaping of deafness, gender, language, body—is a key process taken up in the chapters of this section. Performance and the role of media also figure prominently in these works, as the connections between (Deaf/gendered) language and the (Deaf/gendered) body play on various stages and are delivered via various media. Finally, by emphasizing multidisciplinary and interdisciplinary approaches, the authors of these essays also promote methodological models that blur traditional boundaries, double our critical vision, and encourage us to ask new questions about the implications of gender and deafness.

QUESTIONS TO CONSIDER

- How do *media* affect the representation and expression of identity/ies?
- What are the *relationships* among language, identity, and the body that are highlighted in these essays?
- How is the relationship and space between the *subject* of these essays and the *self* (of the author/scholar writing the essay) negotiated methodologically and stylistically?

- What roles do the *audiences* play in the performance of gender, identity, language, and deafness in these essays? How is deafness or gender *performed* and also *read* visually in the spaces and scenes presented by these authors?

Deaf Eyes
The Allen Sisters' Photography, 1885–1920

Brenda Jo Brueggemann

"The Misses Allen" they were most often called—personally, by
those who knew them in Deerfield, Massachusetts, and also pro-
fessionally, by those critics who wrote about their photography at the
time. Although their individual names appear in relationship to a few of
their photographs, more often than not they appear as a unit, Mary and
Frances Allen together: The Misses Allen. For nearly fifty years they were
companions in art, work, communication, and everyday life.

A "Well-Rounded Life, in the Chiefest of Things"

Frances and Mary Allen were born to a successful farmer, Josiah Allen,
and his wife, Mary Stebbins, in the town of Deerfield, Massachusetts.[1]
Frances, born in 1854, was the oldest of four children, and Mary was

This essay is based on a lecture given at the Columbus, Ohio, Museum of Art
on February 17, 2005. The lecture was in conjunction with an exhibition of the
Allen sisters' photography at the Columbus Art Museum sponsored in part by
the Ohio Humanities Council and the Collaborative Public Humanities Institute
at The Ohio State University, directed by Dr. Christian Zacher. Dr. Zacher,
Kristina Torres, and Bobbi Bedinghaus were integral in making the lecture successful (and accessible to Deaf and hearing audiences alike); I acknowledge and
thank them for their collaboration and support. Photographs by the Allen Sisters
appear courtesy of the Pocumtuck Valley Memorial Association, Memorial Hall
Museum, Deerfield, Massachusetts.

Mary Electa Allen

Frances Stebbins Allen

born four years later in 1858. They had two younger brothers. The Josiah Allen family was an extended one; numerous close relatives were always stopping by. They also housed many boarders during the children's younger years—especially young, unmarried, female teachers for the local school. In the fall of 1874—when Frances (often called "Fanny" at that time) was twenty years old and Mary (known sometimes as "Mame") was sixteen—they began, together, a two-year program at the State Normal School teacher's college in Westfield, Massachusetts. Upon graduation from the normal school, Frances spent the next ten years, from 1876 to 1886, teaching school. Mary's health was reportedly poor during this period so her teaching was rather sporadic.

By 1886 their hearing loss had become great enough that they both gave up teaching. The specific source of the loss is as yet unknown, and the sisters did not develop significant problems until they were in their early thirties. The best medical guess we have today is that their loss might have been the result of otosclerosis, a hardening of the bones of the ear. This condition, once thought to be the result of chronic ear infections or the toll of typical childhood illnesses, is now known to be largely genetic.

True to the pattern of the Allen sisters, it may not appear in a significant way until the middle years of a person's life. In 1893—when they would have been thirty-nine and thirty-five, respectively—the two sisters took a hundred-mile trip by train to Boston to be examined at the Massachusetts Eye and Ear Infirmary. The doctors determined that Frances would not benefit from surgery on her ears but that Mary might. Thus, surgery was performed on Mary but proved unsuccessful. Mary Allen apparently made use of an ear trumpet for some time. However, she eventually complained that it did not work very well, and so she gave it to her neighbor, Lucy Andrews, who was also deaf (and who had ten children). Even with two owners, the ear tube—which was sold as a "conversation tube" in the 1902 Sears, Roebuck catalog—survives in apparently excellent condition (see figure 1) (Flynt 56). Those of us who have used hearing aids with the same lack of overall utility as Mary Allen and Lucy Andrews experienced, and who thus eventually retired them to our sock drawers, might well imagine Mary Allen's "conversation tube" nestled among the knickers of either of these two women at the time.

In 1897, after they had already embarked on their second career as photographers, Mary—who was often writing letters—corresponded with her friend and cousin, Ellen Gates Starr, about their position and life in

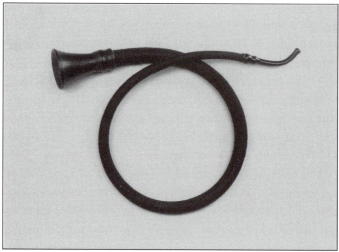

FIGURE 1. Mary Allen's ear trumpet, c. 1902.

relation to their hearing loss.[2] Starr responded with words that are remarkably wise and forward thinking given the reality of what it must have
been like for two single women who had just lost their first careers (and
one of the few careers available to women at all during this time): "No, it
isn't a maimed life. It is a difficult one—hard & trying often; but those
who having eyes see not & having ears hear not, they live the maimed
life. Yours is a well rounded one, in the chiefest of things" (Flynt 22).

Although certainly their hearing loss could not have been heartening,
the fact remains that it did foster their new careers in photography just as
it added to their mutual support of each other. Although the official historical records state that Mary and Frances "remained single" all of their
lives, in fact nothing could be further from the truth. Not only did they
have each other in an obviously rich and rewarding nonsingular relationship, but they also had thick and multiple relationships with their Deerfield neighbors, their extended family, and several key women of the
time—most notably Ellen Gates Starr; the social reformer Jane Addams,
who cofounded the Hull House in Chicago; and Frances Benjamin Johnston, a foremost photographer and critic of the "pictorial" school of photography that was becoming so popular at this time. Finally, out of their
deafness and their close relationships, they generated a kind of "life of the
eye" through the lens of photography.

It is likely that the Allen sisters learned about photography from their
brother, Edmund Allen, who often took photographs for his job as a civil
engineer in the 1880s, the same time that they were going deaf and leaving their careers as teachers. Edmund himself began using the camera
outside of his engineer's job when his four daughters were born, between
1888 and 1895. By at least 1884, Frances and Mary were photographing
using a view camera and creating albumen prints. There is, for example,
a wonderful image taken by Frances of Mary standing beside a view camera in 1885, which would have been at the very beginning of their photographic careers.[3]

The Allen sisters had been taking pictures, using photography as both
art and income, for nearly fifteen years before their moment of national
and international fame. Brought along with thirty other American women
photographers to be featured in the 1900 Universal Exposition in Paris,
the Allen sisters found themselves the center of considerable attention

when the exhibition organizer, Frances Benjamin Johnston—herself a well-known photographer and critic—declared the sisters two of the "Foremost Women Photographers in America" in a July 1901 issue of *Ladies Home Journal* (Flynt 42).

Despite their popularity as photographers even in their local area (neighbors reported having to put signs on their own doors warding off lost Allen sister visitors),[4] and despite their considerable artistic and competitive success, when they did choose to exhibit their work in larger public exhibits and contests, the Misses Allen remained remarkably modest about their work. In a March 1894 article in the photography journal the *Photo-Beacon*, the sisters present a quite unpretentious "Prize-Winners' Account of Themselves." This account contextualizes well the sisters' own vision of their work and is worth repeating, at least in part:

> Our methods are too simple to have much interest for the skilled amateur photographer who tries all the new processes. We use the camera simply as a quick way of sketching, and regard all the technical part, which comes after the exposure is made, as a necessary evil. . . .
>
> In pictures, artistic excellence is usually entirely at variance with what is called a perfect photograph. The eye cannot focus itself on every object in its field of vision at the same time. If a photograph does this, the effect is hard and unnatural. But there must be method in this madness. A picture is not necessarily beautiful because it is blurred, and there's need of all one's technical skill, even after a negative is made, in adapting the print to its peculiar individual qualities.
>
> The merit of posing, which you kindly give us credit for, belongs rather to the models. Our chief virtue is in letting them alone. We usually have better success with children who are not too highly civilized, or too conventionally clothed, or who are too young to be conscious. We give them a general idea of the picture we want, and then let them alone until they forget about us and the drop catches an unconscious pose. They consider it a game, as we are always ready to play at it. (Flynt 27)

As their modest comment on their art demonstrates here, the sisters' particular success at the kind of art "pictorial" photography being made popular at this time was chiefly with children, although they also excelled at photographing colonial recreated scenes of work and home, local citizens at work or play, and local landscapes. Throughout their photographic career Mary repeatedly described their work as somewhere between "art" and "craft." This midway designation may have been in part because their photography served at least a dual function for them as both artistic expression and basic income. For even while their images garnered attention in competitions and art-focused publications, the Allen sisters also used it as a source of income. Their income-producing photography can be divided into two categories: portrait photography (including sittings arranged for people who traveled to have their portraits done by the sisters) and photographic illustrations for magazine articles.

They opened their own formal studio in 1901 by converting an upstairs bedroom into their darkroom; the parlor downstairs became the salesroom. The conversion of a typically "hearing" social space, the parlor, into their salesroom, a place now dominated by the eye—a space centered around visual communication—seems particularly appropriate. In 1904 they began publishing catalogs of their images. Their last catalog was published in 1920. Mary apparently went on with some of the business throughout the 1920s—well into her sixties—but Frances's sight began to deteriorate considerably during that decade. Although she became both deaf and blind, Frances continued to work in her garden, and she walked the equivalent of a mile every day on their front porch. Frances died first, at the age of eighty-seven, on Valentine's Day, February 14, 1941. Always but always together, Mary died only four days later, February 18, at the age of eighty-three.

In a Community: The Arts and Crafts Movement in Deerfield

Some part of the Allen sisters' success at photography—whether as art or craft, income or aesthetics—would have been due to their local historical circumstance as citizens of Deerfield, Massachusetts, at the turn of the past century. Deerfield was a town deeply engaged in the local arts and crafts movement that swept much of America at the turn of the century, and it was regarded for "its four-fold aspect which makes up the background for human happiness,—rural peace and plenty, historical associations, artistic expression, and intellectual alertness" ("Deerfield," 53).

Mary Allen herself was one of the original four members of the Deerfield Society of Blue and White Needlework; in fact, she designed its trademark, a blue "D" within a flax wheel (see figure 2). This society of embroiderers was held up as a kind of model community for arts and crafts at the time, as was noted by the *Chicago Daily News* in 1897: "The Deerfield Society of Blue and White Needlework is a national product of our awakened interest in things colonial and in handsome things rather than in those turned out by the dozen from machines; it is also an example of the Ruskin notion of establishing village industries and promoting rural crafts" (Flynt 32).

In fact, for a number of years Mary was often torn between embroidery and photography. In a 1898 letter to Francis Benjamin Johnston she

FIGURE 2. Deerfield Society of Blue and White Needlework.

wrote that the two "still elbow each other, & I am no nearer deciding which master to serve" (Flynt 33). But by 1900, when Johnston convinced the Allen sisters to exhibit some of their prints in the famous Universal Exposition in Paris, photography seems to have become the dominant elbow for her. Yet the relationship between their photography and the larger arts and crafts movement was still often two handed, as their biographer Suzanne Flynt has noted: "Frances and Mary Allen served two critical, but distinct, roles in the Deerfield Arts and Crafts movements: their handcrafted photographs were among the town's artistic offerings and their images of craft workers publicized the town's activities" (Flynt 33). The photographic work of the Misses Allen was always handcrafted, aesthetic, subtle, careful, and yet simple, and these qualities matched and advanced those of the overall Arts and Crafts movement in America at the time.

What is more, their location in Deerfield, Massachusetts, was crucial to the content and composition of their photography as they made the most of their local subjects.[5] The Allen sisters excelled, for example, at four overlapping kinds of photographic compositions that all somehow made use of local scenes and subjects. First, their images often capitalized on the still potential nostalgia of farming in the area (see figures 3 and 4). Second, they often recreated colonial life (another form of nostalgia of the time) through the portraits of local subjects (their friends, neighbors, and family most often) who willingly posed for them in colonial scenes and costumes and through their photographic documentation of annual pageants that often featured colonial themes (see figures 5–8). Third, they excelled and capturing and composing nature's paradoxical grandeur and simplicity in their local environment as well as through some foreign travel and a trip to the western United States (see figures 9 and 10). Fourth, and perhaps most successfully, their photography often exhibited the simple yet rich lives of children (see figures 11–13).

Living in Deerfield had additional relevance for the Allen sisters. Deerfield is located only twelve miles from Northampton, Massachusetts, which is home to the Clarke School for the Deaf. Founded in 1867, this school was the first permanent oral school for the deaf in America, and to this day it remains one of the premier oral-focused educational centers for deaf and hard of hearing children in America, if not the world. The Allen

FIGURE 3. Onion Harvest.

FIGURE 4. Sharpening the Scythe

FIGURE 5. Betty at the Churn.   FIGURE 6. The Letter of the Law

FIGURE 7. Spirit of the Wheat.

FIGURE 8. Anachronism.

FIGURE 9. Snowstorm.

FIGURE 10. Red Winter Sunset.

FIGURE 11. Eleanor Brown
Stebbins (1875–1955)
(Mrs. Benjamin Stebbins)
Washing a Child's Hand.

FIGURE 12. Making a Dam.

FIGURE 13. Little Girl & Doll at a Tea Party.

sisters both took some lipreading lessons at the Clarke School; however, they did not do well at them. Although Mary continued to give lipreading some effort and practice, Frances—who was also apparently more deaf than Mary—abandoned lipreading and oral efforts altogether and relied primarily on writing to communicate with others. (There is, for example, a wonderful image taken by Mary Allen of her sister, Frances, exchanging a written note with one of their young nephews.) But given that the oral method dominated in the education of deaf children (and adults) at this time, the sisters' proximity to the very center of American deaf oral education certainly would have affected the way they went about being "deaf" and interacting in a hearing world.

WOMEN AND PHOTOGRAPHY: A TURN OF THE TWENTIETH CENTURY SNAPSHOT

Alfred Stieglitz, father of the pictorial movement in photography and instigator of the renegade "photo-secession" movement at the turn of the twentieth century, wrote to Frances Benjamin Johnston in summer 1900 that "the women in this country are certainly doing great photographic work & deserve much commendation for their efforts." Commendation was indeed quick in coming, as Johnston organized, on very short notice, the history-making exhibit of thirty-one American women photographers at the Universal Exposition in Paris in both 1900 and 1901. The exhibit was so successful that it went even more international when W. I. Sreznewsky of St. Petersburg commissioned the exhibit to travel to Russia.

Johnston herself was a formidable figure in American photography; she compiled a string of impressive firsts: the first White House photographer, the first woman member of the Washington D.C. Camera Club, the first woman really involved in underground photography, and a prolific critic and author (on the subject of photography and art) (Curtis 24). For the Universal Exposition in Paris, Johnston particularly sought out and encouraged those women doing what she deemed as "art photography." Furthermore, records of her correspondence indicate that she believed that the inclusion of professional photographic work by three American women photographers in particular was essential to the exhibit: Zaida Ben Yusuf from New York, Mabel Osgood Wright from Connecticut, and the

Allen sisters of Deerfield, Massachusetts. From the outset, photography developed as a field that offered women multiple and previously unmatched possibilities. Here, at some necessary and illuminating length, is how contemporary photography scholar Verna Posever Curtis explains these possibilities in an essay about Francis Benjamin Johnston's role in "staking the sisterhood's claim in American photography":

> It was true that the field of photography, in particular, offered women life-fulfilling possibilities. The will to experiment in a promising endeavor motivated those seeking their independence in the last quarter of the century. Photography allowed women to show their mettle in socially acceptable ways without being bound to predominantly male patronage or to the academic tradition of the fine arts. Qualities that were advantageous to the picture-taking, developing and mounting processes—such as deftness, attention to detail, good taste, patience and perseverance—were regarded as innately female, or at least were reinforced through training in such household arts and crafts as spinning or needlework. Indeed, mastery of photography required what was then expected of the female sex. In photographic portraiture, to cite one area, women who radiated graciousness and tact were at a great advantage with sitters. (29–30)

It is striking how Curtis's list of advantageous qualities for success at photography mirrors, in essence, those qualities deemed most desired for teachers: deftness, attention to detail, good taste, patience, and perseverance. Yet teaching was clearly a hearing vocation (at that time, if not always), and photography, quite conveniently, could facilitate the deaf and "silent," but ultraobservant, faculties of the photographer's "eye."

In their thirties, the Misses Allen, who trained first as teachers and who earned their own income as well as their independence, found themselves struggling to communicate in an oral and aural world. In fact, when Johnston wrote to the Allen sisters early in 1900, requesting that they submit some photographs and a biographical sketch for consideration as part of the famous Paris exhibition, Mary Allen responded modestly about their work and their biographies. Although Mary hints at the role of their deafness in coming to photography, she does not, of course, directly name it:

I will send you a few prints to show what sort of work we have
done in a few days. I should be glad to compose an autobiography
also, but you know already all there is to know. We have no
"methods" and no "conditions." We have had not training either—technical or artistic—and we have no theories. We take
what work comes to hand—and it fits itself as it can into the intervals of other duties, for it still has to take a secondary place.
   We took to it [photography] ten years ago as a resource, when
we were obliged to give up teaching. (Flynt 39)

As this passage from Mary Allen's own letter indicates, they were talented and resourceful, yet they also lived with the limitations in career
options imposed upon them as members of the female sex at this particular time and place. Quite craftily, quite artfully, however, they found their
place and success behind the shutter of the camera's eye. With a camera
in their hands and an artful eye, the Allen sisters passed in a hearing
world.

DEAF EYES: THE ALLEN SISTERS AS DEAF/ WOMEN/PHOTOGRAPHERS

The Allen sisters grew up in a unique period and place in American deaf
history. It was also a hard place, to be sure. For deaf people in America,
the first half of the nineteenth century had been a significant period of
educational and social growth as the first school for deaf children opened
in Hartford, Connecticut, in 1817—the American School for the Deaf
(ASD). Education for the students at ASD was delivered and encouraged
in both oral English and manual sign language—a method that not only
worked to meet the linguistic capabilities of all the students but that also
allowed deaf adults to be teachers of deaf children. But by midcentury
things began to shift considerably. Oral education grew to be the favored
method of education. The first major oral school in the United States, the
Clarke School for the Deaf in Northampton, Massachusetts, opened in
1867. Although the first college for deaf and hard of hearing people in
the world opened in 1864—then known as the Columbia Institution for
the Deaf in Washington, D.C., and now known as Gallaudet Univer-

sity—oral education was still fast taking hold as *the* method of instruction for deaf children in the United States.

The influence of Alexander Graham Bell was substantial in these oral-focused efforts. Bell's mother and his wife, Mabel Hubbard Bell, were both deaf and in fact Bell began his adult career as an oral educator of deaf children. Mabel had been one of his students. He stumbled onto the telephone—his most famous invention—because he was actually looking for a device that would help deaf people hear better and that would help him use, with more success, a method of teaching deaf pupils that he and his father had developed called "visible speech." Bell also developed the first audiometer—a machine to measure hearing loss. Furthermore, Bell was also known as one of the leading eugenicists of the day, and he even wrote and published a eugenicist tract, *Graphical Studies of Marriages of the Deaf*, attempting to prove that when deaf people marry other deaf people they often produced deaf children. Using his "positive" eugenics philosophy as his rationale, Bell concluded that deaf people should thus be greatly discouraged from marrying other deaf people.

The eradication of sign languages and the support for, and dominance of, oral/speech-based means of communication and education for deaf people was crucial to Bell's eugenicist argument. Bell believed that when deaf people had sign languages to share with each other they were all the more likely to associate exclusively with each other and marry. He supposed that deaf children raised orally would be more likely to mix, mingle, and marry in the hearing world, thereby eventually decreasing (if not eradicating) the birth of deaf children. At a famous international conference on the subject of deaf education, the Milan Conference of 1880, Bell himself spoke strongly in favor of oral-only education. When the vote was taken at the Milan Conference regarding the oral-manual debate, sign language was declared forbidden as a method of educating (or communicating with) deaf children.[6]

The Allen sisters grew up in the middle of this period of significant stigma over deafness, when staunch oral methods came to dominate deaf education and when eugenics "science" declared deafness (and thereby deaf people) an aberration worthy of eradication and not deserving of marriage, particularly if the cause of deafness was unknown (as it was for the Allen sisters) and potentially genetically transmissible. Perhaps they felt the stigma even more palpably because they were well educated and well off financially, because they began young adulthood with a career that depended significantly on their hearing, and also because they lived in such close proximity to the nation's premier (and elite) school for oral education. One effect of the focus on oral education was that deaf women found themselves without employment opportunities at a time when America's women were entering the teaching force in great numbers. Although deaf men, being men, had other kinds of work they could do, the possibilities were quite limited for deaf women. Once teaching—along with the focus on oral education—was taken from them, the limits were staggering. As historian and Deaf studies scholar Susan Burch has written, the combined trends of oralism and the overall feminization of the teaching force in America "ultimately displaced educated Deaf women to an even greater extent, depriving them of both educational and career opportunities, as well as of social choices. Thus, as oralism and other reform movements opened more opportunities for women in general, they closed doors for Deaf women" (19). If Deaf Americans overall were the subjects of "illusions of equality," as historian Robert Buchanan suggests, deaf women were not even allowed the illusions.

Yet clearly Mary and Frances Allen had something—or rather, some things: a camera; a failed career at teaching and new time on their hands; a knack with children; a sensitivity to the soul of a pose; an educated and worldly sense of art and culture that was quite forward-looking, yet a strong sense of local flavor and understanding that also centered on saving and savoring the past (nostalgia, we might call it); and a community that embraced them and their work. And, of course, they had each other. With two pair of deaf eyes, they looked out for each other. Mary often assisted Frances, for example, whose hearing loss was considerably greater, when they traveled and also when they met with people to do their portraits.

As time went on and the sisters aged and became even more deaf (Frances was also mostly blind in the last ten years of her life), their photos move back and away from their earlier people-centered and posed portraits. These portraits would have surely been hard to do well the more their deafness overtook them. Frances especially withdrew and communicated less and less with people in Deerfield; while Mary would still sometimes take the actual portraits or pose the subjects, Frances would complete the technical work and focus on other business-related tasks. In the later years, especially in the last five, from 1915–20, most of their photography is either of landscape—something they would not really need to listen to or interact socially with—or an image that positions them as the distant history-recording observers who chronicled the many pageants and events in the Deerfield community. From these positions, their camera and their photographers' eyes—deaf eyes—allowed them to remain in the scene, however distant. Whether they were watching and recording from close up or afar, the deaf eyes of the Misses Allen behind their cameras were serving, in effect, as tools of communication and social interaction, art and income, history and hope.

Notes

1. Much of my autobiographical information about the Allen sisters comes from Suzanne L. Flynt's thorough and remarkable book about them and their photography: Suzanne L. Flynt, *The Allen Sisters: Pictorial Photographers 1885–1920.*

2. Ellen Gates Starr founded the Hull House settlement in Chicago with Jane Addams in 1889, where she also lived for nearly thirty years. She is known for her significant social reform efforts aimed at child labor laws and improving the working wages and conditions for immigrant factory workers, as well as her strong support of and belief in the value of arts and crafts for communities and individuals alike.

3. Throughout their photographic careers, the sisters often took portrait images of each other.

4. Biographer Suzanne Flynt notes that the Allen sisters' neighbors were said to have had to direct "lost" visitors and portrait seekers to the home of Mary and Frances Allen. On this matter, I speculate that it is quite possible that the visitors may well have first shown up at the correct address. But given the fact that the sisters were, of course, deaf and may well have been in the darkroom, elsewhere in the house, or busy with a sitting, it is quite possible they did not hear the first knocks of their visitors. And when they did not answer the initial knocking, their visitors likely wandered off to another nearby house—a house where someone actually did answer the door—and inquired about the correct address of the sisters.

5. A good number of the Allen sisters' photographs are available digitally at the Old Deerfield Memorial Hall Museum online collections.

6. For further reading about this era and the effects of oralism and A. G. Bell on the Deaf community, see the works by Baynton, Van Cleve and Crouch, Van Cleve, and Winefield.

Works Cited

Baynton, Douglas C. *Forbidden Signs: American Culture and the Campaign against Sign Language.* Chicago: U Chicago P, 1996.

Buchanan, Robert. *Illusions of Equality: Deaf Americans in School and Factory, 1850–1950.* Washington, D.C.: Gallaudet UP, 1999.

Burch, Susan. *Signs of Resistance: American Deaf Cultural History, 1900 to World War II.* New York: New York UP, 2002.

Curtis, Verna Posever. "Frances Benjamin Johnston in 1900: Staking the Sisterhood's Claim in American Photography." *Ambassadors of Progress: American Women Photographers in Paris, 1900–1901.* Ed. Bronwyn A. E. Griffith. Hanover: Musée d'Art Américain (dist. UP New England), 2001.

"Deerfield," *Handicraft* 5, no. 4 (July 1912): 53.

Flynt, Suzanne L. *The Allen Sisters: Pictorial Photographers, 1885–1920.* Deerfield, Mass.: Pocumtuck Valley Memorial Assn. (dist. UP New England), 2002.

Old Deerfield, Massachusetts Memorial Hall Museum. <http://memori alhall.mass.edu/home.html> and <http://www.americancenturies .mass.edu/home.html>. Accessed February 20, 2006.

Van Cleve, John V., and Barry A. Crouch. *A Place of Their Own: Creating the Deaf Community in America.* Washington, D.C.: Gallaudet UP, 1989.

Van Cleve, John V., ed. *Deaf History Unveiled: Interpretations from the New Scholarship.* Washington, D.C.: Gallaudet UP, 1993.

Winefield, Richard. *Never the Twain Shall Meet: Bell, Gallaudet, and the Communications Debate.* Washington, D.C.: Gallaudet UP, 1987.

The Aesthetics of Linguistic Envy
Deafness and Muteness in
Children of a Lesser God and *The Piano*

Jennifer L. Nelson

Deaf and Dumb: A Group by Woolner

Only the prism's obstruction shows aright
The secret of a sunbeam, breaks its light
Into the jewelled bow from blankest white;
So may a glory from defect arise:
Only by Deafness may the vexed Love wreak
Its insuppressive sense on brow and cheek,
Only by Dumbness adequately speak
As favoured mouth could never, through the eyes.
—*Robert Browning (105)*

I n Robert Browning's poem "Deaf and Dumb: A Group by Woolner,"
the qualities of deafness and dumbness are physical obstructions that
nevertheless reveal something—"the secret of a sunbeam."[1] In Browning's
revelation, the qualities of deafness and dumbness thus function to facilitate the expression of abstract concepts such as love and language, as the
secret "breaks its light / Into the jeweled bow from blankest white." The
prism's obstruction leads to enlightenment, and then attention becomes
focused on the glory revealed as well as the physical mechanism for this
revelation. Bodies become enviable sites of language production and expression: "Only by Deafness may the vexed Love wreak / Its insuppressive

189

sense on brow and cheek, / Only by Dumbness adequately speak / As favoured mouth could never, through the eyes." Even as the mouth or speech are "favoured" in society, Browning expresses muteness or deafness as obstacles. Yet as an obstructing deaf/mute body becomes the locus of attention, it also becomes the "prism" that refracts an aesthetic and abstract ideal.

The body as enabling something ideal seems to be a tradition in poetry, as seen (for example) in Thomas Traherne's poetry, which celebrates elective muteness and deafness in order to reach spiritual enlightenment.[2] We also see this tradition in the French Enlightenment, where silence is seen as more natural via the Rousseauesque expression/articulation of bodily gestures as closer to nature and the ideal than speech.[3]

Paul De Man also writes about the concept of an obstacle leading to a greater aesthetic ideal, as in "a glory from defect" in *Blindness and Insight*, where the critic's "blindness" sparks or leads to insights (xx, and "The Rhetoric of Blindness," 102–41). Lennard Davis, a cultural and literary critic, also writes of the "deafened moment" when one reads (mutely) the printed page; as such, deafness enables the act of reading (4, 104). Ironically, though, such metaphors reinforce the disabilities themselves; for example, when Davis stresses that the act of reading is a "deaf" act because one doesn't need a voice, thus making the voice less dominant, he also incidentally reinforces the idea of deafness as being cut off from the world and as such perpetuates this stereotype. In addition to De Man, Davis, and others, critic Barbara Johnson also articulates this poetic tradition, and she names it "muteness envy" in her critical essay on Keats's "Ode to a Grecian Urn" poem and Jane Campion's film *The Piano*. Johnson notes, "The ego-ideal of poetic voice would seem, then, to reside in the muteness of things" (129).

These ideas of bodily obstruction and then aesthetic expression have particular resonance as applied to the deaf and/or mute female bodies in the films *Children of a Lesser God* (1986) and *The Piano* (1993). Deaf and/or mute women, when they "speak" (their art, their will, their resistance, their expression) differently and beautifully using their bodies via sign language or pianos (to name two of the modes of expression featured in these films) become particularly prone to sexual, bodily interpretation and sometimes violence or coercion. This interpretation and resulting coercion colonizes, because there is often a desire to gain or control the "secret" Browning refers to in his poem by seizing, observing, and coercing the body. These films go further than Browning's explication of the body as leading to "insuppressive sense," in that they illustrate what happens when observers (in these films, the male protagonists or agonists) try to grasp and control the "secret of the sunbeam" for themselves; further, the deaf and/or mute female is oddly positioned because there is the double bind of attraction yet pressure to conform and change on their parts. Browning's "favoured mouth" indicates a whisper of this attitude in his acknowledgment of the value society places on the mouth, or speech, even as he celebrates deafness and muteness.

When I outlined this topic to a deaf friend of mine, not in the literature field, she laughed and said, "That old fantasy of the silent woman." Not only does this common stereotype of the silent female body invite possession, but it also suggests a writing-upon by a controlling agency. One can theoretically write one's own desires and thoughts onto a silent woman, as it were, and issues of control arise when that silent woman expresses herself in an unsanctioned way, no matter how beautiful. Art or expression as a bodily quality (Johnson 130) thus becomes allied with the sexual body/urn/other signifier for the cultural male gaze. Barbara Johnson herself stresses this aspect of the mute tradition in poetry: "The parodic edge to these poems seems only to confirm the normative image of a beautiful, silent woman addressed by the idealizing rhetoric of a male poet for whom she 'seems a thing' "(132). For Browning, too, deafness and muteness are things or "prisms" that refract different aesthetic means of expression other than the "favoured mouth."

Yet what happens when the silent idealized body resists and speaks itself in the face of such possession and control? When Keats's urn responds to the speaker's questions, it "answers with chiasmus, tautology, abstraction. The speaker asks for history; the urn resists with theory" (Johnson 142). While attracting the gaze theoretically draws attention to the individuality within "disability" or Browning's "defects," this act of looking also invites a pressure to conform or change; this double bind catches the aesthetic mute and/or deaf body, particularly the female one. As Rosemarie Garland Thomson notes, "the physically disabled body becomes a repository for social anxieties about such troubling concerns as vulnerability, control, and identity" (6). In this essay, I explore the anxiety expressed in relation to the mute and/or deaf woman and how that anxiety arises from issues of "vulnerability, control, and identity" in relation to language and culture.

In the films *Children of a Lesser God* and *The Piano*, the deaf and/or mute women represent or allude to music, art, or language within/expressed by mute, contained bodies, even as their bodies "speak" differently or deviantly in resistance; these women are seen as "urns" or Browningian "obstacles" or "prisms" capable of refracting poetry or culture (in the larger sense). Inscriptions of language or allusions to something aesthetic, to something made on their mute bodies, is desirable yet distancing and invites male colonization and control of their bodies, often via sexual possession (which can also often be seen or read as aesthetic possession) or through sexual violence/coercion. Johnson's essay comes to focus on this last point: "The aesthetic of silence turns out to involve a male appropriation of female muteness as aesthetic trophy accompanied by an elision of sexual violence" (136).

Extending Johnson's claim here, I argue that this process of idealizing a silence that leads to coercion in *The Piano* and *Children of a Lesser God* works more as a function of controlling the aesthetic parameters of language and normativity than it docs as a cultural clision of the difference between physical female pleasure and violation in order to reinforce patriarchy. Muteness is not just a function of the cultural desire for the blurring of the line between female pleasure and rape.[4] It also blurs the difference between linguistic/artistic autonomy and coercion/colonialism of women and other marginalized groups such as deaf people and the Maori of New Zealand. To push the parallel further, one might call such "muteness envy" a rape/coercion of language and art, not merely of the sexualized body. Metonymically, the body and language may function similarly, but a focus on sexual violence actually "mutes" the additional aspect of language and cultural coercion. If we look more to the idea of linguistic domination, we may now be able to explain why mute and/or deaf people are frequently presented as objects of desire, specifically because aesthetic language in all its "voices," sanctioned or not, is often conflated with body issues. And it is easy to focus on the body when there are other "voices," as it is a common misperception—Derrida and others have noted this misperception—that the voice is bodiless and essentially separate from the body, whereas hands, which deaf people often use in/ for language, clearly are not.

As examples of "muteness envy" and resulting attempts at control in relation to both language and sexuality, the films *Children of a Lesser God* and *The Piano* portray mute women (one deaf, both willingly mute) who resist domination in various forms and who attract the gaze of the would-be poet/appreciator of aesthetic principles. Both women—Sarah in *Children of a Lesser God* and Ada in *The Piano*—are in relationships with men who see them as something "poetic" and potential, as embodied examples of the glories arising from "defects," to use Browning's terminology. As sites of both aesthetic and linguistic "muteness envy," Sarah and Ada's expressive bodies are sexualized as loci of language and power even as they try to resist the controlling agency of men through various forms of resistance.

RANDA HAINES'S *CHILDREN OF A LESSER GOD*

Muteness and the need to categorize it, contain it, and cure it as a condition cover up the conflation between poetic/linguistic pleasure and its colonization in *Children of a Lesser God*. In this film, deaf Sarah has a power over hearing James that is more than just the power of sexual attraction. She has the power of a variant yet beautiful sign language in the face of his own language, and he seeks to impose his own poetic ideal, speech, in all its "prism"atic colors on her, even as she already (much as Ada does with her piano) refracts something beautiful with her body and sign language. When James sees Sarah for the first time, angry at someone for their incompetence and using strong, spirited sign language, he marvels at her beauty and her will. Yet he also sees her language—one that is expressed with her face, hands, and body—as an obstacle and a "defect," and so the first thing he does is try to convince her to let him give her speech lessons. In response, she smokes in front of him, defying the school's fire laws. She also mocks his pathetically slow signing and is savagely sarcastic. He asks her, "And you don't want to speak?" She bitterly responds, "Brilliant."[4]

James is actually the odd one out even as he is on a mission to teach speech to those who can't hear it. For example, he is pathetically thrilled after he begs one deaf student, Glenn, to "just give me one sound." Glenn struggles, and finally says "tw . . ." in trying to say "Twisted Sister," his favorite band. James's reaction to this partial—and twisted—utterance is as if all is well with the world: "That's great!" he enthuses. His reaction indicates that one pathetic sound produced is worth all those years of speech therapy and manipulation, more important even than mathematics and written English. A focus on the body and its possibilities is further shown in James's fascination with Johnny, a deaf student who, like Sarah, refuses to talk. Johnny is in a sense marginalized in his resistance because of his position as one who refuses to talk, who only signs, much like Sarah. James tries to overcome Johnny's resistance to speech but fails; at the end of the movie, Johnny turns James's gaze back onto himself, and James has no words, for once.

Throughout the movie, however, using the mechanisms of speech and speech therapy, James attempts to get inside deaf people, to understand them and to change them. He is fascinated with silent Sarah and all that she represents—the "other" existing outside speech. When she dances at the restaurant on their first date to her own music inside her head, not to the external music, he is fascinated by this aesthetic subversiveness as well as her body. She dances to her own inner aesthetic, not James's, and this is one source of his attention. Sarah presents her world, her language, her mode of interiority as a beautiful thing. James's response is, at first, just a watchful gaze, but eventually he tries to control her by coercing her to create (deaf) speech. For example, when they are on the beach, Sarah tells him that she knows the sound of the waves. She then translates the "sound" on her body, beautifully. He watches her artistic creation, comments on her stubbornness, and then says to her, "What am I saying?" without signs, thus forcing her to attempt to lipread him. Later in the film a similar, but reverse, scene occurs. In this role-reversed scene, Sarah asks James to show her Bach's music "sounds" and although he tries, he cannot. Thus, she succeeds in translation and communication whereas he fails. Yet despite his own failure, James still wants them to meet on a common ground in terms of language modality—*his* common ground. He projects that desire onto Sarah, as when he says to her, after a fight where it becomes clear that they have different linguistic realities and desires, "Let's crawl under the covers and pretend we are in some romantic, distant place." She replies, simply, "We're not. We're here."

James persists in trying to master and mirror his (speech) ideals on Sarah's linguistic body. Haines reinforces this idea by frequently posing the actors in front of mirrors, especially in several speech instruction sessions. There is also one significant point toward the end of the film where Sarah looks in a mirror herself and moves her lips to see what she would look like talking, and she sees that her mouth movements do not look normal. What James proposes and desires then is to make her sound and look abnormal, in a mockery of his ideal, though he doesn't yet realize that. His attraction to her then is of a Pygmalion type, resting on linguistic envy masked as linguistic "improvement" and dominance. Sarah is onto this, however, and she accuses him of wanting her to be a deaf person so that he can change her into a hearing person. Her resistance to this colonizing attraction is exemplified by a school play in which James's students "share" music by signing and singing to their parents. Though this is hardly an aesthetic experience, speech/signing and music are both used, which makes the performance acceptable to the ears of the parents. James is thrilled with his students, especially Lydia, who sings and signs; he then looks at Sarah, who has been watching this performance, to share his feelings. She does not share them but instead stalks off, upset and jealous of Lydia and her spoken language. Sarah's linguistic envy becomes evident then, too. She looks in a mirror, breaks it, and hurts her hand in front of the parents. This mirror-breaking scene marks precisely the moment in the film when James takes her out of the (deaf) school and moves her in with him, paternalistically taking care of her and continuing his speech-centered project.

Always concerned most with speaking and hearing, James asks Sarah at one point what she hears, and she says, "No one has ever gotten in there to find out." James asks if she will ever let him in. They look quizzically at each other and turn their gaze on each other; in this gazing exchange, they both become "other" to each other. We must recognize, for example, that Sarah is similarly attracted to James instead of someone like Orin Dennis, who is also deaf and seems to understand Sarah's motivations. Thus, the attraction of the "other" also functions both ways. Whereas a nonspeaking deaf person would be a challenge to a speech teacher, a speech teacher and his views might also be a challenge to the deaf person who is the target. This reversed challenge is represented in the film with repeated small parodies on the concept of silence in that deaf people are not actually silent—the music blares, the phone rings, the TV screams, grunts and certain verbalizations are made while signing; the result of this tower of Babel is that hearing people such as James are "deafened." James is the Other here as well, not just Sarah, and both try to win the other to their way of seeing and being linguistically in the world. The romanticizing and sexualizing of this double "othering" bind also serves to gloss over the linguistic envy and colonization that occurs in the film.

James's speech-centered idealism within the deaf world of the school where he works leads him into a few unintentionally self-mocking situations. James is proud of teaching swear words just to get his students to voice more, and ironically, one of them learns this lesson well, sequentially calling James "asshole," "dickbrain," and finally, in crowning summit, "fuckface." James has pushed speech itself as the goal, regardless of its quality or context. He fails to see the joke on him even as he tells the student, William, that "language skills can be dangerous." But William already has language skills in the form of sign language, and so he responds, "So long, Fuckface." William has the last word here, not James. James is out of place, as always, but he is "deaf" to this fact. At a deaf party, for example, he is again the odd one out, as Sarah and her friends are the ones inclusively talking and enjoying themselves; he is self-excluded (even though he can see their sign language and participate if he wishes—and not vice versa), standing by the table, bored, resentful (even though deaf people endure this type of alienating linguistic experience every day of their lives). There is an ironic poster on the wall behind him: "A Sound Beginning: The First Conference for the Hard of Hearing." He complains, instead: "I just feel like everyone is talking in some far north Hungarian dialect over there."

The principal himself satirizes James as a representative of deaf education/speech education at several points throughout the movie. At one point, for example, he says, "Yelling at the back of a deaf person? Very good, James. [Aside to another] He's been at all the best schools." Sarah, too, cleverly turns the tables, even on the principal: when the principal teases her about deaf people's propensity to cheat in poker via secret signs and how she and James will win everything because of that, she responds by saying that they can't cheat because James is hearing. She also twits James by rolling her eyes when he says, "Well, maybe I like to hear myself talk." It is clear that they are on separate sides of an aesthetic, communicative, linguistic divide. Sarah also mocks James's own aesthetic: at one point she apes a deaf student, probably Lydia, in speech therapy, and makes herself look grotesque, like a dog panting and begging for favors.

Language and the body meet in envy and resistance in James's home (where Sarah now also lives). As such, their "shared" language becomes metonymic for sex with the two both trying to get something—some connection, some communication—from the other. There is no physical rape or coercion in the film; in fact, it is Sarah who often initiates sex or pushes James into bodily intimacy. Sex as a way of "speaking" concerns James, too, as when they have sex at one point and he can't help asking her to say his name because he wants to get closer to her (she sees no need for this). She responds with anger because he had promised not to ask her to speak. The utterance of his own name is ultimate consummation for James, and this is what drives a wedge between them. For James, to claim names, especially in speech, is to claim bodies, in a sense. Or is it vice versa?

JANE CAMPION'S *THE PIANO*

The Piano opens with a clear statement that Ada McGrath chose not to speak from an early age. Ada notes that her narration is her mind voice, not her speaking voice. As critic Barbara Johnson notes in her essay about this film, Ada's father referred to this refusal to speak as a "dark talent." Thus, this designation of her "dark talent" sites her muteness in the aesthetic, artistic realm, and she says that her father recognized it as such. Ada says, "Silence affects everyone in the end. . . . The strange thing is I don't think myself silent. That is because of my piano." Her piano becomes her voice, the body of her voice, and as such there is an implicit connection between the three—Ada, piano, and voice. She is a passionate piano player, and George Baines is transfixed by both the spectacle and sound of her playing. Later in the movie, we see George Baines, who desires Ada and her piano/voice, standing naked and caressing the piano in her absence; here the piano is metonymic of Ada's expression, as well as her body. Significantly, Ada later writes her feelings for George on a piano key: Ada, piano, body, and "voice" all come together.

With her "voices," Ada is not silent at all; she has paper, her sign language, and her piano as her "speaking" instruments. Still, her physical muteness attracts the attention of Alisdair Stewart, her mail-order husband, who sees her as a problem to work with (while waiting on the beach where they arrive, he complains that she's so small, and he asks her if she can hear him), even though he wrote to her that her muteness would not bother him. Before he meets her for the first time, he looks at a photograph of her and sees her in that medium as a silent woman, as an art form. Yet he is bothered because she resists as a photo would not, and in answer to her resistance, he tries to sever her art from her body, her piano from her person, her voice from herself—committing linguistic coercion and violence in the process. Ada's resistance to him is transgressive in his eyes when she insists on taking her piano, and he says no; he then leaves her piano alone on the beach. Ada's response to Stewart is, "It's mine." Stewart is then obdurate in taking her voice away from her.

In this taking, he invalidates other forms of expression outside the norm; music as voice is not part of his personal aesthetic. It is unclear, however, what he might substitute for the piano's voice; wifely attentions and obedience, perhaps, to the Victorian aesthetic of Coventry Patmore's "Angel" in the house? Later, it is no surprise that the play Stewart's relatives enact is Bluebeard, a play on women's obedience to husbands. In this play, wives who don't behave properly get their heads cut off. Prophetically, Stewart will later cut of Ada's finger in anger when he finds out she is sleeping with Baines. Her finger is of her body, and it is of her (linguistic) voice as well; thus, her disobedience to Stewart results in his linguistic envy and attempt at control through the amputation of her finger.

Because Ada's muteness alludes to something beyond Stewart's ken, she becomes an object of confounded desire for him. For example, when Ada carves piano keys into the table in the absence of her piano, Stewart thinks there is something wrong with her, as "it doesn't make a sound" when Ada plays on the carved table keys. He can't "get" her; her music is in her head at this point, even without her piano. Yet he cannot attain her interiority. Stewart then sells her "voice," her piano, to Baines, who cleverly recognizes it as a way to get into Ada's interiority. To not listen to someone or to mark someone inscribes a position of power, and Ada exercises this power on Stewart. Her resistance galls him, especially because he cannot "turn a deaf ear" to her as she does to him, more or less. Later, when Stewart sees Baines in possession of Ada's body and her love—attained, however, by coercing/accepting (there is a fine line here) her "voice" in a barter between piano keys for sexual favors—Stewart locks her body in an attempt to control her body, her "voice," and her will.

Yet her piano does not totalize her voice or her will, as she expresses them in other ways as well, even though Stewart has unknowingly sold it off to George Baines. She closes herself off to Stewart, and when she finally gets her piano back from Baines, Ada won't play it for Stewart. Instead, Ada plays with Stewart's body later, caressing it all over and gazing on him but not letting him touch her or play with her body. He himself then resists her will when she tries to pull his pants off (without letting him touch her), by pulling away from her and yanking his pants back up. Stewart wants her subjectivity, her "voice" and her self within her body that she holds off from him; he wants to control her voice (her will, her attention) and yet he is also ultimately envious—and scared—of it. Finally, he is so scared of it that he tells Baines to take her away: he has heard her voice in his head, silent, with no movement on her lips, as he took care of her while she was sick—after he cut her finger off. As Barbara Johnson notes, her voice is a projection of his fears (143), of something greater and beyond himself and his control: "She said, I'm afraid of my will, of what it might do. It is so strange and so strong. I have to go. Let me go. Let Baines take me away. Let him try and save me." "Hearing" her "voice" then, Stewart has to let go of his control of Ada, but it must, for him, be couched within letting another man "save" her and her will. For Stewart, Ada's errant poetic voice—and body—must seem within the control of someone else—another man—regardless of whether it really is.

Baines is fascinated with Ada's passionate music playing, her piano, and her body, all in one; he seeks not to learn how to play the piano but to listen to it, to take it in. Ada's piano playing makes her body open and vulnerable to Baines—much as Sarah's sign language makes her an object of desire for James in *Children of a Lesser God*. Baines uses the piano as a way to try to gain something from Ada. She becomes an object of his desire because he cannot read her totally in her interiority, her "difference." It is not merely Ada's body and her pleasure or coercion that Baines is so fascinated with; it is the aesthetics of her piano playing and/as her mode of expression. Also from a position of linguistic envy, Baines seeks to control and initiate her piano-playing "voice" by bartering piano keys for sexual favors.

However, Baines does not desire Ada in the destructive way that Stewart does. Whereas Stewart cuts off Ada's finger, Baines simply tells her to leave if she does not love him. In the end, he is also the one who wants to keep the piano as they leave for their new settlement, and Ada is the one who insists on throwing it overboard. After this, she starts to learn to talk again with Baines in their new settlement in Nelson, New Zealand. The film ends with Ada making noises, much like Glenn in *Children of a Lesser God*: "va va va," she articulates, even as Baines stops her mouth with kisses, silencing her developing voice.

Conclusion

In *The Piano*, Baines serves an "other" function, much like James in *Children of a Lesser God*: he is the "other" to Stewart and as such Ada is attracted to that, imperfect and somewhat controlling as Baines is. Also, like James in *Children of a Lesser God*, Baines uses Ada's "language" to try to get closer to her and what she represents. Additionally, as James is friendly with his students and other deaf people, Baines is friendly with the Maori—he knows their language and ways and even has Maori tattoos on his face. But in his manipulation of Maori land and Ada's piano, Baines, like James, reinforces the hegemony of a colonial culture in the end, although this hegemony is glossed over in both movies. James himself is in a similar colonial mindset; he signs and tries to linguistically become like Sarah in order to appropriate Sarah and her mode of expression—to further *his* ideal of speech. James also appropriates the bodies of the other deaf students at the school to inculcate his speech ideal. On a similar level, *The Piano* also glosses over the colonized situation of the Maori in terms of land appropriation, as Baines himself appropriates

Maori land and deals with Stewart in land brokering even as he becomes almost like one of them.

At one point in each film both James and Baines realize that what they have been pushing for is not what they want at all. James stops trying to make Sarah use her voice after she finally speaks in response to his demand to "Speak! Speak to me!" She finally screams/speaks at him, but her voice sounds rough and harsh. The sound of her voice is a slap in the face for James, and he then realizes that he's been romanticizing speech all along. Thus, Sarah's attempt/attainment of speech for James is anticlimactic. He crumples, and Sarah leaves him. He lets her go. He realizes he's been obtuse all along, interpreting Sarah through her *lack* of speech rather than as herself and through her sign language. When he watches her from a distance in her new job as a manicurist, he sees that she manages just fine without his help. Throughout the movie, he has said things such as "I'll take care of you" and "Don't you want to be able to get along in the world?" to Sarah's back when she can't see him. He now finds that, in fact, she can, so he leaves her alone. His paternalistic, linguistically envious, and speech-centered gaze is broken—he looks away and leaves. The same can be said for Baines, when he realizes he can't get inside of Ada to her feelings: his sexualized aesthetic and linguistically envious gaze is also broken. Baines stops using the piano to get sexual favors from Ada when he realizes it is more than her playing and her body he wants. Instead, he wants her feelings and her choice—such as it is—to be with him. He tells her to leave if she has no feelings for him, and he ends his sexual coercion of her by returning her piano to her.

These two films are ultimately about the colonial struggle over the envy of language, art, body, voice, and self, as played out on a gendered stage—through Sarah and Ada's deaf/mute bodies and language (as well as on the deaf students at the school and the Maori). Sarah and Ada are both made to speak at some point, even though poetic silence is an ideal, and even though they make their expressions and their desires, albeit structured by an already existing patriarchal society, clear. The men in these films go beyond Browning's poem, where he is content to observe the prism break "the secret of a sunbeam . . . Into the jewelled bow from blankest white." As linguistic and gendered members of a dominant culture, James, Baines, and Stewart are not content merely to observe the "jewelled bow" of difference in the aesthetic and linguistically difference "voices" of Ada and Sarah. In their linguistic, aesthetic, and gendered bodily envy, they must also try to control the mechanism—the female body, language, and "voice"—that carries this difference.

Notes

1. My thanks go to Sidney Fine for corresponding with me about this poem. The statue was apparently exhibited in London's "Great International Exhibition" in 1862, and there are two photos that Mr. Fine referred to: one in the *Browning Newsletter* 6 (1971), p. 38 and the other (showing the statue marking the children's grave) in *Victorian Sculpture* by B. Read.

2. In his poem "Dumnesse," divinity is best achieved through the qualities of deafness and silence, because these qualities are what enable one to take in God's works and to develop oneself in preparation for later invasion by external breaths that carry poisonous voices. Only by being first mute can one shore oneself up in the face of the evils of the outside world, which are carried on verbal symbols:

> Sure Man was born to Meditat on Things,
> And to Contemplat the Eternal Springs
> Of God and Nature, Glory, Bliss and Pleasure;
> That Life and Love might be his Heavnly Treasure:
> And therfore Speechless made at first, that he
> Might in himself profoundly Busied be:
> And not vent out, before he hath t'ane in
> Those Antidots that guard his Soul from Sin. (lines 1–8)

Speechlessness is a necessary preparation for later salvation; in such a way can "Man" contemplate the wisdom and glory of God in nature. From this comes a reliance on the self, as in "in himself profoundly Busied be"; with such a strong foundation anchored in the mute self, rather than business outside, come the "Antidots" that will help when one must finally "vent out" or speak. Deafness, allied with silence, is another necessary prerequisite for the development of the divine character in a person:

> Wise Nature made him Deaf too, that he might
> Not be disturbd, wile he doth take Delight
> In inward Things, nor be depravd with Tongues

Nor Injurd by the Errors and the Wrongs
That Mortal words convey. For Sin and Death
Are most infused by accursed Breath
That flowing from Corrupted Intrails, bear
Those hidden Plagues that Souls alone may fear. (lines 9–16)

Human speech carries within itself the possibility of a corrupting influence on the soul and is akin to a "Plague" or sickness. Initial deafness is one way to keep this mental disease at bay, at least until the soul is fortified enough to withstand the onslaught of the voice breathing out from the "Corrupted Intrails." He notes that God's "Work . . . did in me lurk" (37–38) and that this work comprised seeing "all Creatures full of Deities" (40) with "Cleerer Eys" (39). Silence, solitude, inwardness: all are required to protect onself from later assault or ravishment ("ravishd") by the world:

To reign in Silence, and to Sing alone
To see, love, Covet, hav, Enjoy and Prais, in one:
To Prize and to be ravishd: to be true,
Sincere and Single in a Blessed View
Of all his Gifts. (lines 49–53)

3. For more historical information on silence and idealization in the French Enlightenment, see Nicholas Mirzoeff's *Silent Poetry*. Also see Jonathan Ree's *I See a Voice*. In addition to poetry and the French Enlightenment, the ideal of female deafness and/or muteness is well entrenched via the Victorian ideal of the silent angel in the house and has actually been applied to a number of literary deaf and/or mute female characters. In film studies, it has been well established that Victorian literature informs twentieth-century films. Alfred de Musset's Camille, in "Pierre et Camille," and Sophy in Charles Dickens's "Doctor Marigold" fit this tradition, to name only a couple, and echoes of stories such as these can later be seen in the twentieth-century film tradition of the mute and/or deaf female character. The women in these stories are mute silent "angels in the house," and they eventually learn language via sign language with the ultimate goal of writing and reading the majority language. Their final redeeming quality is often to create a hearing child, usually a boy.

4. Please note that all quotations I use from both movies are based on the captioned text, not the voicing in the movies.

Works Cited

Browning, Robert. *Dramatis Personae*. Ed. F. B. Pinion. London: Collins, 1969.

Davis, Lennard. *Enforcing Normalcy*. London and New York: Verso, 1995.

DeMan, Paul. *Blindness and Insight: Essays in the Rhetoric of Contemporary Criticism*. 2nd ed, rev. Minneapolis: U of Minnesota P, 1983.

Garland-Thomson, Rosemarie. *Extraordinary Bodies: Figuring Physical Disability in American Culture and Literature*. New York: Columbia UP, 1997.

———. "Integrating Disability, Transforming Feminist Theory." *NWSA Journal* 14.3 (2002): 1–32.

———. "Feminist Theory, the Body, and the Disabled Figure." *The Disability Studies Reader*. Ed. Lennard J. Davis. New York: Routledge, 1997.

Johnson, Barbara. "Muteness Envy." *The Feminist Difference: Literature, Psychoanalysis, Race, and Gender*. Cambridge, Mass.: Harvard UP, 1998.

Traherne, Thomas. *Centuries, Poems, and Thanksgivings*. Ed. H. M. Margoliouth. Oxford: Clarendon, 1958.

"Slain in the Spirit"

Kristen Harmon

You have to look hard, but if you drive on the interstate that slices through the head of Columbia, Missouri, you can see a red, brick building flash through the trees: Praise Assembly of God. Praise is a Christian charismatic, Pentecostalist church, and in 1991, Praise became the host site for a small Deaf ministry within its congregation.

In 1995, I am in graduate school in Columbia, half-heartedly working toward a PhD in English. I already know English. It doesn't explain anything to me anymore. What I need to know is American Sign Language (ASL). I feel that it will fill in the blanks for me. I decide that this ministry sounds like an awfully good place to do an ethnographic study. I will be a participant-observer, so the side benefit, of course, will be ASL.

Entering that red brick church and the white-painted drywall of its sanctuary, I am a hopeful ethnographer and an oral deaf woman full of dread. I have a head full of French feminist theory. I am not a "believer."

What I am: exhausted from the exigencies of lipreading and ear molds.

If religion is essentially a question of the Other, I want this red-brick/white-drywall space, these (Deaf and hearing) people "speaking" in tongues, to explain how being works, in an Other language.[1] I want to know the systematic constraints of signifying practices in language but more importantly, how these processes work for "specifying just what, within [that] practice, falls outside the system and characterizes the specificity of the practice as such."[2]

What lies outside of speech and spoken female bodies? I have to know.

Pseudonyms are used throughout for some participants at their request.

As an ethnographer, I also want to know if so much of religious feeling is speechless, without words, and if so much of women's subjectivity is theorized—particularly in French feminist theory—as being peripheral or marginal to patriarchal spoken languages, how do women using ASL change the relationship, change the experience with language, and, in doing so, change God?

On that first Wednesday night service in October 1995, I set out with (1) paper and pen for field notes, (2) a tape recorder for interviews with hearing participants, and (3) shaky hands and a pounding heart. I feel intrepid and nervous. I had not met many signing, Deaf adults in my life, thus far.

On Wednesday nights, the Deaf ministry group—ten to fifteen Deaf adults—meets separately for their own Bible study. The primary language used in these gatherings is ASL, mixed with some "contact" signing. Occasionally present at these gatherings is Adeline, a white, hearing woman. Adeline learned ASL for evangelizing purposes, and she is sometimes called upon to interpret the main service on Sundays.

Adeline is a member of the church, as is her seventeen-year-old daughter, Marcia. Adeline is in her early forties, with long, straight, brown-gray hair that she pulls tightly back. This, with her smooth, well-scrubbed face, gives her the look of a double-exposed photograph, a child's round face superimposed on the body of an adult. Adeline's daughter, Marcia, is an intense teenager with "dishwater blonde" hair, and she is sometimes awkward and shy with her peers. Yet she is confident, even a little bossy, when she signs with her mother and with some of the Deaf adults and their hearing children.

I start with Adeline and Marcia because they are hearing women and, without exception, what we lump together and label as "French Feminist" theory is written by and about hearing women. In this explorative endeavor, I start with interviews with this mother-daughter pair, in spoken English and by doing so become, in effect, a "voiced body" speaking with other such voiced bodies. After all, that's what I am, had been, up until the winter of 1995.

ADELINE: I used to think that I could only worship God through
            my voice, but even when there's signing like we were

tonight . . . you know you just find your hands worshiping God and singing just as a form of worship. . . . You
can get totally lost in the Spirit doing that. A lot of times
after I've been singing for awhile, I'll just start signing,
and then I'll quit using my voice, and kind of get lost in
it. And I can hear the music, but it's like, I'm in there,
I'm just kind of carried away with the Spirit, you know.
And I just use it, it's unexplainable. It really is. It really
is unexplainable.[3]

After service one Wednesday night, I lipread Adeline and Marcia while
we sit around the tape recorder, set up in the middle of a rickety long
table in the fellowship hall. They fingerspell terms for me that I don't
understand on their lips, and I appreciate this new, and visually legible,
component to spoken conversation.

As a "voiced body," marked with years of speech therapy, I have
thought through some of the theoretical ramifications of what it must
mean to come to ASL as a second language. I have had waking fantasies
of "quit[ing] using my voice, and kind of get[ing] lost" in a visual and
expressive experience that, as of yet, still lies outside of my spoken experience. But it is still not clear to me how much of Adeline's "unexplainable"
experience is due to the nature of the trance state and how much of it is
due to the untranslatability of an alternative modality of expression, an
expressive outlet that arguably—especially in the iconic elements—is
closer to representing the experience itself.

It has been assumed—most often by hearing nonsigners—that ASL, a
visual-gestural language, must be able to articulate the body in ways that
speech cannot; surely, such "expressing the body" must be closer to the
utopian ideal of a "women's language" as expressed by Cixous and Irigaray. Some, including American feminist scholar Elaine Showalter, assume that ASL must be a "semiotic" rather than a symbolic language.

By way of illustration, Showalter once described—in a theoretical article—witnessing at an academic conference a young woman who she later
realized was an ASL interpreter: "In this context, her signs seemed uncan-
nily feminine and Other, as if we were watching a Kristevan ambassador
from the semiotic, or the ghost of a Freudian hysteric from the beyond.

Anna O. is alive and well in Georgetown!"[4] Although Showalter's description is startling (and dismaying) in its erasure of Deaf people and a particular linguistic history, this reaction is not unique. For some hearing/nonsigning people, watching ASL feels like a revolutionary and immediate creation of language that is only legible in the deepest cells of the body.

Watching an interpreter, they note that this language feels unsettling, sexy, and in a dim, half-perceived way, almost, but not quite, comprehensible. They see the act of ASL—in the moment—as language in the midst of the semiotic *chora*, "the rhythmic space, which has no thesis or position, the process by which significance is constituted . . . nourishing and maternal."[5] They imagine that ASL has the capacity for envisioning the body's disruptive drives in language; they imagine that ASL is textless, that the message is embodied in ways that spoken languages cannot parallel, and furthermore, that this embodiment is revolutionary: "for there to be a transgression of the symbolic, there must be an irruption of the drives in the universal signifying order, that of 'natural' language which binds together the social unit."[6]

This romanticized "reading" of interpreters is ever hopeful; projecting, or superimposing, the presence of the semiotic echoes Kristeva's theories concerning the possibility for sociolinguistic revolution from within and from without spoken language. What Showalter and others remember, upon seeing ASL, is that the semiotic is "a kinetic functional stage . . . [that] precedes the establishment of the sign; it is not, therefore, cognitive in the sense of being assumed by a knowing, already constituted subject."[7] It is also theorized as "a pre-verbal functional state that governs the connections between the body (in the process of constituting itself as a body proper), objects and the protagonists in the family structure."[8] Later, once the speaking/writing subject enters the "symbolic" order, then the semiotic shows up only as a "pulsional pressure" on the symbolic language, as contradiction, meaninglessness, disruptions, silences, and absences.[9]

These spectators of ASL are hopeful because paying attention to the semiotic in written or spoken language reveals "a transgression of position, a reversed reactivation of the contradiction that instituted this very position."[10] Kristeva extrapolates her theories for revolution in poetic language from avant-garde poets and modernist writers who illustrate a willingness to exert such a "pulsional pressure" upon language because "art—this semiotization of the symbolic—thus represents the flow of jouissance into language."[11] By *jouissance*, Kristeva means an ecstatic state which is "sexual, spiritual, physical, conceptual at one and the same time . . . total joy or ecstasy (without the mystical connotation) . . . [that which] implies the presence of meaning . . . requiring it by going beyond it."[12] Most important for social revolution through language, however, are the ways in which such "poetic language" calls into question the "very principle of the ideological because they unfold the *unicity* of the thetic (the precondition for meaning and signification)."[13] As a result, poetic language sets in motion "what dogma represses . . . [and] thus, its complexity unfolded by its practices, the signifying process joins social revolution."[14]

It is no wonder, then, that the desire for an embodied, "text-less," and semiotic language is so powerful; "in so doing, [poetic language and mimesis] no longer act as instinctual floodgates within the enclosure of the sacred and become instead protesters against its posturing."[15] Through the semiotic presence in the symbolic order, the patriarchal God is unmade, as are systems of social signification that insist upon categorization and hierarchy.

However, for the purposes of the sociolinguistic feminist revolutionary project that Showalter and others imagine, ASL is not the language. Kristeva makes this clear by noting that "this [semiotic] functioning [is distinct] from symbolic operations that depend upon language as a sign system—whether the language [*langue*] is vocalized or gestural, as with deaf-mutes."[16]

Even so, despite such a bald decision, for a nonsigner/spectator, there remains that sense of tantalizing embodiment. What these academic interpreters of conference sign language perceive as dimly comprehended and embodied meaning are the gestural and iconic elements of ASL. ASL does have many signs that are iconic, in that they do resemble their referents, but there are just as many signs that do not resemble their referents and are arbitrary signifiers. Despite the irrupting presence of the iconic, ASL is constituted like other symbolic languages, as an interplay between the symbolic and semiotic modalities: "These two modalities are inseparable within the *signifying process*. . . . the dialectic between them determines the type of discourse (narrative, metalanguage, theory, poetry, etc.) involved."[17] This process works to constitute the limits and excesses of the speaking/nonsigning subject. With an eye to sightings of "poetic language," a quick perusal of ASL morphology and usage confirms that, like spoken languages, users of ASL encode artifacts of symbolic social ordering through inflections and phrasings that reveal gender, age, race, sexual orientation, and so forth.

However, I think that maybe these feminist "readings" of female ASL interpreters at academic conferences—however myopic and misleading they are in erasing actual Deaf people—may be on to something, if only to point out the necessity of doing away with sound to envision a revolutionary language *moment.*

Kristeva is, like many feminists and the other "French feminists," grounded firmly in sound, even at the moment when language is essentially unmade, prefigured, amorphous, and mobile: "the semiotic is heard in rhythms, intonation, and children's echolalia as well as in artistic practice and in discourse that signifies less an object than a *jouissance.*"[18] For Kristeva, the representation of female *jouissance* is compelled, instigated, by sound; sound determines both the subject and the practices that signify the limits of the signifying processes as such. In an essay about Christianity and the Virgin Mary as a source of discourse on motherhood, she writes of the fetishization of parts of the Virgin's maternal body and notes that according to this system of fragmentation, in both religious art and practice, such a "cult of the mother" leads to a reification of the signs of divine maternity, that is, the Virgin Mary's "ear, . . . tears, and . . . breast," and in so doing denies her agency and sexuality. As a result, "With the female sexual organ changed into an innocent shell, holder of sound, there arises a possible tendency to eroticize hearing, voice, or even understanding."[19]

In effect, then, for Kristeva "feminine sexual experience is thus rooted in the universality of sound, since it is distributed *equally* among all men, all women."[20] Women then face a choice to live life "hyper-abstractly," as an idealization, or as "merely *different,* other, fallen."[21] When faced with overdetermined bodies and fictions of love and death at the source of (Christian) religion, the only exit is available through *jouissance* or an anguished identification/collapse into "love itself and what he is in fact—a fire of tongues, an exit from representation."[22] Both exits from representation are instigated by/embedded within sound.

While Adeline is speaking more about trance states than about ecstatic, glossolaliac states, Adeline demonstrates this "exit" from representational fictions when she says that "I can hear the music, but it's like, I'm in there, I'm just kind of carried away with the Spirit, you know. And I just use it, it's unexplainable. It really is. It really is unexplainable." Tellingly, Adeline says that she can "hear" the music, but it is as if she is *in* there, carried away, beyond words and representation other than "unexplainable."

Given that Adeline, my participant, is hearing and that "poetic language" (with its tendency toward the semiotic impulse) and the possibility of *jouissance* are "profoundly a-theological," I am having some difficulty teasing out the difference between a mystic or religious subjugation to a divine being that is without oneself and a revolutionary act of undoing language, anything that "breaks the symbolic chain, the taboo, the mastery."[23, 24] This heady exercise with Kristevan theory begins to feel circular, like an ontological argument for the existence of God by defining the thesis and antithesis of the word "God."

During Sunday services, my feelings of both titillation and startled nervousness—do they really expect *me* to do this, too?—are only slightly repressed by my need to take field notes and to take in everything around me. For God's sake, I think, when the hands go up around me, I just wanted to learn sign language.

KRISTEN: What's interesting to me is that it seems that—from the way you talk about it—you're somehow closer to God by speaking through the body rather than speaking through the voice. . . . is this the case?

ADELINE: It's another expression, if you will, another opening; it would be like the deaf being able to hear. We use our voice, we use our hands, we use our body when we lift our hands to praise God. It's just another form, it's another expression of worship that's, I don't know, it's just sort of too awesome to explain.

How does Adeline feel about me, about the adults in the Deaf ministry? I wonder, when I am pretty sure I have lipread correctly "another opening; it would be like the deaf being able to hear." It is unsettling that she has taken a fact of my body and used it to describe her experience. For a split second, I feel startled and resentful, as though my hidden agenda has been revealed: I came to Praise to learn other ways of being, to become Deaf.

I am also surprised at the unexpected eroticism of *another opening* and then intrigued by the possibility of the double meaning of her analogy; she could mean being able "hear again," in the literal sense of being "healed," through a laying on of hands. She could also mean being able to "hear"—or rather, sense/apprehend/take in—in a different way.

Interestingly, however, she complicates this by emphasizing the multiple expressive components of the experience: "We use our voice, we use our hands, we use our body when we lift our hands to praise." For Adeline, the use of sign language has the same experiential meaning as the concept of *l'ecriture feminine* idealized in Helene Cixous's "Laugh of the Medusa": "In fact, she physically materializes what she's thinking; she signifies it with her body."[25] The French feminist and writer Helene Cixous describes women's language as a state where "senses flow, circulate, messages as divinely complicated as the strange microphonetic signals conveyed to the ears from the blood, tumults, calls, inaudible answers vibrate, mysterious connections are established."[26] In this particular women's language, Adeline's analogy points to an experience of being filled with an apprehended presence, a source of a message intelligible only when turned inside out, or outward in, through another opening, much like a "deaf[ened body] being able to hear [apprehend]."

Obviously, once again, the sense of hearing is privileged as the source for the irrupting message, but the description of the body as a source of sensory information aligns with the goals of "women's language." Let me reiterate: ASL is not a utopian "women's language" and is very much a "symbolic" language, but this sense of recuperation or another "opening" might explain why some hearing women are drawn to learning sign language.

Turning away from voice toward an alternative expressive and experiential language also signifies a material, sensual body positioned in opposition to the voiced body and its memory. Such a juxtaposition reveals the "desire for the escape from the constructions and commodifications of the body . . . furthermore, a desire to produce those bodies elsewhere, in some other cultural space, where bodies might be returned upon, and so touched upon, on different terms and in different ways."[27] It becomes another opening, as Adeline said, in her unintentionally Irigarian analogy.

After talking with Adeline and Marcia, it becomes clear to me that even though the reasons for hearing women to learn sign language are varied and individually compelling, for the two of them, there is little room for fully realized Deaf people in this construct of signed words and sign language as "another opening":

MARCIA: I can't sing. That's the main reason why I do it [perform signed renditions of Christian songs before the congregation]. Because that's my way of worshipping God because I can't sing. I can't carry a tune. . . . That's what a lot of people say, you sing terribly. You shouldn't get up there and sing. So that's my way of worshiping *and when I started signing, there weren't any deaf here to sign for. So I was just kind of signing for the hearing people in our church. And it got started kind of like that because there were, when I started signing, no deaf here at all.* So I started signing, and it's kind of stuck. [emphasis mine][28]

Without a Deaf audience, a comprehending audience, then sign language becomes a performance of the socially delimited "feminine," and when set to the tune of contemporary Christian pop music, becomes yet another scripting of the female body. The signs are made legible (and thus constrained) by being set to words, and then the performance, with gesture, swaying, and expressive body movements is read as stereotypically feminine.

There are no hearing men or boys volunteering to sign along with music. One Sunday morning, the preacher makes a joking insinuation from the pulpit about the perceived effeminacy of a hearing male interpreter. The Deaf members of the congregation offer a sign language class on Wednesdays that's overwhelmingly attended by women and children.

Adeline's husband, Marcia's father, reluctantly signs a very few words, usually only after quite a bit of prodding from Adeline. The preacher, clearly bored or impatient during the ASL classes, learns a few signs, one of which he—with a boyish grin—pulls out again and again, to much laughter and applause, like a hat trick: ILU, or I LOVE YOU.

In this context, there's little possibility for empowerment through the performed or impromptu use of signed words or signed language among the hearing/speaking women; it becomes another socially accepted way to be female for these women. Whenever some of the hearing women use signed words along with their speech, when they raise their hands to the ceiling and sign, "YOU POWERFUL," it startles no one in this church congregation. (It only surprises a sleepy hearing boy, who startles wide awake at the sight of moving hands and, once he sees he's not in trouble, stares with a suspicious frown on his face.)

On November 19, 1995, I attend a Sunday evening service at Praise Assembly of God and witness Jeanna, a white Deaf woman in her late twenties, and Pat, a white Deaf woman in her forties, being "slain in the Spirit." ("Slain in the spirit" is the term used in the charismatic churches to describe "movement of the Holy Spirit upon a person. The claim is that the Holy Spirit moves with such power on a person, that the person is 'slain.' . . . he/she is so overcome by the presence of the Spirit that he/she falls down to the ground being completely overcome."[29])

Jeanna is chubby and cute, with long, dark, thick hair that she wears cut in a long bob with bangs cut straight across in front like a ruler. Her eyeglasses cover the circles under her eyes when she's just worked a long shift at a wholesale book warehouse.

Pat is pear-shaped, with thin, graying hair. During church services, she watches the hearing congregation members in a pleasant and blank way that belies the mischievous side that comes out when church is over. When church is done, she is an ironic mimic of hearing people's awkward and revealing behavior when "confronted" with a Deaf person. (Once, Pat teases the preacher about a sign he had "mispronounced" in the last Wednesday night sign language class, but he doesn't take the time to pay attention to what she is trying to tease him about; he tries to joke his way around and away from her and waves goodbye while Pat is still trying to explain.) Pat and Jeanna laugh often together, and they pull me into their rollicking conversations. Because Jeanna is only a few years older than me, she takes it upon herself to be my guide in this church setting and often comments on the unfamiliar proceedings for me.

After the altar call at that Sunday evening service in late November, Jeanna and Pat walk forward and kneel together at a low wooden bench near the pulpit and the drum set. After a few moments with her eyes closed, Jeanna rocks back and forth, one hand on Pat's back, the other pushing and pushing against the air in front of her. A few more congregation members come forward to kneel, and Jeanna makes collecting motions with her upraised hand as if there is a lightning bug or a gnat above her head.

After ten or fifteen minutes, Jeanna signs, sporadically at first with OH, JESUS and YOU POWERFUL, with LORD in between. Then, with quick, jerky signs, she prays specifically for Pat. HEAL HER, GIVE HER STRENGTH, KICK DEVIL OUT, OUT, OUT.[30] By this time, Pat, her eyes closed and head lowered, holds her arms outstretched before her, palms held upward as if she is waiting to catch something.

Then, with a sudden jerking movement, Pat falls backward, and Jeanna, shaken out of her own movement toward a trance state, catches her. While Jeanna holds Pat, she and Rosalie, another Deaf woman, discuss Pat, signing that she has gotten the FIRE. Because Pat lies across Jeanna's arm and leg, Rosalie tells Jeanna to WAIT rather than to move and risk waking Pat before she is ready to come back out. Pat's hands are still outstretched, her fingers spread and stiff. She lies there, eyes closed, and a small smile appears on her face. Her hands close into fists, and five more minutes pass. Her lips do not move, like those of the hearing worshipers near them. Finally, she awakens, shakes her head blissfully, and sits down next to me and Jeanna in the pew.

ME HURT YOU? Pat asks Jeanna.

NO, Jeanna signs back, BUT WHEN SPIRIT DESCEND/STRIKE, I FEEL, FAST! SCARED ME. SHOCK RIPPLE ACROSS YOUR BACK. Pat nods and smiles again, sleepy looking.

I ask Jeanna if this is being "slain by the Spirit," and she explains that WHEN FEEL GUILTY, SET UPON, WEIGHED DOWN, ASK LORD THESE THINGS, FOR FAMILY, FOR SELF. HE SEND PEACE, BLESSING. EYES CLOSE, FEEL TINGLING—here, she trails her fingers up her arms, shivering—IN ARMS, FACE,

SPIRIT COME, STRIKE—IN THE HEART—LIFT UP, FEEL GOOD, AT PEACE.
WHEN PAT FALL, ME FEEL SPARK-ELECTRICITY, IN HER BACK, SO FAST! She
then signs the sensation as a shivering shock transmitted from Pat to her.
After the service, Pat lingers, chatting, and she tells us that she had
been feeling so heavy, so weighed down; in praying, she felt hot, wanted
to take off her jacket, but found that she could not move. She prayed to
get up, but signed that H-E kept her there, PINNED DOWN.

TRUE, I FALL, she signs, her eyes relaxed.

For both Jeanna and Pat, the signs for and description of the visiting/
descending Spirit are different from those of the hearing and signing congregation members. For Adeline and the other hearing and signing members, the description of the Holy Spirit is literally SPIRIT or GHOST. When
Jeannna and Pat describe the mobile, encountering Spirit, one index finger points upward and moves downward and toward the body in a zigzag
fashion until it strikes the heart. That movement conceptualizes the relationship embedded in the trance state for these women in a very different
manner than used by the hearing women to articulate their experiences.

Alternately, Adeline's characterization of the trance state in spoken English draws upon a community-based formula for describing the experience of being "slain in the spirit": "I remember one time when I was
healed. I know what the Spirit of God felt like at that particular time. He
healed me, it felt hot, not burning, but hot oil from the top of my head
to the tip of my toes and then back up. . . . yeah, you can feel the fire of
the Holy Spirit." For Adeline, the Holy Spirit descends upon her in the
form of holy oil, the kind of blessing described in the Old Testament.
Other hearing women in the congregation also use this analogy, describing their encounters with the Spirit as the anointing, or blessing, of oil.
After experiencing this *mystic?* moment, Adeline uses symbolic language,
as Kristeva means it, and she arranges the sensory experience into a hierarchical relationship with the divine, moving from head to toe and back
up.

ADELINE: It could be when God slays people in the Spirit, there's
           a reason for it, you know, and he might do it for a differ-
           ent reason. If he's going to slay you in the Spirit, he's
           going to talk to you about something. He doesn't just

do it just to do it. He'll do it for a reason. Like he might slay somebody and then fill them with the Holy Ghost. Maybe he'll slay somebody over here and talk to them about something in their life they need to get straightened out. He usually does it for a reason.

Adeline's description of the trance state known as being "slain in the spirit" and its origin in a divine imperative seems remarkably paternalistic in comparison to Jeanna's much more direct and body-based explanation. With her description of certain physiological signs of relief and relaxation—clearly benefits of an induced meditative state—Jeanna's explanation sounds like a possible layman's psychology of religion. In contrast, "Maybe he'll slay somebody over there and talk to them about something they need to get straightened out" explains God as a chastising Father, very much in keeping with the Western model of hierarchical family structure.

Jeanna's explanation seems to describe a different God at work, one that offers peace and consolation: WHEN FEEL GUILTY, SET UPON, WEIGHED DOWN, ASK LORD THESE THINGS, FOR FAMILY, FOR SELF. HE SEND PEACE, BLESSING. EYES CLOSE, FEEL TINGLING—here, she trails her fingers up her arms, shivering—IN ARMS, FACE . . . SPIRIT COME, STRIKE—in the heart—LIFT UP, FEEL GOOD, AT PEACE. Could this be a God made different through an Other language, a more *feminine, maternal* God?

Because of my own secret desire to let go, to find a God who apprehends my body, who comforts and explains and helps me sleep at night, I am tempted to accept Jeanna's God as a refashioning, an embodied God who transcends gendered familial structures. Even so, I cannot ignore the immediate context in which these trance states occurred, a church that insists upon categorization of male and female roles and upon the primacy of the heterosexual family unit as emblematic of all that is right and proper.

This is, after all, a church in which the pastor has, from the pulpit, relayed messages "from God" expressly intended for the pastor's wife. (And one day when the preacher, with even more shouting and gesturing than usual, describes the "abomination" of two lesbians holding hands as they walk in front of his car, I realize from his detailed description that he's likely talking about two friends of mine.)

I feel torn open at this church.

"Thank you for this opportunity for compassion for those of us who are not as perfect as the rest of us," the preacher once said, in a prayer just before the Wednesday night ASL class began. Not as perfect? I look around to see if any of the Deaf adults react, but they politely watch the interpreter.

And so I don't say anything and keep going back. Each time my tires kick up a gravel cloud on the driveway leading up to this church, I feel like I have breathed in something poisonous.

Christmas 1995

I have been going to Praise Assembly for more than a month. After I turn in my grades and my term papers, I escape to Chicago and back to the comfort of my family and my hard-won communication with my mother, who often serves as my oral interpreter. We go downtown to a reading given by a male poet. We go to dinner with a group of women from the reading. No one really knows the others, and so there is a jittery, flashy brightness that overtakes conversation; there is no obligation to ever see each other again.

I sit through dinner conversation, numb and anxious, hoping both that no one will try to talk to me and that someone will rescue me from having to try to lipread everything. Then I notice signing at a nearby table. I watch over the talking heads at my table—it is a hearing woman who signs and her Deaf husband. The woman waits while her husband points out his order on the menu and then speaks and signs her own choices to the waitress.

Later, when they finish eating, they stand and shrug on their winter coats, and one of the women at my table leans over. She tells the signing woman, "Thank you. That was so beautiful." The signing woman just nods—polite—but you can tell she is annoyed.

I flush, filled with embarrassment and rage at this woman at my table and her appropriation—however unintended—of what should be *my* language. ASL is not a dinner show! I shake with anger because I don't quite yet fully have it—sign language—and I need it. At Praise Assembly of God and at the Greater Columbia Association of the Deaf club gatherings, I halt along in sign language, cringing and praying.

One night, at Praise, I am asked to help translate a verse from Corinthians, and I try: LOVE WHAT? PATIENT. LOVE WHAT? and I can't think of the right translation for "kind." Only later do I realize that I had signed SUFFER instead of its near neighbor on the chin, PATIENT. Every mistake I make feels twisted out of my skin, a reminder of time running out. This does not feel beautiful.

Not hearing, and not yet Deaf, I entered this church, wanting to know what lay outside of spoken language, what was possible outside the tradition of self and God grounded in sound. This is a "charismatic" church, and through Jeanna and Pat, I witness again and again something that I have no idea how to comprehend. In all my training as an academic, as an oral deaf woman, and as a Southern "good girl," I was not prepared to deal with the yearning subtext of *charisma*. My life has been about control, about not ever slipping and losing my place in the lipread conversation. It has never been about an encountering spirit, one who lifts up and provides peace. It has never been about communication that comes easily or that strikes directly.

"Charismatics" are neo-Pentecostalists who have formed congregations like the Assemblies of God that incorporate traditionally Pentecostal elements such as speaking in tongues and prayers for healing.[31] Despite the contemporary association with denominations who espouse socially and politically conservative beliefs, historically, "charisma" has been considered a subversive force. Philosopher Andrea Nye notes, "Certainly the church of our fathers, as the inspiring mystic Mary Daly would call it, learned the lesson fast that charisma was divisive and fragmenting and that the church would survive only if inspiration was replaced with dogma and with an organization."[32] Nye's distinction between inspiration and dogma is an important recognition of the social systems regulating religion. Nye's description also echoes Kristeva's categorization of the semiotic and the symbolic as a system regulating language and Cixous's Realms of the Proper and of the Gift as a similar system that also regulates gender.

Helene Cixous reinterprets the Lacanian libidinal female and male economies as the Realm of the Gift and the Realm of the Proper. The

Realm of the Gift opposes the Realm of the Proper (representative of the law, classification, property, and hierarchy). The "gift is perceived as establishing an inequality—a difference—in that it seems to open up an imbalance of power."[33] As such, the Realm of the Gift is "a deconstructive place of pleasure and orgasmic exchange with the other" and can open up a new space for *l'ecriture féminine*.[34] If, in this context, the "other" is the Holy Spirit, then it is certainly appropriate that charisma supplies a subversive "gift" or rejoicing, something that Pat, Jeanna, and Adeline do in their encounters with the divine.

Given the specificity of their relationships with a theologically defined and gendered male Spirit, I am confused by the *jouissance*, the real and completely unselfconscious pleasure I see on Pat's face and on the faces of the hearing women surrounding me. Jeanna and Pat both agree that Pat has experienced an encountering and electric spirit who knocks her over, literally, pervades her body with heat, and keeps her PINNED DOWN.

However, because of the bodily insistence of Pat's experience, I wonder if these encounters with the Other, in the name of the Father, are instead examples of what Kristeva describes as a "masochistic *jouissance*," or a woman's "only means of gaining access to the symbolic paternal order . . . by engaging in an endless struggle between the orgasmic maternal body and the symbolic prohibition—a struggle that will take the form of guilt and mortification and culminate in a form of masochistic *jouissance*."[35] The female ecstatic is one of several female archetypes, one that is ultimately tied to the "feminine," yet another stage in the process of participating within the symbolic.[36] In this particular church setting, there are no alternative descriptions of a female or even gender-neutral Spirit, and so in their use of male pronouns, Pat and Adeline reference and frame their experience within the rhetoric common to religious and mystic discourse. As a result, their male God is necessarily paternal and overpowering in their encounters.

Mystic discourse is contingent upon what has been called an "annihilation of consciousness," in which the discovery of the Other is essential, a "blow that both wounds and delights."[37] In this mystic discourse, one sees repeated references to loss of self, an expulsion of self, and transcendence. They martyr their sense of self and sacrifice it to a presence. The implication of this is, as Kristeva notes, that the conditioning of the symbolic order implicit within Christianity acts as a means by which women can "atone for their carnal *jouissance* with their martyrdom."[38] Interestingly, Pat's description of her trance states is quite a bit more bound to the carnal, in the embodied sense of the word, as she describes feeling pinned down, burning hot, and unable to move.

The French philosopher and psycholinguist Luce Irigaray would not be surprised by my confusion at the kind of *jouissance* expressed here. She argues that female mystics are immersed in yet another master discourse, one that denies representation except as a negative reflection of the male, and that includes interactions with a male God: "And if God, who thus has re-proved the fact of her non-value, still loves her, this means she exists all the same, beyond what anyone may think of her."[39] The female in this discourse is overdetermined as a negative space, an absence. Even as she makes self-abnegating proclamations during or after a mystic state, "that pleasure is still hemmed in by representations—however metaphysical—and by prescriptions—still ethically onto-theological—which determined it (and her) and thus limit their extension."[40]

By declaring, "Now I know it/myself and by knowing, I love it/myself, and by loving, I desire it/myself," the female mystic is complicit in the same system that allows *jouissance* but cannot grant her subjectivity.[41]

As an oral deaf woman, that is exactly it. That is exactly how I feel, in spoken English. I am allowed to move through the hearing world, to speak, but I can never be real. I have been faking it.

I entered this church filled with hope and dread, hoping for what exactly? Freedom from my old life? A new, emancipated body? It disappoints me to the edge of nihilism to realize that these hearing and Deaf women's ecstatic and trance experiences are not necessarily liberating or emancipating but act instead to once again limit and constrain, especially in Pat's descriptions of the "spirit." So, once again, there is the recognition that "speaking [or articulating experience through a symbolic language] will always involve a sacrificial contract. Lived experience may shatter that contract, but a new contract must be made as exclusive of lived experience as the old."[42]

But, even so, there is something about that annihilating moment when you are in between contracts. In between languages. When you fall.

I don't quite understand what I am feeling, at this church. I am failing as an ethnographer. Badly. Each time I go to Praise Assembly of God, I feel something crack, and afterward I cannot walk as well.

One day in early spring, I board the city bus and see Janet, a Deaf woman I have met at the deaf club in town. She waves me over to her, and I sit beside her. She tells me about her work as a dishwasher, bowling last night, her fiancé from Fulton. I nod and sign something about my stop coming up soon; I am headed to work at the university.

RIGHT, YOU INTERPRETER, I FORGOT, she tells me. I shouldn't—I know—but I feel slapped across the face.

NO, I yank out my hearing aid and angrily show her the proof. I AM DEAF.

BUT YOU SPEAK she signs, using a derisive inflection on the sign for speaking.

I give up. I am a failure. I nearly throw my hearing aid through the window. YES, I SPEAK. NO CHOICE. DON'T BLAME ME, I snap at her, holding my eyes wide open so she cannot tell she has made me cry. She mocks me, then laughs and shrugs.

ADELINE: I heard a story one time of a woman who was deaf in one ear, totally deaf, could not hear a thing in that ear. She went through a healing line to receive healing for that. And when she started, she really didn't believe she was going to be healed. But she began hearing the music that was being played on this side of her, 'cause this was the ear. Then blood poured out of her ears, like all over her clothes. She had on like a bright yellow outfit and it was just red by the time she walked out of there. She started hearing after that. So, she really, she really was doubtful at first, but she really began to believe that it could happen and God healed her.

As a doubtful girl—a participant-observer—I chose to do an ethnography of a Deaf ministry because I thought that would be an easier way into learning how to be Deaf.

I lose too much weight, cannot sleep, and don't make sense to myself or anyone else when I try to describe this cracking open. I dream of crucifixions, of stopwatches.

In late March 1996, I quit. I am finished. I put away my field notes, now semaphoric in their brevity and chaos. Trudy, a professor at the university, pulls me aside to talk about my stalled progress in the PhD program and my future as an academic and as a writer; "you seem so . . . discouraged," she tells me. I almost cry, but it is too late. At this point, I. Just. Don't. Care.

Suddenly, through Elaine, another professor, and a surprise chain of people stretching across the eastern half of the United States, there is an e-mail with an invitation to visit Gallaudet University, to see the Deaf university in Washington, D.C. When I board the eastbound train in Chicago, my mother, my oral interpreter of twenty-six years, hugs me and tells me to go find my life.

When I return from Gallaudet, I have a dream where I wander, a ghost, in between speech and sign language, and it's only until a Deaf person—no one I recognize even now—tells me that I'm who you are/a person that I become real and feel relief, crashing, flooding, satisfying relief.

true I respond, no longer doubtful.

Notes

1. Ross Guberman, ed., *Julia Kristeva: Interviews* (New York: Columbia University Press, 1996), 41.

2. Julia Kristeva, "The System and the Speaking Subject," in *The Kristeva Reader*, ed. Toril Moi (New York: Columbia University Press, 1986), 27.

3. Adeline Hardt, interview by Kristen Harmon, (5 November 1995.)

4. Elaine Showalter, "A Criticism of Our Own: Autonomy and Assimilation in Afro-American and Feminist Literary Theory," in *Feminisms: An Anthology of Literary Theory and Criticism* (New Brunswick, N.J.: , 1997), 213.

5. Julia Kristeva, *Revolution in Poetic Language* (New York: Columbia University Press, 1984), 26.

6. Kristeva, *Revolution*, 62.

7. Ibid., 27.

8. Ibid.

9. Toril Moi, *Sexual/Textual Politics* (New York: Routledge, 1988), 162.

10. Kristeva, *Revolution*, 69.

11. Ibid., 79.

12. Kristeva, *Desire in Language* (New York: Columbia University Press, 1980), 16.

13. Kristeva, *Revolution*, 61.

14. Ibid.

15. Ibid.

16. Ibid., 27.

17. Ibid., 24.

18. Guberman, ed., *Interviews*, 105.

19. Julia Kristeva, "Stabat Mater," in *Kristeva Reader*, 173.

20. Ibid.

21. Ibid.

22. Ibid., 177.

23. Kristeva, *Revolution*, 61.

24. Kristeva, "About Chinese Women," in *Kristeva Reader*, 154.

25. Helene Cixous, "Laugh of the Medusa," in *Feminisms*, 351.

26. Quoted in Anu Aneja, "The Mystic Aspect of *l'ecriture feminine*: Helene Cixous' *Vivre L'Orange*," *Qui Parle: Journal of Literary Studies* 3, no. 1 (1989): 190.

27. Kathryn Bond Stockton, "Bodies and God: Poststructuralist Feminists Return to the Fold of Spiritual Materialism," *Boundary 2* 19, no. 2 (1992): 119.

28. Marcia Hardt, interview by Kristen Harmon, November 5, 1995.

29. Christian Apologetics and Research Ministry, "What Does It Mean to Be Slain in the Spirit?" http://www.carm.org/questions/slain_spirit.htm (accessed February 2, 2005).

30. Kristen Harmon, "Field Notes" (November 19, 1995). Words in small capital letters represent ASL signs.

31. Harvey Cox, *Fire from Heaven: The Rise of Pentecostal Spirituality and the Reshaping of Religion in the Twenty-First Century* (Reading: Addison-Wesley, 1995), 106.

32. Andrea Nye, "Woman Clothed with the Sun: Julia Kristeva and the Escape from/to Language," *Signs: Journal of Women in Culture and Society* 12, no. 4 (1987): 672.

33. Moi, *Sexual/Textual Politics*, 112.

34. Ibid., 113.

35. Kristeva, "About Chinese Women," 27.

36. Ibid.

37. Michel deCerteau, "Mysticism," *diacritics* 22, no. 2 (1992): 17–18.

38. Kristeva, "About Chinese Women," 146.

39. Luce Irigaray, *Speculum of the Other Woman* (Ithaca, N.Y.: Cornell University Press, 1985), 199.

40. Ibid., 201.

41. Ibid., 200.

42. Nye, 679.

How Deaf Women Produce Gendered Signs

Arlene Blumenthal Kelly

Unfortunately, feminist perspectives on disability are not widely discussed in feminist theory, nor have the insights offered by women writing about disability been integrated into feminist theorizing about the body.

—*Susan Wendell, 1997*

D eaf female teachers of mostly hearing American Sign Language (ASL) learners must attempt to bridge the gap between Deaf culture and the mainstream hearing culture through teaching ASL and Deaf culture. To find out how they construct gender and feminism and then name the cultural sources of their constructions, I conducted an ethnographic study of five ASL teachers, whom I call Helen, Sadie, Gina, Jenny, and Lee. All of the women were born deaf, and all except Lee had hearing parents and learned ASL as their primary language when they entered school (between the ages of three and six).[1]

Although Lee began acquiring signs at birth, she hesitates to label this as ASL because the term did not appear until much later in her life and because her parents were both hard of hearing and oral.[2] In fact, her parents did not sign until they had two deaf children and began to socialize with other signing Deaf people. Furthermore, because both parents were hard of hearing, they used voice to communicate with each other. Lee's own signing fluency did not surface until sometime between high school and college. Lee was often the bridge between her parents and the Deaf world, much like a hearing child who usually interprets the hearing world for Deaf parents. Lee explains, I OFTEN CALL MYSELF DEAF CODA [child of deaf adults], ALWAYS HAVE TO EXPLAIN THINGS TO MY PARENTS, I THEIR INTERPRETER, HELP TEACH THEM. MY PARENTS NOT THAT EDUCATED. HAVE TO EXPLAIN TO THEM.[3]

For most of the women in this study, communication at home with hearing parents was mediocre at best. Three reported that none of their parents learned to sign; thus as children, they relied on lipreading, gesturing, or writing. Communication with other hearing relatives varied. For example, Jenny, who has a younger Deaf brother, used gestures in her family. Some of her hearing siblings could sign and finger spell fairly well. Often family members resorted to writing. Jenny recalled that during family gatherings, she and her Deaf brother would pair off to chat or to play. Now that both Jenny and her brother are married, their Deaf spouses have joined their small circle at family gatherings.

At the time of the study, the participants ranged in age from thirty-five to sixty. They grew up from the 1960s to the late 1980s. Although they had varied educational backgrounds, Deaf institutes (residential schools for deaf children) were clearly prominent in most of their lives.[4] During this time period, the United States underwent significant changes that resulted in the recognition of equal rights for racial and cultural minorities and for women. These changes occurred both within and outside the Deaf world.

Two of the women were in their twenties when ASL was recognized as a bona fide language and when the women's movement reemerged in 1965. Even after ASL gained recognition as a language, many hearing teachers believed it was an inferior language and that it was inadequate as the language of instruction. As a result, manually coded English systems that incorporated elements of ASL and English emerged. Many Deaf people found themselves on a linguistic seesaw, including most of my participants.

Because Gallaudet College (now University) was (and still is) the world's only liberal arts college for Deaf people, and most other colleges did not provide interpreters at that time, the women in this study attended and graduated from Gallaudet between 1961 and 1983. Each woman was positive about her Gallaudet experience, finding it an explosion both of cultural awareness and personal growth. All but one received a masters degree from Western Maryland College (now McDaniel College), in either Deaf Education or the Teaching ASL Program (TAP) between 1976 and 1994, and all of them had been teaching ASL for at least five years.

Religion became a topic of interest after the first round of interviews when Gina and Lee both mentioned their links to Judaism. One was born into it, and the other married into it after a Presbyterian upbringing. I then wondered if religion had an influence on their willingness to reach across cultures. In the second round of interviews, I learned that Helen, who was raised as a Lutheran, married into Judaism as well. Sadie's parents were of different faiths, and she was further influenced by a third religion imposed by her Deaf institute. Because of this mishmash of beliefs, Sadie has chosen not to practice a specific religion. Jenny, raised as a Catholic, views her being deaf as a "gift from God" because this characteristic allows her to make an important difference in people's lives. Although we discussed religion and the notion of bridging cultures, it seems religion plays a relatively minor role in the lives of four of the women and a major role for only one.

Defining Gender Terms

The life experiences of these five women reveal both similarities and dissimilarities in how each was raised and how each identifies as a Deaf woman. I explored how the informants' life experiences shaped their perceptions of "gender" and "feminism." I also studied how they signed terms such as "sex" and "patriarchy" to determine if the productions were linguistically constrained and/or socially influenced. Examining these terms with the women highlighted how these terms bridged, or not, the Deaf and hearing worlds. I discovered that although they taught gendered signs in their classrooms, gender roles and issues were not significant factors in bridging the two worlds.

During the second round of interviews, I was curious to discover whether the informants had signs for two terms common in the Women's studies field: *gender* and *feminism*. As Doe (1993) suggests in her dissertation, there are no known official ASL signs for "gender" and "feminism."

From this point, concepts such as "sex," "gay and lesbian," and "mother and father" emerged as natural evolutions in the informant's dialogues with me. These terms, especially the concept of "patriarchy" within the Deaf community, were significant during the third round of interviews. Our discussions highlighted how the women's Deaf and female experiences influenced their constructions and perceptions of these terms. Some signs were either linguistically constrained or socially influenced.

Gender: MAN^WOMAN

The women defined "gender" to mean male and female. They offered finger spelling as an alternative to signing MAN^WOMAN, advising that there were no semantic differences between the signed and finger-spelled forms. Their definition(s) were illuminated by how they signed it even if there are no official signs for this term.

The sign MAN originates at the forehead and ends on the chest, and the sign WOMAN begins at the chin and also ends on the chest (see figure 1).

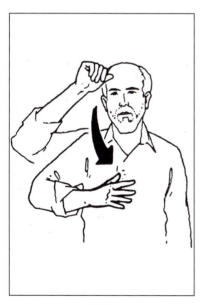
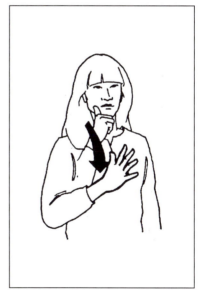

MAN   WOMAN

FIGURE I.

A 5 handshape is used, with the thumb in contact with the forehead or
the chin, respectively, and then the chest. At times, the sign begins with
a closed fist with an extended thumb at either the forehead or chin, yet it
consistently ends with a 5 handshape at the chest. This phonological difference does not suggest any semantic alternations. As often happens in
compounding, the movement of the first sign in MAN^WOMAN is short-
ened so that the thumb may not contact the chest for MAN.

For the five women, *gender* simply connotes male and female. When
asked for a sign for this English word, each informant invariably signed
the compounded form, MAN^WOMAN. At first, Lee signed MAN THEIRS,
WOMAN THEIRS, but quickly added MAN^WOMAN (see figure 2).[5] Finger
spelling G-E-N-D-E-R was also offered as an alternative, although this form
suggested no semantic shift from the signed form.

I noticed that each woman offered MAN^WOMAN to define gender, but
they never transposed the order to WOMAN^MAN. Thus, in the third round
of interviews, I inquired whether the sign order was influenced by an
internalized stereotyped social notion that men are superior to women, or
if the ASL production was a physical linguistic constraint. Upon being
asked the question, most informants experimented on the spot with both
forms before discussing it any further. Initially, some reported that societal views about gender may have influenced how they sign. I then finger-

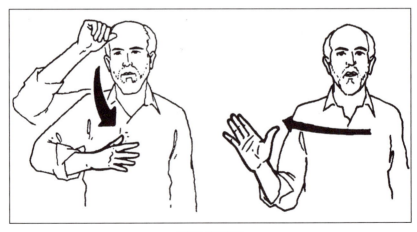

MAN THEIRS

FIGURE 2.

spelled P-A-R-E-N-T and asked how they signed that concept. *Parent* is often signed as MOTHER^FATHER, with the female noun at the head of the compound, and it is rarely signed in reverse (see figure 3). This changed the informants' minds, and they cited location or comfort level as factors in signing MAN^WOMAN rather than WOMAN^MAN.

Sadie initially offered that she might have been brainwashed about male superiority, conceding quickly that it indeed is oppressive. She then offered the example of GAY^LESBIAN, which is never signed LESBIAN^GAY. I, as a heterosexual woman, had been advised against signing GAY because it is an in-group sign, so I asked her about this. Sadie explained that although this production was once widely accepted, it is now an utterance used by gay men themselves (see figure 4).[6] Then when I ask her to sign P-A-R-E-N-T, she automatically signed MOTHER^FATHER. This episode propelled Sadie to cancel the notion about male superiority and realize that the order of MAN^WOMAN is more a result of physical comfort than anything else.

In addition, Gina suspected that the English phrase "he and she" might have influenced her signing of MAN^WOMAN. Nevertheless, after discussing and experimenting with the form, she finally decided that location

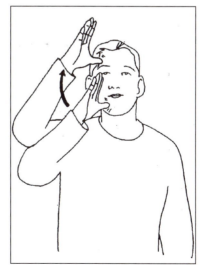

PARENTS

FIGURE 3.

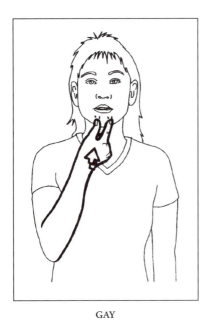 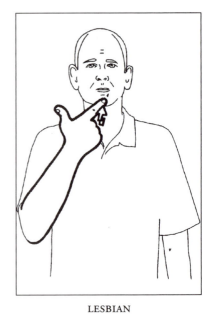

GAY   LESBIAN

FIGURE 4.

and physical comfort, not sociolinguistic influence, is the overriding factor in the sign sequence.[7]

Jenny cited harmony, rather than social views, in executing MAN^WOMAN. Like Jenny, Lee did not suggest societal views for this ASL production. Instead, she insisted that it was based on the comfort of moving downward from the forehead to the chin. She was, however, dumbfounded when she caught herself using an upward movement for MOTHER^FATHER. All informants offered that they never use the word *gender* in their ASL teaching because the need simply never arises. They teach gendered signs such as MAN, WOMAN, BOY, and GIRL and other signs such as AUNT and GRANDMOTHER. Helen took advantage of the locations of these gendered signs, using them as memory aids for ASL learners. As my interviews with these informants illustrate, the sign order of MAN^WOMAN warrants further sociolinguistic investigation. Why is it signed this way and not the other? What are the implications for this particular sign sequence?

During the second round of interviews, four informants independently began a dialogue about the term *sex*, discussing its English and ASL definitions. The topic of sex and the signs used to convey this concept, #SEX and SEX (see figure 5) then became one of the focal points in the third round.[8] Three informants offered that *sex* has two meanings in ASL and English—as a noun to describe biological attributions and as a verb to denote physical intercourse. Two other informants agreed on the English definitions but wavered on ASL productions.

The origin of the sign SEX, although obscure, dates from sometime in the 1970s. Sadie, however, claimed that a hearing biology teacher in an American Deaf institute invented this sign. Because the sex chromosome for males is Y and for females is X, this teacher created this sign. Over time, the Y handshape underwent a lexicalization into an X. On the other hand, someone not in this study told me that SEX was created in the mid-1970s by a hearing husband-and-wife counseling team who perceived that finger spelling S-E-X was too obvious, thus having a sign would be a good cover-up, like a euphemism. However, unlike many English words that have origins described in the *Oxford English Dictionary*, there is no known published literature about the origin of the sign SEX or many other ASL signs.

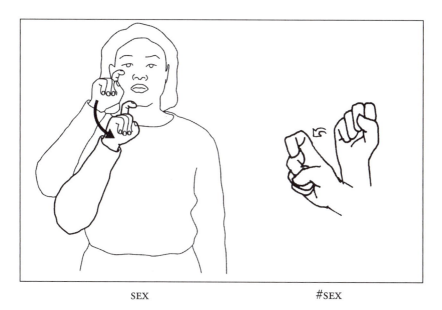

SEX   #SEX

FIGURE 5.

In the second round of interviews, Helen, Sadie, and Gina discussed the implications and meanings behind the sign SEX, offering that it actually meant biological differences. The general Deaf population, however, today uses this sign to indicate both biological attributions and sexual intercourse—which was erroneous according to these three informants.

In the final round, the semantics of signing and finger spelling *sex* was explored further. Helen, Sadie, and Gina reiterated that SEX is not in their sign vocabulary because #SEX is not difficult to execute. They were also adamant that SEX is a noun and that #SEX can be either a noun or a verb. Jenny claimed that both forms, SEX and #SEX, are interchangeable as either a noun or a verb. She, however, preferred to finger spell it, suggesting that it is more appropriate to ask "which gender" than "which sex." In addition, Lee suggested that either form could signify a noun or a verb.

The topic of signed and finger-spelled forms for "sex" was raised by the four informants in the second round of interviews, becoming one of the focal points in the final round. Jenny and Lee seemed uncomfortable in discussing this as evidenced by nervous laughs and pauses. On the other hand, the three other informants were not at all embarrassed. Did this discomfort stem from uncertainty of the usage of the sign SEX? There also seemed to be a general confusion in regard to the usage of the signed form. Clarification may be needed to establish uniformity for its usage. Determining the exact origin of SEX, although not of utmost urgency, might be of interest to historical linguists.

Feminism: WOMAN^SUPPORT

In discussing the term *feminism*, I finger spelled the word to the five informants. First, Helen responded that her childhood was tomboyish, thus she was not feminine. I then recalled that feminist literature has consistently suggested that feminism is a difficult notion. So perhaps this was true for Helen. However, it turned out that she did not know the difference between "feminism" and "feminine." Because Helen was the first to be interviewed in this round, I fretted that I would face similar difficulties in discussing feminism with the remaining women. This, however, was not the case with how Sadie, Jenny, and Lee defined the term:

Sadie: I VISUALIZE WOMAN STRONG BELIEVE ABOUT WOMEN, AS A WOMAN, WHO I AM. EMPOWER MYSELF. HOW I WANT TO SAY, THINK, BEHAVE, BELIEVE. THAT WOMAN'S THINKING, NOT LIKE MAN'S THINKING. ENOUGH OF BOWING TO MAN'S WAYS, NO THANKS. THAT WHAT I VISUALIZE.

Jenny: WOMEN HAVE THEIR OWN RIGHTS, POWER, CONTROL, RE-SENT MAN ABOVE THEM, PREFER WOMEN NEAR #OR ABOVE MEN. THEIR CULTURE, EXPERIENCES, GROW UP, OPPRESSION + + +. NOW WOMAN CAN DO ANYTHING IN WORK WORLD.

Lee: MAYBE POLITICAL ACTION, #OR SOCIAL ACTION, FIGHTING FOR RIGHTS, CAN BE DAINTY, FEMININE. WOMEN'S RIGHTS TO VOTE, FEMININE RIGHTS, EQUALITY. #OR DEPENDING WHICH PER-SPECTIVE, (shifts role) FEMININE, #OR (shifts role) THAT WOMAN NOT FEMININE, MORE M-A-S-C-U-L-I-N-E, MAN^WAY. (Shifts back to self.) I NOT SURE WHAT YOU LOOKING FOR.
A: LET'S LOOK AT WORD F-E-M-I-N-I-S-M, NOT F-E-M-I-N-I-N-E.
L: OH O-K, UMMM, WOMAN ROLE IN SOCIETY. MOVEMENT. COULD BE, AGAIN, POLITICAL MOVEMENT, SOCIAL MOVEMENT.

Gina recalled struggling to understand the word *feminism*. In her ado-lescence, she learned about the word and equated it with being masculine. Gina also associated the term with noted feminist Gloria Steinem, imag-ining her to be manly. However, when Gina attended the National Asso-ciation of the Deaf convention in Miami, the 1970 National Democratic Convention was taking place nearby. Steinem was in attendance and ap-peared in public. Upon seeing her, Gina was surprised to see how femi-nine Steinem was.

In addition, Gina continued to be unsure about the difference between *feminism* and *feminist* until we made an analogy with *oralism* and *oralist*.[9] Not only did this analogy help Gina grasp the difference between "-ism" and "-ist," but it was interesting that we used the oralism concept to facilitate understanding.

None of the five women knew a formal or established sign for femi-nism. But they experimented on the spot with several possible signs, in-cluding WOMAN with an emphatic nonmanual grammatical marker denoting assertiveness, power, or strength; WOMAN^UNITY; and finger spelling. When I said that I have seen WOMAN^REBEL, Sadie and Jenny reacted adversely, declaring it had a negative connotation. Lee did not like it either, saying that the production is too much like "revolution." Jenny offered that REBEL could imply "disobedient." Sadie then suggested that Deaf women need to get together to discuss feminism, its sign, and semantics.

When I showed the sign WOMAN^SUPPORT, all liked it (see figure 5). I explained that this sign emerged in my doctoral classes with interpreters. In the beginning, we used WOMAN^REBEL, but as the interpreters and I came to understand the complicated issues surrounding feminism, that sign was no longer appropriate. So we came up with WOMAN^SUPPORT. Sadie said she has seen some people use that sign. After more discussion, the participants came up with other possible ASL compounds—WOMAN^EMPOWER, WOMAN^RIGHTS, and WOMAN^EQUAL.

Sadie, Jenny, and Lee agreed that men can be feminists, in the same way that there are hearing allies in the Deaf community. Lee offered the following explanation: SUPPORT OF WOMAN RIGHTS, IDEAS, MOVEMENT, YES. EVEN IF NOT WOMAN. FOR EXAMPLE, HEARING PEOPLE CAN'T BE IN CORE, HEART O-F DEAF CULTURE, BUT CAN SUPPORT COMMUNITY. SAME IDEA FOR MEN SUPPORT WOMEN.

Feminist social scientist Margaret L. Anderson (1997) suggests that *feminism* means different things to different people. People are often reluctant to call themselves feminists because of a misunderstanding about what it means. Common misconceptions include lesbianism, man-hating, and an inability to be gentle, kind, and reasonable. Actually, feminism is a way of both thinking and acting (Anderson 1997, 8). It allows us to look at how women's and men's positions in society result from social institutions and attitudes. Thus, it became interesting to see how the five female participants presented ASL signs for gendered terms.

The fact that feminism itself is already a difficult notion to grasp underscores the appreciation of four of my five informants. Yet it was interesting to see that feminism was associated primarily with fighting for equality and rights as Sadie, Jenny, and Lee suggested, as well as being masculine as in Gina's case. Although there are no known signs for feminism, the informants were ingenious in devising possible ASL compounds for it.

Patriarchy: MAN CONTROL

Because the informants consistently signed MAN OPPRESS, MAN CONTROL, or MAN^CONTROL^ME in the second round of interviews, I took these to signify patriarchy (see figure 6). I then became curious if they knew any English equivalents for these signs. In the third round of interviews, I used these glosses to elicit English versions.

Helen, Sadie, and Lee claimed not to know the English word(s) for these signs. But when I finger spelled P-A-T-R-I-A-R-C-H-Y to them, they nodded their heads in the manner among signers denoting "oh of course I knew, I just forgot." In addition to this head nod, both Sadie and Lee offered the female counterpart, by finger spelling M-A-T-R-I-A-R-C-H-Y. *Patriarchy* was a new word for Gina and Jenny. I wondered if they had actually seen this word in print but never found out its meaning, but I did not probe them. Jenny was pleased to learn this new word as well as. *matriarchy*, asking me to write them down for her.

Although three of the women admitted later that they actually knew this English equivalent, none of them used the word on their own. It became obvious that the English counterpart was clearly not in their consciousness. Is it because they have not been exposed to it on a frequent basis, even if they used the ASL equivalent eloquently and frequently in this study? If this word is not in their consciousness, I have come to believe that it, like the sign denoting gender, is not taught in their ASL classes. This is not to suggest that not teaching some specific gendered signs would jeopardize the learning of ASL or bridging the two worlds. It is just interesting that the teachers who are female do not teach some

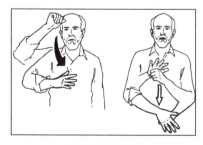
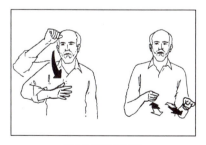

MAN OPPRESS   MAN CONTROL

FIGURE 6.

specific gendered signs, aside from those that signify female familial or
social roles such as mother, aunt, sister, teacher, and nurse.

CONCLUSION

As a result of my interviews with the five Deaf ASL teachers, I concluded
that the signed forms for *gender*, *feminism*, and the English version of
patriarchy are not part of these women's active vocabulary. The informants themselves admitted that they rarely thought in these terms and
they never used the word "gender" in their ASL classes because the need
simply never arose.

Sociolinguists suggest that the lexicon may be separated by form or by
function. *Form* refers to the absence of significant meanings attached to a
specific lexical term. In this study, MAN^WOMAN and #SEX fall into this
category because the signs for these terms are straightforward and can be
applied to any parts of speech. #SEX can be a noun or a verb. *Functional*
terms suggest a correlation between semantics and form. The ASL signs
for "feminism," MAN OPPRESS, MAN^CONTROL^ME, are functionally linguistic because specific semantics (meanings) come to mind.

In addition, *patriarchy* leans more toward being a linguistic construction for the informants because they either never used or heard of it before. In short, you clearly cannot begin an insightful dialogue if you do
not know the terminology (Doe 1993). Does this lack of knowledge cause
gender issues to stay on the back burner within the community of Deaf
women? Though the answer to that question was not part of this, it seems
that it would be difficult to have an insightful dialogue on the issues if the
informants in this study identified themselves as Deaf more than as women
and not even as Deaf women. Their lives revolved around experiences of
being Deaf, such as facing communication barriers in various social con-
texts. As teachers of ASL and Deaf culture, their Deaf identity/ies are much
more salient than their gender identity. After participating in this study,
they were moved to reconsider the role of gender issues in their lives.

In general, the Deaf female experience is excluded from cultural studies. Although Deaf women generally do not view themselves as disabled,
literature about Deaf people is usually found within fields such as, but
not limited to, psychology and audiology. There is a severe absence of

scholarly literature written from and/or about the cultural perspective of Deaf people (Schuchman 1988). Most of the literature focuses on the physical deficit of hearing impairment, rather than the social experiences associated with being Deaf (Padden and Humphries 1988; Paranis 1996). Even more discouraging is that most of this literature neglects the Deaf female experience. It is hoped that this study, along with Doe's dissertation, will prompt Deaf women to write and publish their life experiences. Such stories would enrich cultural studies, Deaf studies, American studies, women's studies, and disability studies.

When I began my research, I speculated that ASL teachers became empowered after ASL teacher preparation, that this form of empowerment was tied to their Deaf identity/ies, that Deaf women rarely addressed gender issues in depth, and that the dialogue emerging from this study would promote a reconsideration for the role of gender issues in Deaf women's lives. As it turned out, these speculations were proven true. Before becoming ASL teachers, the participants took their life experiences for granted. As they came to understand the marriage of language and culture, their identity/ies as Deaf people became much more salient. In other words, they became empowered. Their physical identity/ies as women, however, were not salient. Although they were physically female, their experiences as women were not as prominent as their Deaf experiences. Toward the end of this study, each participant confessed that she rarely considered gender issues and roles within her own life and the Deaf community.

NOTES

1. This essay is based on my dissertation, "How Deaf Women Construct Teaching, Language and Culture, and Gender: An Ethnographic Study of ASL Teachers" (in American Studies, University of Maryland, College Park, December 2000). I collected my data from the women's responses to written demographic forms, videotaped interviews, videotaped classroom participant observations, and follow-up e-mail communiqués.

2. This hesitancy is common; see chapter 5 in Padden and Humphries (1988) for further explanation.

3. Using English words to represent ASL signs is known as glossing. These words appear in small capital letters. The symbol ⌃ is used to signify ASL compounds. A hyphen is used between two glosses that represent one

sign. Hyphens are also used between the letters of finger-spelled words (Valli and Lucas, 1995).

4. The first permanent American school for the Deaf was founded in 1817 in Hartford, Connecticut. It was, and still is, a residential school where students lived for the majority of their childhood. Other such schools were established across the nation. It was then the norm for the majority of American Deaf children to go to such schools for an average of eighteen years. However, since the 1975 passage of the PL 94-142 promoting mainstreaming in public schools, residential schools are facing extinction. Helen and Jenny attended signing residential schools all their lives. Sadie went to an oral residential school all her life, learning signs informally from her peers. Gina had the widest variety of experiences, from a signing day school to a boarding oral school to two different public schools. Lee, who is hard of hearing, attended public schools.

5. THEIRS in this context means "pertaining to."

6. GAY is executed with the tips of the index finger and thumb of the G handshape tapping two or three times on the chin. I was curious about the use of GAY among Deaf gay men, so I asked students, ranging from eighteen to thirty in age, in my fall 2000 Deaf culture class about it. Perplexed by Sadie's suggestion that only gay men used this sign, they proposed that GAY may be a generational issue, warranting a sociolinguistic investigation.

7. Location and physical comfort as understood in sign language linguistics refer to the production of signs. There are signs that are not comfortable either for the signer or the signee. In addition, the semantics very often can and do change.

8. The crosshatch signifies a lexicalized finger-spelled form in which one or more of the letters are dropped and the resulting hand configurations and movement become a recognized sign (see Valli and Lucas 1995). In the case of #SEX, the middle letter is dropped and the hand twists. SEX is executed with an X handshape originating at the temple, moving downward, and ending at the cheek.

9. Oralism is a philosophy that espouses speaking over signing, and an oralist refers to a person who practices this philosophy.

WORKS CITED

Akmajian, A., R. A. Demers, and R. M. Harnish. 1988. *Linguistics: An introduction to language and communication*. Cambridge, Mass.: MIT Press.

Andersen, M. L. 1997. *Thinking about women: Sociological perspectives on sex and gender.* Boston: Allyn and Bacon.

Doe, T. M. 1993. Exploring gender with Deaf women and their hearing sisters. PhD diss., Univ. of Alberta, Edmonton.

Fasold, Ralph. 1987. *The sociolinguistics of society.* New York: Basil Blackwell.

Padden, Carol, and Tom Humphries. 1988. *Deaf in America: Voices from a culture.* Cambridge, Mass.: Harvard University Press.

Parasnis, I., ed. 1996. *Cultural and language diversity and the Deaf experience.* New York: Cambridge University Press.

Schuchman, John S. 1988. *Hollywood Speaks: Deafness and the Film Entertainment Industry.* Champaign, Ill.: University of Illinois Press.

Valli, Clayton, and Ceil Lucas. 1995. *Linguistics of American Sign Language: An introduction.* 2nd ed. Washington, D.C.: Gallaudet Univ. Press,

Wendell, S. 1997. Towards a Feminist Theory of Disability. In *The disability studies reader*, ed. L. J. Davis, 260–69. New York: Routledge.

"Beautiful, though Deaf"
The Deaf American Beauty Pageant

Susan Burch

The rise and continued popularity of beauty contests in the Deaf world reflect the differing notions of cultural deafness and beauty, both within the Deaf world and in mainstream society.[1] These pageants have primarily emphasized the physicality of women, while often downplaying or denying their Deaf cultural identity. At the same time, Deaf male spectators herald cultural deafness at these competitions, and with their Deaf female peers they challenge the prevalent notion of "the perfect body" exhibited by mainstream beauty contests. Although certain aspects of displaying cultural Deafness in such pageants have changed since the Deaf President Now! Movement (DPN) and the greater politicization of the community in the 1990s, gendered Deafness has remained relatively static in significant ways.[2]

Several scholars have elegantly shown that the mainstream beauty pageants of the twentieth century responded to the rise of eugenics and social-scientific constructions of physical fitness and normalcy.[3] In one such provocative work, *The Black Stork*, historian Martin Pernick demonstrated that eugenics promised to make humanity not just strong and smart but beautiful as well. Being hereditarily fit included being visually attractive. Ugliness, according to these scientists, was a hereditary disease. Good grooming was commonly linked to good breeding.[4]

Articles in Deaf newspapers reflected a similar notion. A 1925 *Silent Worker* article noted, for example, that "good health is so radiant an attribute that mere 'irregular fatures'[sic] are almost, if not entirely, unnoticed in their possessor. . . . is it not logical, therefore, that . . . the entire body can be developed to that physical perfection which is genuine beauty?"[5] A 1927 article in the same paper, entitled "Beauty Is Health Deep," claimed that "no one can be truly handsome unless she [sic] is truly healthy."[6] The article goes on to describe the discipline needed to maintain an appropriate regimen to show women's inner beauty by perfecting their outer beauty.

Deaf people have long accepted the hierarchy of "handicaps" expressed by early eugenicists and have rejected such negative classifications for only their own population. Deaf leaders and advocates consistently focused on their "normal" intelligence and ability to work—their "able-bodiness"—in public relations campaigns and in expressions to each other.[7] Yet mainstream society commonly perceived deaf people as similar to if not identical with "defectives" like feebleminded people, undercutting community members' citizenship status. As eugenic ideology intensified during the twentieth century, Deaf activists sought to preserve and protect their society by distancing themselves from other disabled people and emphasizing their commonality with mainstream, middle-class society.[8] Deaf beauty contests exemplify this strategy. Women's beauty, as projected by the Deaf media and pageants, enforced the notion of normalcy in two ways: the sense of commonality with (able-bodied) others, and the sense that beauty specifically suggests healthiness and vitality. The issues of "passing" (as able bodied), normalcy, and beauty strongly inform the popularity of Deaf beauty pageants.[9]

Deaf beauty pageants are ubiquitous. Since the 1920s, they have flourished at the local, state, and national level. Inspired in part by the early Miss America competitions, local, state, and national Deaf organizations began sponsoring Deaf beauty pageants in the 1920s.[10] Deaf newspapers, films, and eventually television programs frequently celebrated such victors, usually with greater frequency than other groups or types of women.

Commentary on Deaf beauty pageants in the Deaf and mainstream press reveals an intimate connection between women's beauty and oralism (as both a symbol and practice of "normalcy" in the period before DPN). Articles from the 1920s on deaf dancer Helen Heckman epitomize this. One entitled "Overcoming the Handicap of Deafness" asked readers whether they had ever witnessed a deaf girl play the piano compellingly or sing and dance eloquently. Praising Heckman's ability to perform musical numbers—via instruments, her voice, and her body—the article alludes to the many obstacles overcome by the deaf prodigy: her "handicap of deafness," the loss of her mother at a young age, and her physical awkwardness. Repeatedly citing Heckman's ability to speak and dance as the means as well as the symbol of her success, the author instructs readers to learn from her example: "The results in this direction may be taken as a convincing demonstration not only of the value of the training of the body, but of the possibilities in the way of development of the mental faculties through the training of the body."[11] In other words, a beautiful, fit body reflects a beautiful, fit mind. The article originally ran in a mainstream publication (*Physical Culture Magazine*) and thus instructed presumably hearing women to take note from Heckman's experience, but its placement in the prominent Deaf magazine, the *Silent Worker*, takes on added meaning. Presenting Heckman as the model of a successful *deaf* woman specifically encouraged female deaf readers to emulate her physical beauty and poise as well as her efforts to speak vocally. The general absence of articles explicitly describing women who could not voice articulately or perform like Heckman (and hearing women) compounded the powerful message sent by the essay on the oral "overcomer": deaf female beauty required oralism. Other articles echoed this point.

Three years later, the November 1922 cover of the *Silent Worker* displayed a profile of Helen Heckman under the banner "Our Beautiful Deaf Women." Heckman had placed second in a mainstream national contest of beauty of face and figure. The extended article on Heckman not only celebrated her good looks but also highlighted her strict oral training and complete separation from Deaf people and Deaf culture. The newspaper again praised and embraced her "overcoming" story. Later, writing from Italian Switzerland in 1928, Heckman spoke directly to Deaf readers of the *Silent Worker*. Contrasting her deaf childhood with her oral adulthood, she said, "I think of myself at the age of twelve, a fat, lazy, ignorant girl, without speech or learning, using signs in lieu of words, deficient in the sense of balance, unable to eat without smacking or to exert myself at all without making unnatural sounds." With oral training she could "converse freely with hearing persons through the natural medium of speech; read the lips of others so easily that I do not sense

the absence of hearing . . . [and] move about in the hearing world as a normal, happy being without the finger of pity being pointed toward me."[12]

Her point, like her speech, was clear. Success, normalcy, and beauty depended on oral ability. Although Heckman may have pitched her message to the broader Deaf community, it resonated mostly with women. Throughout the 1920s the *Silent Worker* (and its peers during and since) vilified deaf men who advocated oralism, limiting Heckman's example to female consumers. The paper, which was the premier Deaf newspaper of its time, consistently delineated success according to gender, and feminine deaf achievement was closely allied with oralism. Heckman, perhaps the most visible oral example of her time, appears to be the only deaf female to be honored twice on the front cover of the *Silent Worker*, the premier paper of its time.[13]

Other Deaf magazines echoed this message. For example, a 1935 *American Deaf Citizen* front page article celebrated Miss Deaf Chicago, Esther Dettinger. Repeatedly referred to as "the oralist," Dettinger walked away with the crown from the Kansas City pageant.[14] Four years later, two

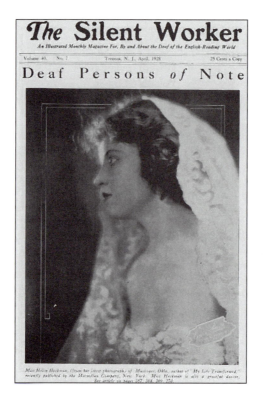

The Silent Worker
An Illustrated Monthly Magazine For, By and About the Deaf of the English-Reading World
Volume 40.   No. 7   Trenton, N. J., April, 1928   25 Cents a Copy
Deaf   Persons   of   Note

Miss Helen Heckman, (from her latest photograph) of Muskogee, Okla., author of "My Life Transformed," recently published by the Macmillan Company, New York. Miss Heckman is also a graceful dancer. See article on pages 267, 268, 269, 270.

front covers of the popular *Digest of the Deaf* displayed oral beauties. The July 1939 issue claimed that Kansan Beulah Edith Harding enjoyed a "singing childhood" before becoming deaf at age ten and emphasized her speech skills. It later described her as "an excellent speaker and lip reader." A finalist for the Miss Chicago contest in the 1930s, Harding went on to professional modeling under the name Barbara Lee.[15] Marion Rene, the subject of the September 1939 issue, was a night club dancer. "Her success in spite of the critical criteria of the bright lights is yet another proof that deafness need be no bar to undoubted talent." The article continued: "Perhaps a story of her life will bring comfort and help to other young deaf people and make them feel that there indeed is a place for each of them in this hearing world."[16] This "blonde oralist" achieved success by appearing exceptional only in her beauty and dance skills, like Heckman. Subsequent media coverage of deaf winners of mainstream as well as Deaf pageants—especially state and national ones—noted that the lovely ladies had "excellent" or "very good" oral skills.

Articles throughout most of the twentieth century continued to broadcast deaf beauties' ability to "pass" as hearing. In the 1950s Violet Hylton bested her coworkers at the Standard Garment Company beauty pageant, startling the judges when they learned she was deaf. The newspaper report specifically emphasized that the contestants were evaluated according to their poise, personality, and, "of course, how they would look in a bathing suit."[17] The "personality" component likely involved some spoken presentation that Hylton could satisfy with demure responses, whereas the poise and bathing suit competitions allowed Hylton to be seen exactly as the hearing women were seen—posing, sashaying, smiling, and nodding at the audience. In all of these ways, silence was seen as exemplary of femininity. A 1981 article on Miss Deaf America winner Mary Beth Barber noted: "A male patron at a theater once grabbed her and swooned over her sexy 'French' accent." It continued: "A date recently told her, 'Mary Beth, your ears may not work well, but they sure are pretty.'"[18] Barber, who had attended oral and mainstream schools, had overcome her shyness by joining the cheerleading squad and theater groups where she presumably voiced regularly (and successfully). Placed among a crowd of hearing ladies, Hylton, Barber, and others like them distinguished themselves not by their physical or cultural deafness but by their physical beauty. Even the attempt to pass seemed to be important. Although they failed to fully pass as hearing, the women still succeeded. Their attractiveness helped them "overcome" their stigmatized deafness in the eyes of hearing judges. In these cases and many others, authors reveled in the success of deaf women's actual or perceived victory over and among hearing women—in beauty pageants or in extracurricular activities. In the process, they—and presumably many readers—celebrated the approval bestowed on one of their own by the broader hearing world.

Multiple factors tied deaf femaleness to oralism and beauty, while anti-oralism partly defined male cultural deafness. For many—hearing and deaf—oralism had unique feminine qualities. For example, the quintessential oral educator throughout the late nineteenth and twentieth centuries was single, white, and female. The skills she taught fostered "polite"

behavior—speaking over gesturing. Discouraging facial expressions common in signed (visual) communication as "barbaric"—and thus inherently more "masculine"—oral female advocates focused on young girls
more than boys, instilling lipreading and speech skills along with specific
gendered behavioral lessons. Many parents and oral educators hoped that
with speech training, deaf girls might attract hearing suitors; deaf boys, in
contrast, were assumed incapable of landing a hearing girl and thus received more vocational training than speech training. As oralism expanded, female oral educators generally replaced deaf male teachers in
the classroom. Emasculated by this cultural and employment threat, Deaf
men—as "protectors of Deaf society and culture"—specifically fought
oralism and oral educators.

Oralists and Deaf leaders fostered a specific form of deaf female femininity that encouraged deaf women to use oralism to pass as hearing in
their search for beauty. For example, contributors to the *Volta Review*, the
preeminent oral journal, explained to ladies how lipreading in front of
mirrors helped cultivate beauty, including one article entitled "How to
Be Beautiful, Though Deaf." The author goes on to call oralism a miracu-
lous art for deaf ladies seeking femininity. Another article in the same
issue continued, claiming that "Love May Be Blind, but Not Deaf."[19]
Such prescriptive essays conflated love, sex, beauty, and marriage to describe successful deaf women. Especially pervasive was the suggestion that
sexual appeal demanded greater "normality" for deaf women.[20] In other
words, deaf women had to "pass" as hearing in order to be attractive. By
the 1950s some vocational advocates advanced beauty arts, such as
makeup classes and hair styling, for deaf women in particular because "it
is logical to consider the proper use of cosmetics as the final oralist touch
in the scientific care of the well body. The value of good appearance in the
development of personality is frequently emphasized [and necessary]."[21]

Presenting deaf women as "normal" through their beauty and orality
was in fact a conscious decision by some Deaf male leaders. Like many
other minority groups in early twentieth-century America, Deaf elite men
felt compelled to prove their value to society, and thereby earn a place of
equality rather than to demand civil rights or government intervention on
their behalf. In the case of Deaf beauty pageants, men emphasized deaf
women's beauty and oral ability as a way of proving that they were "real"

men—to each other as well as to mainstream society. In essence, the men claimed that "our beautiful deaf women" were as good as hearing women, and therefore they themselves must be worthy men. In this example, deaf women were ornamental tools by which one group of men "spoke" to another. The desire to prove their worthiness and normalcy manifested in additional ways. This particular approach necessitated that the community minimize its difference with mainstream society. In Deaf media and public relations campaigns, Deaf organizations inflated qualities they shared with mainstream society: strong work ethic, patriotism, high moral values, and civic responsibility. In fact, many leaders went further, suggesting that Deaf people surpassed their hearing peers. This "hyper"-American image very specifically challenged the pervasive view of deaf citizens as disabled, different, or "Other."

Beauty pageants presented a public venue to assert deaf worthiness, deaf normalcy. Deaf contestants allowed themselves to be inspected, judged, and admired. This process assumed—implicitly and explicitly—that finalists and winners were the most worthy, the most "perfect" in their normalcy. The structure of these contests reveals both a close alignment with mainstream rituals and complex Deaf cultural expectations for women. Early contests, usually sponsored by local clubs, copied the patterns that prevailed in mainstream society, which highlighted a mixture of fashion modeling, walking, posing, and responding to questions. Various Deaf associations joined together to sponsor larger beauty contests by the 1930s, but a national program occurred roughly forty years later. Proposed by Douglas Burke in 1966, the Miss Deaf America pageant grew from the Cultural Program of the National Association of the Deaf (NAD). As one official website explains:

> There was one aspect of the arts that had yet to be explored—the world of drama. Dr. Burke visualized the need of a "way to recognize deaf actresses at an early age." . . . The main objective of the Miss Deaf America Talent Pageant was ". . . a new concept to help us elevate the image and self-concept of deaf ladies throughout the United States. This is not an ordinary contest. . . . beauty, poise, gracefulness are desirable qualities, but the biggest point is one's cultural talent performance."[22]

As with the Miss America Pageant, four categories of competition have dominated the national Deaf pageant since the 1970s: evening gown, swimsuit, talent, and congeniality (the question and answer—Q&A—interview). At most, two of the categories—talent and interview—encourage expression in ASL, and judges are expected to assess fashion taste in all four sections (as listed on their ballots). Moreover, the talent and congeniality performances occur in the final rounds, after all the contestants have "passed" under the audience gaze, representing themselves solely with their bodies (not using signed or spoken language). Thus, although many claim that such pageants offer deaf women a chance to express themselves, it is a highly physicalized version of expression, and the performative nature of the Q&A leaves a tightly scripted—and muted—personal voice.

The example of Ann Billington, winner of the first Miss Deaf America pageant in 1972, encompasses these complicated notions of "normalcy," beauty, and cultural deafness. Dressed in a trim white sailor suit, Billington signed while vocally singing a piece entitled "Hey, Look Me Over" during the talent competition. Raised orally, she only started to learn signs while attending Gallaudet College.[23] Articles on Billington consistently noted her understandable speech and her ability to read lips well. Many other contestants and subsequent winners had similar backgrounds and abilities and were proud to express them.

Billington's performance of exemplary deaf femininity continued during her reign as "an ambassador who conveys Deaf Awareness in
beauty."[24] Mervin Garretson, president of the NAD in1978, asserted that
Miss Deaf Americas as a group "face an awesome responsibility in projecting a positive and a genuine image of deaf persons, not only from the
standpoint of entertainment, but also in information sharing and in en-
gendering good will and acceptance of deaf people as they are."[25] One
article specifically describing Billington proclaimed: "The Miss Deaf
America winner is a talent queen! As such, she is a capable and beautiful
performer. She can be helpful to your convention by performing a show
whenever you need her talents, maybe at the ball or maybe during the
banquet. She could sing a song at the banquet table, maybe 'The Star
Spangled Banner' or 'America the Beautiful.'"[26]

Miss Deaf America, explicitly described by this ad, serves as an ambassador of beauty and vitality to mainstream society, but she also reflects
cultural Deaf ideals. Billington is "talented and beautiful," challenging
mainstream notions of disabled citizens (including deaf people) as dependent, incapable, and unappealing. Her possible performance of patriotic
songs suggests commonality with mainstream society, of full and equal
citizenship status, while also celebrating a deaf body and sign language.
But gendered expectations also strongly informed her purpose at Deaf
conventions. She was ornamental to the men and appealing to the eyes
more than the mind (for she was not a main "speaker" at these venues).
Additionally, she was a role model for young deaf women, who presumably saw her as successful—as what a deaf female should want to be. As
Miss Deaf America, Billington and her successors held a special place in
the community because they instilled pride and served as a symbol of
unity, vitality, and happiness. Still, these queens, while visually testifying
that deafness can be positive, rarely had the opportunity to "voice" their
opinions on issues that complicated the community. The fact that the
sponsoring organization—the NAD—did not allow female members to
vote until 1964 or that it did not elect a female president until the 1980s
serves to mirror this muted voice, to reflect on this muted place of female
"deaf, though beautiful."

The requirements for contestants in the Miss Deaf America pageant
(and Miss Gallaudet and many other state-level contests) reflect main-

stream pageant rules but also reveal physical and cultural Deaf components. For example, young ladies must be between eighteen and twenty-
eight, never married (and may not marry during their reign if selected),
without any children, free of any criminal record, and must be an American citizen.[27] In addition to having "talent, poise, charm, intelligence,
beauty of face and body, social ability and maturity," a contestant must
submit a certified audiogram and possess a hearing loss of 65 decibels or
more (American Standards Association) or 75 decibels or more (International Organization for Standardization) in both ears. According to official documents, contestants are not required to possess American Sign
Language (ASL) skills or other culturally "Deaf" attributes, such as attendance at a residential school, membership in Deaf clubs or churches, and

so forth. It is nevertheless culturally understood that sign language is the preferred mode of communication at these pageants.

The role of sign language in pageants has specific historical gendered meaning. The most popular talent performances for contests, from the 1920s to the present day, are signed recitations of poems or signed-songs.[28] This kind of signing has been traditional for women in the broader cultural Deaf community, and it is one of the few areas where they received praise for their signing. Frequently at commencements and conventions, Deaf women have signed the national anthem or a piece of poetry. Seen as theatrical-dramatic performances as much as expressions of the splendor of sign language, these cultural expressions linked bodily beauty with artistic and linguistic merit. Deaf women were rarely called "master signers." That status was given only to men (and in some cases, hearing men). Even the NAD's film preservation series, which began in 1910 and included some twenty filmed presentations to capture "the butiful sign language," shows only one woman, Mary Erd. Her performance of Longfellow's "Death of Minnehaha" is one of stunning drama. Dressed in Indian garb and shot from a distance, her work stands in stark contrast to the closely shot, public speech/sermon style of virtually all the male masters' films. George Veditz, a main force behind these sign master films, derided Erd's performance, however, claiming she had not "the film face" and that hers was not "the sign language." Descriptions of women signing, even in the Deaf press, also connect the physical beauty of the woman to the elegance of her signs. No such commentary appears for men. Thus although women display their "talent" of signing, the lines between ASL skill, acting, and beauty are blurred together.

While deaf women's cultural status, when compared to their hearing peers, remains blurry and muted, cultural values regarding oralism and signs—as expressed in beauty pageants—have certainly clarified in the past twenty-five years. Civil rights activism and academic linguistic re-search that "proved" ASL was an authentic language—among other po-tent factors—have provided a more fertile environment for Deaf people to express and celebrate their cultural-linguistic identity. Emboldened by the DPN movement in 1988 and disability/Deaf civil rights activism since, Deaf judges (meaning both the officials and the general commu-nity) of pageants have expressed a more specific ideal of cultural Deaf feminine beauty. An interview with the 1988 Miss Deaf America, Brandi Sculthorpe, for example, noted that the Illinois native's heroes included her mother and I. King Jordan, the Deaf president installed that year at Gallaudet as a consequence of the DPN protests. Several pictures in the article show Sculthorpe signing.[29] Coverage of the 1990 beauty queen, Nancylynn Ward, further demonstrates this enhanced Deaf cultural "read" of Miss Deaf Americas. Showered with photographs throughout, an article on Ward in *Deaf Life* magazine described the twenty-two-year-old auburn beauty's Deaf cultural credentials: she was prelingually deaf, attended a residential school for the deaf in Maryland (as well as other programs), and preferred ASL for communication. The pictures in the article especially mark her as culturally Deaf. Portraits throughout the essay show Ward signing words like "home," "meet," "fine," and "talk."[30] Distinguished from common modeling portraits, these "signing" shots include facial expressions, hand shapes, and hand positioning that resemble pictorial sign dictionary entries. In this way, the photos allowed Ward to "speak for herself" with signing readers, enhancing the common cultural-linguistic bond. Similar "signing" montages commonly appeared in Miss Deaf America interviews during and after the 1990s.[31]

Those who deviated from this model faced increasing challenges. For example, Alexandrea Hermann won the Miss Deaf California pageant in 1991, playing piano for the talent portion. After the pageant, however, members of the community roundly criticized her for "mainstream life-style"—reading lips and speaking, attending a hearing school, and social-izing primarily with hearing people. Hermann was informed that she could not use her piano talent for the national competition.[32] She did not win the national title. In the following year, a *Deaf Life* poll asked readers whether they felt pageant contestants should be allowed to sing or play music as part of their talent routines. Although most (62 percent) an-swered yes, a strong minority (39 percent) disagreed.[33] One former judge in state deaf pageants suggested that contestants be aware that "some kind of fallout [might occur] if they decided to sign or play music." Another opponent of "hearing"-style performances answered with an emphatic "No!" The respondent continued: "Most Deaf audience do not benefit from it [sic]. . . . They will talk to each other until the next contestant comes on stage with respect and pride in her culture!"[34] This attitude pervaded many state and national pageants. As a current description of the pageant notes, "This is not an ordinary contest . . . beauty, poise, gracefulness are desirable qualities, but the biggest point is one's cultural talent performance" and that "the women are judged across a broad spectrum of categories including . . . knowledge of deaf culture."[35]

Heather Whitestone, even before becoming Miss America and igniting a fury, experienced this firsthand. In 1992, she competed in the Miss Deaf Alabama competition, where she was trounced because of her choice to employ Signing Exact English and to voice (SimCom). Unable to fully understand the ASL of the interviewer (or the judges)—and their inability to understand her—ironically "handicapped" Whitestone, certainly posing a barrier to the prize. In addition, the usual camaraderie described by contestants about behind-the-scenes socializing was starkly missing for her at this contest. In fact, on an outing after the competition, Whitestone's peers glared at her and made disparaging remarks because she voiced her order to a waitress while the others used signs and writing.[36] As Whitestone wrote in her autobiography, "Just because I spoke, had a hearing family, danced ballet, and used signing exact English, they decided that I could not fit into the deaf culture, that I was not an 'ideal' deaf person."[37] Members of the Deaf world likely respond: "Exactly." As an "out" oral deaf person, Whitestone was "outted" by the women who claimed cultural Deafness as their common, beautiful, and beautifying bond.

Whitestone's victory at the 1994 Miss America pageant fueled a passionate dialogue within the Deaf community, as well as between Whitestone and Deaf culture activists. As an outspoken oralist advocate, Whitestone represented the exception rather than the norm of deafness. Her "anything is possible," motto—the overcomer image—resonated with mainstream society, making her one of the best-known Miss Americas. Whitestone's deaf "performance" exemplified her "can-do" platform. During the final round, the interview, Whitestone marked herself as deaf by wearing her hearing aids. In fact, her hairstyle—swept up—displayed them prominently. In this way, she specifically acknowledged her physical deafness while distancing herself from cultural Deafness. The latter she perceived as the true disability because it separates and distinguishes individuals from mainstream society. This interesting play among average, normal, and exceptional echoes traditional Deaf cultural strategies regarding the concepts of disability and normalcy. But for many contemporary deaf people, Whitestone's "overcoming" strategy went too far. A *Deaf Life* magazine poll that year claimed that among its readers, 55 percent felt Whitestone did not represent deaf people.[38] In another article, a deaf social worker admitted that many of her peers initially celebrated Whitestone's win, remarking that "it's always a great joy to see a deaf person move on and be treated like the others."[39] The article goes on to claim that such successes are "encouraging: having a disability need not prevent you from being beautiful or glamorous or successful. You can have a disability and still reach the peak of 'perfection,' the 'ideal.'"[40] Belying the ambivalence within the Deaf world about disability, "passing," and oralism, the author asked: "What if the 'deaf heroine' is an oralist?"[41] Excessively virginal, sweet, sheltered, pretty, compliant, and hopeful, and with a disability to overcome that importantly did not hinder her perfection of superficial beauty, Whitestone was at once marked as disabled by her hearing aids and yet also invisibly disabled. By "overcoming" her deafness, too, she remained an ideal mainstream female beauty.

But she was not an ideal to the culturally Deaf world, and they rejected her attempts to "speak" for them. Whitestone lamented:

> I was beginning to think that my bright hopes of influencing the deaf community would vanish like morning mist. . . . I felt that some deaf people looked at me as a sort of freak. . . . I was willing to lend my voice to help them, but they didn't seem to care. No matter how hard I tried to talk about my platform . . . some deaf people always managed to bring up the controversy about speaking versus signing.[42]

Whitestone's similarity to Helen Heckman in the 1920s is striking. They both were dancers and oralists who used their bodies even more than voices—signed or vocal—in a wholesome yet alluring dramatic performance of hyperfemininity; they are the truly assimilated. Yet this so-called "assimilation" is achieved, ironically, by being "pedestaled."[43] Put on a pedestal, they remain, in a sense "outcast" (or rather "up-cast") in a paradoxical distant but "assimilated" position. Their disability—and from a cultural perspective, their deafness—is invisible except as an ornament of their exceptionalness. They were, indeed, the mainstream ideal of a deaf woman.

As a literary and cultural mirror to Whitestone's image, the same 1994 issue of *Deaf Life* also provided an exclusive interview with Maureen Yates, who was crowned Miss Deaf America earlier that year. Yates, a lanky, blond, deaf daughter of deaf parents, embodied contemporary Deaf cultural ideals. She attended a Deaf school, had a masterful command of sign language, and participated in Deaf sporting events and clubs. Two months earlier, Yates had posed for the cover of the *New York Times Magazine,* signing the word FREEDOM for an article entitled "Defiantly Deaf."[44] Eminently comfortable among deaf people, Yates defined "inclusion"—a common term for mainstreaming deaf children into public schools—as "being Deaf in a school for the deaf" and "being Deaf in a Deaf environment."[45] Like Whitestone and all beauty queens, however, Yates accentuated the need for all deaf people to get along, promoting harmony and tolerance.

Deaf people's current outcry against the vision of deafness embodied by a Heckman or a Whitestone—compliant, oral, and assimilated—signifies an important evolution in projected notions of cultural Deafness. Although the community never fully submitted to the oppressive forces of mainstream society, its strategies and attitudes previously accommodated and incorporated significant common values. That is less true today as Deaf citizens publicly celebrate their separate social-linguistic identity and more forcefully reject acculturation.

Deaf society's projected notion of gendered deafness has changed little. Although critical assessments of beauty pageants proliferate in mainstream society and burgeon among many ethnic minorities in America, virtually none appear in the Deaf cultural world. Even as the Deaf community celebrates its gains in mainstream society, it still "reflects the most traditional and conservative attitudes our society holds about women, attitudes that are perpetuated by the communication barrier created by deafness."[46] These barriers undermine Deaf women's status on multiple levels. Deaf and hearing women rarely interact, in large part because of language differences and the related, pervasive misperceptions hearing people have about deafness. Discouraged by inaccessibility, Deaf women frequently do not join mainstream associations, thus limiting the exchange of ideas, experiences, and perspectives on gender and women's issues in general. Moreover, language barriers affect literacy and education, as several other essays in this collection attest. Often limited by lower reading skills, Deaf women may have greater difficulty accessing the dense feminist critiques that proliferate in academic and activist circles. Likewise, historic inaccessibility to popular media such as radio, television, and film have resulted in Deaf women's comparatively limited exposure to diverse expressions of gender, power, and identity. Other factors likely undermine internal reassessments of women's place in the Deaf world. For example, criticism from "outside" the Deaf world is often taken as criticism of the community rather than of a specific issue within the group. This is common for many minority groups, but it may be heightened in this case because of the continued experiences of oppression and discrimination by hearing people. Moreover, those very hearing people have only recently expressed direct recognition and active support for Deaf people's culture and abilities, first and most visibly in the Deaf President Now! Protest in 1988. Perhaps feminist and similar critiques—originating from the "outside"— still appear too radical, threatening a community that still battles broad discrimination based on their auditory condition.

Deaf men and women historically have rejected perceptions of deaf bodies as defective or dependent, yet Deaf beauty pageants still have yet to incorporate more complex expressions of female cultural Deafness. Immensely popular, folksy, and kitschy, Deaf beauty pageants exemplify the subversive conservatism of this minority culture and the ambiguous and ambivalent place of Deaf women within it.

Notes

1. In this work I focus primarily on larger competitions and the National Association of the Deaf's Miss Deaf America Pageant, initiated in 1972 in Miami Beach, Florida. To my knowledge, there have been no historical studies of Deaf beauty pageants and very few on Deaf women in general. Much of my work thus owes a debt to scholars in general women's and gender history. A number of academics have produced excellent works on America's beauty pageants, and I acknowledge two in particular: I draw heavily from Maxine Leeds Craig's work, *Ain't I a Beauty Queen?* (Oxford: Oxford Univer-

sity Press, 2002), which cogently describes the politics and cultural meaning of African American beauty pageants; I also borrow from the model of interpretation provided by Sarah Banet-Weiser's *The Most Beautiful Girl in the World* (Berkeley: University of California Press, 1999), which reveals the intersection of beauty, citizenship, and national identity.

2. Deaf President Now! (DPN) symbolizes the 1988 protest at Gallaudet University, then the world's only liberal arts institution primarily serving deaf and hard of hearing students. DPN activists demanded that the university dismiss its recently elected hearing president and install its first Deaf president. The campaign resulted in the election of I. King Jordan, a Deaf administrator, and symbolically remains the most prominent example of recent Deaf civil rights success.

3. See, for example, Craig, *"Ain't I a Beauty Queen?"*, and Wendy Kline, *Building a Better Race* (Berkeley: University of California Press, 2001).

4. Martin Pernick, *The Black Stork* (New York: Oxford University Press, 1996), 60–61.

5. Helena Lorenz Williams, "Health, the Course to Beauty," *Silent Worker* 38, no. 3 (1925): 136–37

6. Elizabeth Cole, "Beauty Is Health Deep," *Silent Worker* 39, no. 9 (1927): 340.

7. For more on this, see Susan Burch, *Signs of Resistance: American Deaf Cultural History, 1900 to World War II* (New York: New York University Press, 2002).

8. For more on the Deaf community and eugenics, see Burch, *Signs of Resistance.*

9. "Passing" in this sense refers to the ability to be viewed as hearing or otherwise normal.

10. There is anecdotal evidence that national Deaf beauty competitions existed as early as the 1930s, but the official "Miss Deaf America pageant" sponsored by the NAD did not occur until the 1970s. See "Miss Deaf Philadelphia," *Pennsylvania Society News* 11, no. 9 (1936): 10, and "Miss America of Deaf 1955 Selected for First Time Here," July 4, 1955, Washington, D.C., Gallaudet University Archives, Subject file: Beauty Contests.

11. Lloyd Swift Thomas, "Overcoming the Handicap of Deafness," *Silent Worker* 32, no. 3 (1919): 59.

12. Helen Heckman, "Dreams that Come True," *Silent Worker* 40, no. 7 (1928): 267–68.

13. Oralist superintendent of the New Jersey school, Alvin Pope, ultimately shut down this paper, run by George Porter, in 1929 because it chal-

lenged the oralist policies of the school too vehemently. This Little Paper Family (LPF) publication was not generally on the fence about oralism or Deaf values.

14. "Chicago's Queen Challenges K.C.," *American Deaf Citizen*, June 21, 1935, 1

15. *Digest of the Deaf*, July 1939, cover, 10.

16. "Marion Rene: Night Club Dancer," *Digest of the Deaf*, September 1939, 5.

17. Obie A. Nunn, "Virginia Girl Is Beauty Queen," *Silent Worker* 6, no. 3 (1953): 8.

18. "Mary Beth Barber," *Deaf American* 38, no. 8 (1981): 7–8.

19. See B. S__ky, "Matrimony from an Unmarried Girl's Point of View," *Volta Review* 26, no. 4 (1924): 205, and John A. Ferrall, "How to Be Beautiful, Though Deaf," *Volta Review* 26, no. 5 (1924): 258.

20. *Volta Review* (June 1924): 9. Although similar in mindset to hearing contestants, deaf beauties appreciated the contests for added reasons. Because many girls had vocational training in the art of beauty—cosmetology, hairdressing, and dressmaking—the competitions allowed them to demonstrate their own handiwork as well as their figures.

21. Lillian Dorethelia Jenkins, "A Survey of Vocational Training in Cosmetology for Deaf Girls in the United States" (MS thesis, University of Tennessee, 1954).

22. "Miss Deaf America Pageant History," http://www.uad.org/mdup/mdap_history.htm (accessed January 25, 2005). In 1976, the NAD dropped the term "talent" from the title, making it resemble the Miss America contest more.

23. Billington sang vocally and with signs. "Hey, Look Me Over," *Gallaudet News* February 8, 1972, 2. See also Gallaudet University Archives, Biographical file: Ann Billington.

24. Ruthie Sandefur, director, "Welcome to a Starry Night," Gallaudet University Archives, Subject file: Beauty Pageants.

25. July 2, 1978, letter to Miss Deaf America contestants, Brochure, Gallaudet University Archives, Subject file: Beauty Pageants.

26. *Deaf American*, April 1972, 12.

27. Between 1972 and 1984, two of the eight winners gave up their role because of marriage. However, some more local competitions did allow married women to compete.

28. Susan Daviduff, Miss Deaf America, 1976–78, "Sing a Sign," Brochure, Gallaudet University Archives, Subject file: Beauty Pageants.

29. "Exclusive Interview," *Deaf Life*, October 1988, 21–23. Sculthorpe graces the cover of this issue as well, but she is not signing in the picture.

30. "Miss Deaf America: Nancylynn Ward," *Deaf Life*, October 1990, 19–29.

31. See, for example, "Coming through with Flying Colors," *Deaf Life*, October 1992, 24–28.

32. Jane Slama, "Miss Deaf Captures Title, Controversy," *Santa Maria Times*, September 17, 1991, front page, Gallaudet University Archives, Subject file: Beauty Pageants.

33. "Readers' Responses," *Deaf Life*, December 1992, 34.

34. "Readers' Responses," *Deaf Life*, December 1992, 34.

35. "Miss Deaf America Pageant History," http://www.uad.org/mdup/mdap_history.htm (accessed January 10, 2005).

36. Heather Whitestone, with Angela Elwell Hunt, *Listening with My Heart* (New York: Doubleday, 1997), 42.

37. Whitestone with Hunt, *Listening with My Heart*, 42.

38. "Readers' Responses," *Deaf Life*, December 1994, 28.

39. "Mixed Blessings?" *Deaf Life*, October 1994, Plus 2.

40. "Mixed Blessings?" *Deaf Life*, October 1994, Plus 2.

41. "Mixed Blessings?" *Deaf Life*, October 1994, Plus 2.

42. Whitestone with Hunt, *Listening with My Heart*, 94.

43. Many history works examine this symbol. See, for example, Caroll Smith Rosenberg, *Disorderly Conduct* (New York: A.A. Knopf, 1985); Anne Firor Scott, *The Southern Lady: From Pedestal to Politics, 1830–1930* (Charlottesville: University Press of Virginia, 1995); and Maxine Harris, *Down from the Pedestal: Moving beyond Idealized Images of Womanhood* (New York: Doubleday, 1994).

44. Andrew Solomon, "Defiantly Deaf," http://www.ling.upenn.edu/courses/Fall_2000/ling001/nytimes_deaf.htm; "An Exclusive Interview," *Deaf Life*, October 1994, 20.

45. "An Exclusive interview," *Deaf Life*, October 1994, 26.

46. Martha Sheridan, "Deaf Women: A Review of the Literature," (Dayton, Ohio: Wright State University, 1995), citing G. Becker and J. Jauregui, "The Invisible Isolation of Deaf Women: Its Effect on Social Awareness," *Journal of Sociology and Social Welfare* 8, no. 2 (1981): 250.

Bibliography

The following sources have been directly or indirectly used in the essays. This list, although incomplete, offers valuable resources for those interested in research on issues related to women and deafness.

Print Publications

Abel, Emily. *Hearts of Wisdom: American Women Caring for Kin, 1850–1940*. Cambridge, Mass.: Harvard University Press, 2000.

Adler, P. A., and P. Adler. *Membership Roles in Field Research*. Beverly Hills, Calif.: Sage, 1987.

Allen, Anna. "Report of Committee on Necrology: Ellen L. Barton." *Report of the Proceedings of the Fourteenth Convention of American Instructors of the Deaf*, 1895.

Altman, B. "Disabled Women: Doubly Disadvantaged Members of the Social Structure?" Paper presented at the American Sociological Association Annual Meeting, San Francisco, Calif., 1982.

———. "Disabled Women in the Social Structure." In *With the Power of Each Breath: A Disabled Women's Anthology*, edited by S. Browne, D. Connors, and N. Stern. Pittsburgh, Penn.: Cleis Press, 1985.

American Annals of the Deaf and Dumb (1852).

American Association to Promote the Teaching of Speech to the Deaf. "Proceedings (Except Papers and Lectures) of the Sixth Summer Meeting of the AAPTSD, Held at Clarke School for the Deaf, Northampton, Mass., June 22–28, 1899." *Association Review* 1 (1899): 53–106; 162–76.

Andersen, M. L. *Thinking about Women: Sociological Perspectives on Sex and Gender*. Boston: Allyn and Bacon, 1997.

Anderson, N. *The Hobo*. Chicago: University of Chicago Press, 1923.

Aneja, Anu. "The Mystic Aspect of *L'Ecriture feminine*: Helene Cixous' *Vivre l'Orange.*" *Qui Parle* 3, no. 1 (1989): 189–201.

Arenal, Concepción. "Spain." In *The Woman Question in Europe*, edited by Theodore Stanton, 330–53. New York: George Putnam's Sons, 1884.

Baldwin, M., and W. Johnson. "Labor Market Discrimination against Women with Disabilities." *Industrial Relations* 34, no. 4 (1995): 55–77.

Banet-Weiser, Sarah. *The Most Beautiful Girl in the World*. Berkeley: University of California Press, 1999.

Barnartt, Sharon. "The Socioeconomic Status of Deaf Women Workers." Paper presented at the Mid-South Sociological Association Annual Meeting, Shreveport, La., 1981.

———. "Disability as a Socioeconomic Variable: Predicting Deaf Workers' Incomes." Paper presented at the American Sociological Association Annual Meeting, 1986.

———. "Deaf Population: Women." In *Gallaudet Encyclopedia of Deaf People and Deafness*, edited by John Van Cleve. Washington, D.C.: McGraw-Hill, 1987.

———. "Using Role Theory to Describe Disability." In *Exploring Theories and Expanding Methodologies: Where We Are and Where We Need To Go*, edited by S. Barnartt and B. Altman, 53–75. London: Elsevier/ JAI Press, 2001.

———. "Social Structure, Culture, Role, and Disability." Paper presented at the ASA Pre-conference on Sociological Theory and Disability, 2002.

Barnartt, Sharon, and John Christiansen. "The Socioeconomic Status of Deaf Workers: A Minorities Approach." *Social Science Journal* 22, no. 4 (1985): 19–33.

Barnartt, Sharon, and Kate Seelman. "A Comparison of Federal Laws toward Disabled and Racial/Ethnic Groups in the USA." *Disability, Handicap and Society* 3, no. 1 (1988): 37–48.

Baynton, Douglas C. *Forbidden Signs: American Culture and the Campaign against Sign Language*. Chicago: University of Chicago Press, 1996.

Becker, G., and J. Jauregui, "The Invisible Isolation of Deaf Women: Its Effect on Social Awareness." *Journal of Sociology and Social Welfare* 8, no. 2 (July 1981): 249–62.

Bell, A. G., and J. L. Gillett. *Deaf Classes in Connection with the Work in Public Schools.* Washington, D.C.: Gibson Brothers, 1884.

Bergen, Nell M. "The Girl's Athletic Association." *Silent Worker* 30 (January 1918): 66.

Berkeley, K. C. "The Ladies Want to Bring about Reform in the Public Schools: Public Education and Women's Rights in the Post–Civil War South." *History of Education Quarterly* (1984): 24, 45–58.

A Brief History of the American School at Hartford for the Deaf. West Hartford, Conn.: American School for the Deaf Press, 1933.

Berkowitz, M., and A. M. Hill. *Disability and the Labor Market: Economic Problems, Policies and Programs.* Ithaca, N.Y.: ILR Press, 1986.

Best, Harry. *Deafness and the Deaf in the United States.* New York: MacMillan, 1943.

Bianchi, S. "Changing Economic Roles of Men and Women." In *State of the Union: America in the 1990's. Vol. 1, Economic Trends, edited by* R. Farley, 107–54. New York: Russell Sage Foundation, 1995.

Binner, Paul. "Home Training of Deaf-Mute Children." *Histories of American Schools for the Deaf 1817–1893.* III. Washington, D.C.: Volta Review.

Bolander, A. M., and A. N. Renning. *I Was #87: A Deaf Woman's Ordeal of Misdiagnosis, Institutionalization, and Abuse.* Washington, D.C.: Gallaudet University Press, 2000.

Bragg, Lois, ed. *Deaf-World: A Historical Reader and Primary Sourcebook.* New York: New York University Press, 2001.

Brill, R. "A Survey of Credential Requirements for Teachers of the Deaf in the United States." *American Annals of the Deaf* 100 (1955): 321–29.

Brown, Caroline. "The Representation of the Indigenous Other in *Daughters of the Dust* and *The Piano.*" *NWSA Journal* 15, no. 1 (Spring 2003), http://muse.jhu.edu/journals/nwsa_journal/toc/nwsa15.1.html.

Brown, Tamara L., Gregory S. Parks, and Clarenda M. Phillips, eds. *African American Fraternities and Sororities: The Legacy and the Vision.* Lexington: University Press of Kentucky, 2005.

Browning, Robert. *Dramatis Personae*, edited by F. B. Pinion. London: Collins Publishers, 1969.

Bruce, Robert V. *Bell: Alexander Graham Bell and the Conquest of Solitude.* Boston: Little, Brown & Company, 1973.

Brueggemann, Brenda Jo. *Lend Me Your Ear.* Washington, D.C.: Gallaudet University Press, 1999.

Brueggemann, Brenda Jo, ed. *Literacy and Deaf People: Cultural and Contextual Perspectives.* Washington, D.C.: Gallaudet University Press, 2004.

Buchanan, Robert M. *Illusions of Equality: Deaf Americans in School and Factory 1850–1950.* Washington, D.C.: Gallaudet University Press, 1999.

Burch, Susan. Biding the Time: American Deaf Cultural History, 1900 to World War II. PhD diss., Georgetown University, 1999.

————. *Signs of Resistance: American Deaf Cultural History, 1900 to World War II.* New York: New York University Press, 2002.

————. *Beautiful though Deaf: A History of Deaf Women's Bodies as Cultural Capital.* Bethesda, Md.: Society of Disability Studies, 2003.

Burkhauser, R., and R. V. Haveman. *Disability and Work: The Economics of American Policy.* Baltimore, Md.: Johns Hopkins University Press, 1982.

Bush, M. G. "The Handicapped Child Helps All Children in Wisconsin." *Exceptional Children* 9 (1942): 153–55.

Butler, Judith. *Bodies that Matter: On the Discursive Limits of "Sex."* New York: Routledge, 1993.

Campbell, H. M., J. Robinson, and A. Stratiy. *Deaf Women of Canada: A Proud History and Exciting Future.* Canada: Duval House, 2002.

Carroll, C., and S. M. Mather. *Movers and Shakers: Deaf People Who Changed the World.* San Diego: DawnSignPress, 1997.

de Certeau, Michel. "Mysticism." *diacritics* 22, no. 2 (1992): 11–25.

Chafe, William. *The American Woman: Her Changing Social, Economic, and Political Roles, 1920–1970.* New York: Oxford University Press, 1972.

Children of a Lesser God, directed by Haines, Randa. West Hollywood, Calif.: Paramount Studio, 1986.

Christiansen, J. B., and Sharon Barnartt. "The Silent Minority: The So-cioeconomic Status of Deaf People." In *Understanding Deafness Socially*, edited by P. Higgins and J. Nash, 171–96. Springfield, Ill.: Charles C. Thomas, 1987.

Cixous, Helene. "Laugh of the Medusa." *In Feminisms: An Anthology of Literary Theory and Criticism*, edited by Robyn R. Warhol and Diane Price Herndl. New Brunswick, N.J.: Rutgers University Press, 1997.

Clarke, E. P. "An Analysis of the School and Instructors of the Deaf in the U.S." *Annals* 45 (1900): 228–36.

Clifford, J., and G. E. Marcus, eds. *Writing Culture: The Poetics and Politics of Ethnography*. Berkeley: University of California Press, 1986.

Clifford, G. J. "Daughters into Teachers: Educational and Demographic Influences on the Transformation of Teaching into 'women's work' in America." In *Women Who Taught: Perspectives on the History of Women and Teaching*, edited by A. Prentice and M. Theobald, 115–35. Toronto: University of Toronto Press, 1991.

Cole, Elizabeth. "Beauty Is Health Deep," *Silent Worker* 39, no. 9 (1927): 340.

Columbia Institute for the Deaf and Dumb. Columbia Institution for the Deaf and Dumb Thirty-Eighth Annual Report for the Year ended June *30, 1895*. Washington DC: IDD, 1895.

Cox, Harvey. *Fire from Heaven: The Rise of Pentecostal Spirituality and the Reshaping of Religion in the Twenty-First Century*. Reading, Mass.: Addison-Wesley, 1995.

Craig, Maxine Leeds. *Ain't I a Beauty Queen?* Oxford: Oxford University Press, 2002.

Craig, S. B. "Recruitment of Teachers." *Volta Review* 48 (1946): 701–704.

Cressey, P. G. *The Taxi Dance Hall*. Chicago: University of Chicago Press, 1932.

Crouter, A. L. E. "The Organization and Methods of the Pennsylvania Institution for the Deaf and Dumb." In *Proceedings of the International Conference on the Education of the Deaf held in the Training College Buildings, Edinburgh, on 29th, 30th, and 31st July and 1st and 2nd August, 1907*, 125–55. Edinburgh: Darien Press, 1907.

Crouter, A. L. E. "The Training of Teachers of the Deaf." *American Annals of the Deaf* 62: 293–304.

Curtis, Verna Posever. "Frances Benjamin Johnston in 1900: Staking the Sisterhood's Claim in American Photography." In *Ambassadors of Progress: American Women Photographers in Paris, 1900–1901*, 24–37. Hanover: Musée d' Art Américan, 2001. Distributed by University Press of New England.

Cyrus, Bainy, Eileen Katz, Celeste Cheyney, and Frances M Parsons. *Deaf Women's Lives: Three Self-Portraits*. Washington, D.C.: Gallaudet University Press, 2005.

D'aoust, Vicky. *Complications: The Deaf Community, Disability and Being a Lesbian Mom—A Conversation with Myself.* Seattle, Wash.: Seal Press, 1999.

Davis, Lennard. *Enforcing Normalcy.* London and New York: Verso, 1995.

Davis, Lennard, ed. *Shall I Say a Kiss? The Courtship Letters of a Deaf Couple, 1936–1938.* Washington, D.C.: Gallaudet University Press, 1999.

De Beauvoir, Simone. *The Second Sex.* Edited and translated by H. M. Parshley. New York: Knopf, 1953.

De Beauvoir, Simone. "From *The Second Sex.*" In *Gender Space Architecture: An Interdisciplinary Introduction.* Edited by Jane Rendell, Barbara Penner, and Iain Borden, 29–32. New York: Routledge, 2000.

De Cartagena, Teresa. *The Writings of Teresa De Cartagena.* Translated by Dayle Seidenspinner-Núñez. Rochester, N.Y.: D.S. Brewer, 1998.

"Declaration of Principles." *American Annals of the Deaf* 72 (May 1927): 251–54.

Deegan, M. J. "Multiple Minority Groups: A Case Study of Physically Disabled Women." *Journal of Sociology and Social Welfare* 8, no. 2 (1981): 274–95.

De Land, F. "The Real Romance of the Telephone, Or Why Deaf Children in America Need No Longer Be Dumb." *Association Review* 8 (1906): 1–27, 120–35, 205–222, 329–344, 406–27.

DeMan, Paul. *Blindness and Insight: Essays in the Rhetoric of Contemporary Criticism.* 2nd ed., rev. Minneapolis: University of Minnesota Press, 1983.

Doe, T. M. Exploring Gender with Deaf Women and Their Hearing Sisters. PhD diss., University of Alberta, Edmonton, 1993.

Dworkin, Andrea. *Pornography: Men Possessing Women*. New York: Plume, 1989.

Easton, Terry. "Identity and Politics in the *Silent Worker* Newspaper: Print Publication and the Laboring Deaf Body," *Women's Studies Quarterly* 1–2 (1998): 56–71.

Erikson, E. *Childhood and Society*. 2nd ed. New York: Norton Press, 1963.

———. *Identity: Youth and Crisis*. New York: Norton Press, 1968.

Fischer, Renate, and Harlan Lane, eds. *Looking Back: A Reader on the History of Deaf Communities and Their Sign Languages*. Hamburg: Signum Press, 1993.

Foley, Julia A. "Two Deaf Girls." *Silent Worker* 8 (October 1895): 11–12.

Flynt, S. L. *The Allen Sisters: Pictorial Photographers, 1885–1920*. Deerfield, Mass.: Pocumtuck Valley Memorial Association, 2002.

Foster, S. "Examining the Fit between Disability and Deafness." In *Exploring Theories and Expanding Methodologies: Where We Are and Where We Need To Go*, edited by Sharon Barnartt and Barbara Altman, 101–124. London: Elsevier/JAI Press, 2001.

Freeberg, Ernest. *The Education of Laura Bridgman: First Deaf and Blind Person to Learn Language*. Cambridge, Mass.: Harvard University Press, 2001.

———. "The Meanings of Blindness in Nineteenth-Century America." *American Antiquarian Society* (2002): 119–52.

Freeman, J. *The Politics of Women's Liberation*. New York: David McKay, 1975.

Gallaudet, Edward Miner. "Our Profession." *American Annals of the Deaf* 37(1892): 1–9.

———. " President's Address." *American Annals of the Deaf* 74 (1929).

Gannon, Jack. *Deaf Heritage: A Narrative History of Deaf America*. Silver Spring, Md.: National Association of the Deaf, 1981.

Garland-Thomson, Rosemarie. *Extraordinary Bodies: Figuring Physical Disability in American Culture and Literature*. New York: Columbia University Press, 1997.

———. "Feminist Theory, the Body, and the Disabled Figure." In *The Disability Studies Reader*, edited by Lennard J. Davis, 279–92. New York: Routledge, 1997.

———. "Integrating Disability, Transforming Feminist Theory." *NWSA Journal* 14, no. 3 (2002): 1–32.

Garrett, Mary S., J. C. Gordon, and Elizabeth I. Fowler. *Report of the Proceedings of the Fourteenth Convention of American Instructors of the Deaf held at the Michigan School for the Deaf* (1895).

Giddings, Paula. *In Search of Sisterhood: Delta Sigma Theta and the Challenge of the Black Sorority Movement*. New York: William Morrow and Company, 1988.

Gillett. "Remarks." *Proceedings from Conference of American Instructors of the Deaf* 19 (1911): 189–95.

Gilligan, C. *A Different Voice: Psychological Theory and Women's Development*. Cambridge, Mass.: Harvard University Press, 1982.

Gittens, Joan. *Poor Relations: The Children of the State in Illinois, 1818–1990*. Urbana: University of Illinois Press, 1994.

Gitter, Elisabeth. "Deaf-Mutes and Heroines in the Victorian Era." *Victorian Literature and Culture* 20 (1992): 179–96.

———. "The Blind Daughter in Charles Dickens's *Cricket on the Hearth*." *Studies in English Literature, 1500–1900* 39, no. 4 (1999): 675–89.

———. *The Imprisoned Guest: Samuel Howe and Laura Bridgman, the Original Deaf-Blind Girl*. New York: Farrar, Straus and Giroux, 2001.

Glickman, N. "Cultural Identity, Deafness, and Mental Health." *Journal of Rehabilitation of the Deaf* 20 (1986): 1–10.

Goffman, E. *Stigma*. Englewood Cliffs, N.J.: Prentice Hall, 1963.

Goldstein, M. "Excerpts from the Society of Progressive Oral Advocates: Its Origin and Purpose—1917." *Volta Review* 78 (1976): 140–44.

Greenberg, Joanne. *In This Sign*. New York: Avon, 1972.

Gregory, Susan. "Mothering Real Children in Real Circumstances. Challenging Motherhood: Mothers and Their Deaf Children." In *Motherhood: Meanings, Practices, and Ideologies*, edited by Ann Phoenix, Anne Woollett, and Eva Lloyd. London: Sage, 1991.

Griffith, Bronwyn A. E "'Dainty and Artistic or Strong and Forceful—Just as You Wish': American Women Photographers at the Universal

Exposition of 1900." In *Ambassadors of Progress: American Women Photographers in Paris, 1900–1901, 12–23*. France: Musée d' Art Américan Giverny, 2001.

Griffith, Bronwyn A. E., ed. *Ambassadors of Progress: American Women Photographers in Paris, 1900–1901*. Hanover: Musée d' Art Américan, 2001. Distributed by University Press of New England.

Guberman, Ross Mitchell, ed. *Julia Kristeva: Interviews*. New York: Columbia University Press, 1996.

Hairston, Ernest, and Linwood Smith. *Black and Deaf in America: Are We That Different?* Silver Spring, Md.: TJ Publishers, 1983.

Hairston, Ernest. "A Comparative Analysis of Deaf Students' Self-Concept by Race, Gender, and Placement: Implications for School Administrators." PhD diss., Gallaudet University, 1994.

Hall, R. H. *Sociology of Work: Perspectives, Analyses and Issues*. Thousand Oaks, Calif.: Pine Forge Press, 1994.

Haraway, Donna J. *Simians, Cyborgs, and Women: The Reinvention of Nature*. New York: Routledge, 1991.

Heckman, Helen. "Dreams That Come True." *Silent Worker* (April 1928): 267–68.

Holcomb, Mabs, and Sharon Wood. *Deaf Women: A Parade through the Decades*. Berkeley, Calif.: Dawn Sign Press, 1989.

Howard, J. "Men and Women Teachers." *American Annals of the Deaf* 47(1902): 278–81.

Howe, L. *Pink Collar Workers: Inside the World of Women's Work*. New York: G. P. Putnam's Sons, 1977.

Howe, Samuel Gridley. "The Co-education of the Deaf and the Blind." *American Annals of the Deaf and Dumb* 19 (1874): 162.

Hubbard, G. G. "The Origin of the Clarke Institution." *American Annals of the Deaf and Dumb* 21 (1876): 178–83.

Irigaray, Luce. *Speculum of the Other Woman*. Translated by Gillian C. Gill. Ithaca, N.Y.: Cornell University Press, 1985.

Jackson, Peter W., and Raymond Lee, eds. *Deaf Lives: Deaf People in History*. Middlesex, England: British Deaf History Society, 2001.

J. O. D. "Letter about the Death of T. H. Gallaudet." In *Thirty-Sixth Annual Report from the Directors of American Asylum*, 1852, 27–28.

Jenkins, Lillian Dorethelia. A Survey of Vocational Training in Cosmetology for Deaf Girls in the United States. MS thesis, University of Tennessee, 1954.

Johnson, Barbara. "Muteness Envy." In *The Feminist Difference: Literature, Psychoanalysis, Race, and Gender*. Cambridge, Mass.: Harvard University Press, 1998.

Jones, Judy Yaeger, and Jane E. Vallier, eds. *Sweet Bells Jangled: Laura Redden Searing, a Deaf Poet Restored*. Washington, D.C.: Gallaudet University Press, 2003.

Jones, J. "The Training and Certification of Teachers." *American Annals of the Deaf* 74 (1929): 244–315.

Jones, Nancy Carolyn. Don't Take Any Aprons to College! A Study of the Beginning of Coeducation at Gallaudet College. MA thesis, University of Maryland, 1983.

Josselson, R. *Finding Herself: Pathways to Identity Development in Women*. San Francisco: Jossey-Bass, 1987.

———. *The Space between Us: Exploring the Dimensions of Human Relationships*. San Francisco: Jossey-Bass, 2002.

Joyner, Hannah. *From Pity to Pride: Growing Up Deaf in the Old South*. Washington, D.C.: Gallaudet University Press, 2004.

Katzenstein, M., and C. M. Mueller. *The Women's Movements of the United States and Western Europe*. Philadelphia: Temple University Press, 1987.

Keating, E., and Mirus, G. "Examining Interactions across Language Modalities: Deaf Children and Hearing Peers at School." *Anthropology and Education Quarterly* 34, no. 2 (2002): 115–35.

Keller, Helen. *The Story of My Life*. New York: Dover Publications, [1903] 1996.

———. *Midstream: My Later Life*. New York: Greenwood Press, [1929] 1968.

———. *Helen Keller's Journal*. London: Michael Joseph, 1938.

Kelly, Arlene B. How Deaf Women Construct Teaching, Language and Culture, and Gender: An Ethnographic Study of ASL Teachers. PhD diss., University of Maryland, College Park, 2001.

Kelly, E. "The Recruiting of Teachers." *Volta Review* 48 (1946): 689–701.

King, Ynestra. "The Other Body: Reflections on Difference, Disability, and Identity Politics." *Ms* (Spring 1993): 72–75.

Klages, Mary. *Woeful Afflictions: Disability and Sentimentality in Victorian America*. Philadelphia: University of Pennsylvania Press, 1999.

Kline, Wendy. *Building a Better Race*. Berkeley: University of California Press, 2001.

Klobas, Lauri E. *Disability Drama in Television and Film*. London: McFarland & Co., 1988.

Kristeva, Julia. *About Chinese Women*. Translated by Anita Barrows. London: Marian Boyars, 1977.

———. *Desire in Language: A Semiotic Approach to Literature and Art*. New York: Columbia University Press, 1980.

———. *Revolution in Poetic Language*. New York: Columbia University Press, 1984.

Kudlick, Catherine J. Should Blind Girls Marry? Thoughts on Gender, Disability and the Single Life in Modern France and America. Unpublished paper.

Laborit, Emmanuelle. *The Cry of the Gull*. Washington, D.C.: Gallaudet University Press, 1998.

Lane, H. "Recruitment of Teachers of the Deaf." *Volta Review* 48 (1946): 704–705.

Lane, Harlan. *When the Mind Hears: A History of the Deaf*. New York: Vintage Books, 1989.

———. "Do Deaf People Have a Disability?" *Sign Language Studies* 2, no. 4 (2002): 356–79.

Lane, H. S. "Teacher Recruitment and Training: A Summer Meeting Panel Discussion, June 18, 1952." *Volta Review* 54, no. 49(1952): 500, 512–13.

Lang, Harry G., and Bonnie Meath-Lang. *Deaf Persons in the Arts and Sciences: A Biographical Dictionary*. Westport, Conn.: Greenwood Press, 1995.

Lash, Joseph. *Helen and Teacher: The Story of Helen Keller and Anne Sullivan Macy*. New York: Addison-Wesley, 1980.

Lee, J. L. "Problems in Organization of Teacher Training in Special Education." *Journal of Exceptional Children* 3 (1936): 142–43.

Leeson, Lorraine, and Carmel Grehan. "To the Lexicon and Beyond, the Effect of Gender on Variation in Irish Sign Language." In *To the Lexicon and Beyond: Sociolinguistics in European Deaf Communities*, edited by Mieke Van Herreweghe and Myriam Vermeerbergen. Washington, D.C.: Gallaudet University Press, 2004.

Levy, F. "Incomes and Income Inequality." In *State of the Union: America in the 1990's. Vol. 1, Economic Trends*, edited by R. Farley, 1–57. New York: Russell Sage Foundation, 1995.

Longmore, Paul K., and David Goldberger. "The League of the Physically Handicapped and the Great Depression: A Case Study in the New Disability History." *Journal of American History* 87, no. 3 (2000): 888–922.

Longmore, Paul K., and Lauri Umansky, eds. *The New Disability History.* New York: New York University Press, 2001.

Lloyd, W. H. "The Deaf in Their Relations with Others." *American Annals of the Deaf* 62 (March 1917): 112–21.

"Lottie Kirkland Clarke." *Report of Proceedings of the Twentieth Meeting of the American Instructors of the Deaf,* 203–204, 1914.

Lucas, Ceil, ed. *Multicultural Aspects of Sociolinguistics in Deaf Communities.* Washington, D.C.: Gallaudet University Press, 1996.

Luczak, Raymond. *Eyes of Desire: A Deaf Gay and Lesbian Reader.* Boston: Alyson Publications, 1993.

Lunde, A. S., and S. K. Bigman. *Occupational Conditions among the Deaf.* Washington, D.C.: U.S. Government Printing Office, 1959.

Lytle, L. Identity Formation and Developmental Antecedents in Deaf College Women. PhD diss., Catholic University of America, 1987.

MacLeod-Gallainger, J. *The Status of Deaf Women: A Comparative Look at the Labor Force, Educational, and Occupational Attainment of Deaf Female Secondary Graduates.* Rochester, N.Y.: National Technical Institute of the Deaf, 1991.

Marcia, J. "Development and Validation of Ego-Identity Status." *Journal of Personality and Social Psychology* 34 (1966): 551–58.

Mare, R. D. "Changes in Educational Attainment and School Enrollment." In *State of the Union: America in the 1990's. Vol. 1, Economic Trends,* edited by R. Farley, 155–213. New York: Russell Sage Foundation, 1995.

"Marion Rene: Night Club Dancer." *Digest of the Deaf* (September 1939): 5.

McManaway, H. M. "The Proper Training of Shop Teachers as the Solution of Most of Our Problems." *Conference of American Instructors of the Deaf* 24 (July 1925): 113–23.

Menzemer, H. J. "Should the School or the Shop Teach Shop Language?" *Conference of American Instructors of the Deaf* (1925): 106–108.

Mertens, D. *Research Methods in Education and Psychology: Integrating Diversity with Quantitative and Qualitative Approaches.* Thousand Oaks, Calif.: Sage, 1998.

Minkoff, Debra C. *Organizing for Equality: The Evolution of Women's and Racial-Ethnic Organizations in America, 1955–1985.* New Brunswick, N.J.: Rutgers University Press, 1995.

Mirzoeff, Nicholas. "Framed: The Deaf in the Harem." In *Deviant Bodies: Critical Perspectives on Difference in Science and Popular Culture*, edited by Jennifer Terry and Jacqueline Urla. Bloomington: Indiana University Press, 1995.

———. *Silent Poetry: Deafness, Sign, and Visual Culture in Modern France.* Princeton, N.J.: Princeton University Press, 1995.

"Miss Deaf America: Nancylynn Ward." *Deaf Life* (October 1990): 19–29.

"Miss Lula Edgar Wharton." *Mississippi Institute for the Deaf and Dumb Bulletin* 31 (December 1915): 8–9.

Moi, Toril. *Sexual/Textual Politics: Feminist Literary Theory.* New York: Routledge, 1985.

Moi, Toril, ed. *The Kristeva Reader* New York: Columbia University Press, 1986.

Moore, L. M. "Caroline A. Yale—Pioneer and Builder." *American Annals of the Deaf* 79 (1934): 189–96.

Moores, D. *Educating the Deaf: Psychology, Principles and Practices* Boston: Houghton Mifflin, 1978.

Motley, Monica. Gender Identity Development in Black, Deaf College Women. Predissertation research report, Gallaudet University, 2000.

"Mrs. Kate McWillie Powers." *Mississippi Institute for the Deaf and Dumb Bulletin* 31 (October 1915): 12.

N.C.R. News. "A Girl's Complete Education." *Silent Worker* 30 (December 1917): 53.

Nelson, Jennifer, and Bradley Berens. "Spoken Daggers, Deaf Ears, and Silent Mouths: Fantasies of Deafness in Early Modern England." In *The Disability Studies Reader*, edited by Lennard J. Davis, 52–74. New York and London: Routledge, 1997.

New York Institution for the Instruction of the Deaf and Dumb. *Seventy-Second Annual Report for the New York Institution for the Instruction of the Deaf and Dumb.* New York: NYI, 1890.

———. *Seventy-Third Annual Report for the New York Institution for the Instruction of the Deaf and Dumb.* New York: NYI, 1891.

———. *Seventy-Fourth Annual Report for the New York Institution for the Instruction of the Deaf and Dumb.* New York: NYI, 1892.

Nielsen, Kim. *The Radical Lives of Helen Keller.* New York: New York University Press, 2004.

Nielsen, Kim, ed. *Helen Keller: Selected Writings.* New York University Press, 2005.

Norden, Martin. *Cinema of Isolation: A History of Physical Disability in the Movies.* New Brunswick, N.J.: Rutgers University Press, 1994.

Numbers, F. C. "Advantages and Disadvantages of Conducting a Normal Training Class in Connection with School Work." *American Annals of the Deaf* 72 (1927): 341–49.

Numbers, Mary. *My Words Fell on Deaf Ears.* Washington, D.C.: Alexander Graham Bell Association for the Deaf, 1974.

Nye, Andrea. "Woman Clothed with the Sun: Julia Kristeva and the Escape from/to Language." *Signs: Journal of Women in Culture and Society* 12, no. 4 (1987): 664–86.

"Officers of Institutions." *Silent Worker* 3 (September 1889): 4.

Oliva, Gina A. *Alone in the Mainstream: A Deaf Woman Remembers Public School.* Washington, D.C.: Gallaudet University Press, 2004.

Ontario, Department of Education. *Annual Report.* Toronto: Government Printer, 1904.

Ontario Institution for the Education and Instruction of Deaf and Dumb Persons. *Fifth Annual Report.* Belleville, Ont.: Canadian Mute Printing Establishment, 1884.

Oppenheimer, V. *The Female Labor Force in the United States: Demographic and Economic Factors Governing Its Growth and Changing Composition*. Westport, Conn.: Greenwood Press, 1976.

Orenstein, Peggy. *School Girls: Young Women, Self-Esteem, and the Confidence Gap*. New York: Doubleday, 1994.

Osgood, Robert L. "Becoming a Special Educator: Specialized Professional Training for Teachers of Children with Disabilities in Boston, 1870–1930." *Teachers College Record* 161 (1999): 82–105.

O' Toole, Corbett Joan. "The Sexist Inheritance of the Disability Movement." In *Gendering Disability*, edited by Bonnie G. Smith and Beth Hutchison, 294–300. New Brunswick, N.J.: Rutgers University Press, 2004.

Pach, Alexander L. "With the Silent Workers." *Silent Worker* 30 (May 1918): 140–41.

Padden, Carol, and Tom Humphries. *Deaf in America: Voices from a Culture*. Cambridge, Mass.: Harvard University Press, 1988.

Palen, I. "Ears that Hear Not." *Social Welfare* 5 (1923).

Parasnis, I., ed. *Cultural and Language Diversity and the Deaf Experience*. New York: Cambridge University Press, 1996.

Pernick, Martin. *The Black Stork*. New York: Oxford University Press, 1996.

Pettergill, B. D. "The Instruction of the Deaf and Dumb." *American Annals of the Deaf* 17 (1872): 21–33.

The Piano. Directed by Jane Campion. West Hollywood, Calif.: Miramax Films, 1993.

Pipher, Mary. *Rescuing Ophelia: Saving the Selves of Adolescent Girls*. New York: Ballantine Books, 1994.

Plann, Susan. "Pedro Ponce: Myth and Reality." In *Deaf History Unveiled: Interpretations from the New Scholarship*, edited by John V. Van Cleve, 1–12. Washington, D.C.: Gallaudet University Press, 1993.

———. "Roberto Prádez: Spain's First Deaf Teacher of the Deaf." In *Looking Back: A Reader on the History of the Deaf Communities and Their Sign Languages*, edited by Renate Fischer and Harlan Lane, 53–74. Hamburg: Sig Verlag, 1992.

———. *A Silent Minority: Deaf Education in Spain, 1550–1835*. Berkeley and Los Angeles: University of California Press, 1997. [Spanish ver-

sion: *Una minoría silenciosa: La educación sorda en España, 1550–1835.*
Madrid: Fundación CNSC, 2004.]

———. "Three Early Spanish Teachers of the Deaf." In *The Deaf Way: Perspectives from the International Conference on Deaf Culture,* edited by Carol J. Erting, Robert C. Johnson, Dorothy L. Smith, and Bruce D. Snider, 203–207. Washington, D.C.: Gallaudet University Press, 1994.

———. "Manuel Tinoco." *Sign Language Studies* 1, no. 1 (2000): 65–92.

———. "Patricio García." *Sign Language Studies* 1, no. 2 (2001): 125–46.

Preston, Paul. *Mother Father Deaf: Living between Sound and Silence.* Cambridge, Mass.: Harvard University Press, 1994.

Quartararo, Anne. "The Perils of Assimilation in Modern France: The Deaf Community, Social Status, and Educational Opportunity, 1815–1870." *Journal of Social History* 29, no. 1 (1965): 5–23.

———. "The Life and Times of the French Deaf Leader Ferdinand Berthier: An Analysis of His Early Career." *Sign Language Studies* 2, no. 3 (2002): 182–96.

Ragna, Edward E. "Limitations of the Marriage Market of the Young Deaf Girl." *Silent Worker* 33 (March 1921): 214–16.

Ramsey, Claire. *Deaf Children in Public Schools: Placement, Content, and Consequences.* Washington, D.C.: Gallaudet University Press, 1997.

Ree, Jonathan. *I See a Voice: Deafness, Language, and the Senses: A Philosophical History.* New York: Henry Holt and Company, 1999.

Rimm, S. See Jane Win: *The Rimm Report on How 1,000 Girls Became Successful Women.* New York: Three Rivers Press, 1999.

Robinson, Warren. "Girl's Basketball Teams, Wisconsin School for the Deaf." *Silent Worker* 24 (June 1912): 160.

Ross, Lawrence C. *The Divine Nine: The History of African American Fraternities and Sororities.* New York: Kensington, 2000.

Ryan, James Emmett. "The Blind Authoress of New York: Helen De Kroyft and the Uses of Disability in Antebellum America." *American Quarterly* 51, no. 2 (1999): 385–418.

"The Salary Question." *American Annals of the Deaf* 74 (1929): 260–272.

Saville-Troike, M. *The Ethnography of Communication: An Introduction.* Cambridge, Mass.: Blackwell, 1990.

Schein, J. D., and M. T. Delk, Jr. *The Deaf Population of the United States.* Silver Spring, Md.: National Association of the Deaf, 1974.

Schor, Naomi. "Blindness as Metaphor." *Differences* 11, no. 2 (1999): 76–105.

Schriempf, Alexa. "(Re)fusing the Amputated Body: An Interactionist Bridge for Feminism and Disability." *Hypatia* 16, no. 4 (2001): 53–78.

Schroedel, J., and D. Watson. "Postsecondary Education for Students Who Are Deaf: A Summary of a National Study." *OSERS News in Print* 4, no. 1 (1991): 7–13.

Schuchman, John S. *Hollywood Speaks: Deafness and the Film Entertainment Industry.* Champaign, Ill.: University of Illinois Press, 1988.

Seguin, E. "Education of the Deaf and Mute." In *Commissioners of the United States, Report to the International Exhibition Held in Vienna, 1873,* vol. 2. Washington, D.C.: Government Printing Office, 1876.

"Seminary for Female Teachers." *American Annals of Education* 1 (1831): 341–45.

Sheridan, Laura C. "The Higher Education of Deaf-Mute Women." *American Annals of the Deaf* 20 (October 1875): 249–52.

Sheridan, Martha A. "Deaf Women Now: Establishing Our Niche." *Deaf World: A Historical Reader and Primary Sourcebook,* edited by Lois Bragg, 380–89. New York: New York University Press, 2001.

Showalter, Elaine. "A Criticism of Our Own: Autonomy and Assimilation in Afro-American and Feminist Literary Theory." In *Feminisms: An Anthology of Literary Theory and Criticism,* edited by Robyn R. Warhol and Diane Price Herndl. New Brunswick, N.J.: Rutgers University Press, 1997.

Sims, Anastasia. *The Power of Femininity in the New South: Women's Organizations and Politics in North Carolina, 1880–1930.* Columbia: University of South Carolina Press, 1997.

Smith, Bonnie, and Beth Hutchinson, eds. *Gendering Disability.* New Brunswick, N.J.: Rutgers University Press, 2004.

Sonnestrahl, D. M. *Deaf Artists in America: Colonial to Contemporary.* San Diego: DawnSignPress, 2002.

"Statistics of Speech Teaching in American Schools for the Deaf." *Association Review* 2 (1900): 298–315.

Stevens, Kelly H. "Freehand Drawing and Applied Art: Their Place in Vocational Training," *Conference of American Instructors of the Deaf* 24 (July 1925): 110–12.

Stockton, Kathryn Bond. "Bodies of God: Postructuralist Feminists Return to the Fold of Spiritual Materialism." *boundary 2* 19, no. 2 (1992): 113–49.

Taylor H. "The Ichthyosaurus, the Cave Bear and the Male Teacher." *Association Review* 2 (1900): 361–66.

A teacher in a small school. "Is the Small School a Boon to the Deaf?" *American Annals of the Deaf* 47 (1902): 455–63.

Terry, Jennifer, and Jacqueline Urla, eds. *Deviant Bodies: Critical Perspectives on Difference in Science and Popular Culture.* Bloomington: Indiana University Press, 1995.

"Thomas Lewis Brown." *Report of Proceedings of the Nineteenth Meeting of the Convention of the American Instructors of the Deaf,* 230. 1911.

Thomas, Lloyd Swift. "Overcoming the Handicap of Deafness." *Silent Worker* 32, no. 3 (1919): 59.

Traherne, Thomas. *Centuries, Poems, and Thanksgivings,* edited by H. M. Margoliouth. Oxford: Clarendon Press, 1958.

Thrasher, F. M. *The Gang.* Chicago: University of Chicago Press, 1927.

Tomaskovic-Devey, D. *Gender and Racial Inequality at Work: The Sources and Consequences of Job Segregation.* Ithaca, N.Y.: ILR Press, 1993.

Toward, Lilias M. *Mabel Bell, Alexander's Silent Partner.* New York: Methuen, 1984.

Tucker, Bonnie P. *The Feel of Silence.* Philadelphia: Temple University Press, 1995.

Turk, Diana B. *Bound by a Mighty Vow: Sisterhood and Women's Fraternities, 1870–1920.* New York: New York University Press, 2004.

Tyler, Joseph D. "Letter to Tillinghast Family." In *A Place of Their Own,* edited by John Vickery Van Cleve and Barry A. Crouch. Washington, D.C.: Gallaudet University Press, 1989.

U.S. Department of the Interior. *The Deaf and the Hard-of-Hearing in the Occupational World* (Bulletin 1936 #13). Washington, D.C.: U.S. Government Printing Office, 1936.

Valentine, Phyllis. "Thomas Hopkins Gallaudet: Benevolent Paternalism and the Origins of the American Asylum." In *Deaf History Unveiled:*

Interpretations from the New Scholarship, edited by John Van Cleve. Washington, D.C.: Gallaudet University Press, 1999.

Valli, Clayton, and Ceil Lucas. *Linguistics of American Sign Language: An Introduction*. 2nd ed. Washington, D.C.: Gallaudet University Press, 1995.

Van Cleve, John Vickrey, ed. *The Gallaudet Encyclopedia of Deaf People and Deafness*. 3 vols. New York: McGraw-Hill, 1987.

————. *Deaf History Unveiled: Interpretations from the New Scholarship*. Washington, D.C.: Gallaudet University Press, 1993.

Van Cleve, John Vickrey, and Barry A. Crouch. *A Place of Their Own*. Washington, D.C.: Gallaudet University Press, 1989.

Vidich, A. J., and S. M. Lyman. "Qualitative Methods: Their History in Sociology and Anthropology." In *Handbook of Qualitative Research*, edited by N. K. Denzin and Y. S. Lincoln, 23–59. Thousand Oaks, Calif.: Sage, 1994.

Wait, Gary E. "Julia Brace." *Dartmouth College Library Bulletin* 33, no. 1 (November 1992).

Waterhouse, Edward J. "Education of the Deaf-Blind in the United States of America, 1837–1896." In *State of the Art: Perspectives on Serving Deaf-Blind Children*, edited by Edgar Lowell and Carole Rouin, 5–17. United States Department of Education, 1967.

Weaver, C. *Disability and Work: Incentives, Rights and Opportunities*. Washington, D.C.: AEI Press.

Wendell, Susan. *The Rejected Body: Feminist Philosophical Reflections on Disability*. New York: Routledge, 1996.

————."Towards a Feminist Theory of Disability." In *The Disability Studies Reader*, edited by L. J. Davis, 260–69. New York: Routledge, 1997.

Wenger, Arthur. "Distinctive Features of Schools for the Deaf." *Silent Worker* 33 (January 1921): 111–14.

Wetzel, J. R. "Labor force, Unemployment and Earnings." In *State of the Union: America in the 1990's. Vol. 1, Economic Trends*, edited by R. Farley, 59–105. New York: Russell Sage Foundation, 1995.

"What Does It Mean to Be Slain in the Spirit?" *Christian Apologetics and Research Ministry*, 2003. http://www.carm.org/questions/slain_spirit.htm (accessed February 2, 2005).

Wheeler, F. "Growth of American Schools for the Deaf." *American Annals of the Deaf* 65 (1920): 367–78.

Whitestone, Heather. *Listening with My Heart.* New York: Doubleday, 1997.

Wilkinson, W. "Segregate Buildings." *American Annals of the Deaf* 21 (October 1876): 226–31.

Wilkinson, Warring. "Harriet B. Willard." *Report of the Proceedings of the Twelfth Convention of American Instructors of the Deaf held at New York Institution of Deaf and Dumb.* 1890.

Williamson, Mary M. "Glimpses around the Michigan School." *Silent Worker* 18 (May 1906): 113–14.

Winakur, I. The Income Determinants of Gallaudet College Alumni. PhD diss., American University, 1973.

Williams, Helena Lorenz. "Health, the Course to Beauty." *Silent Worker* 38, no. 3 (1925): 136–37.

Winefield, Richard. *Never the Twain Shall Meet: Bell, Gallaudet, and the Communications Debate.* Washington, D.C.: Gallaudet University Press, 1987.

Wing, "The Associative Feature in the Education of the Deaf." *American Annals of the Deaf and Dumb* 31 (1886): 22–35.

Winzer, Margret A. *Talking Deaf Mutes: The Special Role of Women in the Methodological Conflict Regarding the Deaf, 1867–1900.* Halifax, Canada: Mount Saint Vincent University, 1981.

———. *The History of Special Education: From Isolation to Integration.* Washington, D.C.: Gallaudet University Press, 1993.

Withrow, F. B. "Public Law 87-276: Its Effects on the Supply of Trained Teachers of the Deaf." *Volta Review* (1967): 656–63.

Wittig, Monique. "One Is Not Born a Woman." In *Feminims,* edited by Sandra Kemp and Judith Squires. Oxford: Oxford University Press, 1997.

Wood, Kathleen M. "Coherent Identities amid Heterosexist Ideologies: Deaf and Hearing Lesbian Coming-Out Stories." In *Reinventing Identities: The Gendered Self in Discourse,* edited by Mary Bucholtz, A. C. Liang, and Laurel A. Sutton. New York: Oxford University Press, 1999.

Woodward, J. "Implications for Sociolinguistics Research among the Deaf." *Sign Language Studies* 1 (1972): 1–7.

Wright, A. "The Manual and Oral Combination." *American Annals of the Deaf* 60 (1915): 219.

Wright, Mary Herring. *Sounds Like Home: Growing Up Black and Deaf in the South*. Washington, D.C.: Gallaudet University Press, 1999.

Yale, C. *Years of Building: Memoirs of a Pioneer in a Special Field of Education*. New York: Dial Press, 1931.

WEBSITES/DATABASES

American Foundation for the Blind Helen Keller Archives: http://www.afb.org/

Database of films: http://www.disabilityfilms.co.uk/deaftoc.htm

Deaf Women United: http://www.dwu.org/links.htm

Deerfield, Massachusetts, Memorial Hall Museum: http://www.americancenturies.mass.edu/home.html

Disability History Museum: http://www.disabilitymuseum.org/

Gallaudet Index to Deaf Periodicals

Gallaudet Index to Deaf Biographies

RIT Deaf Women Bibliography: http://wally.rit.edu/pubs/guides/Deafwomen.html#v

Silent Worker, Gallaudet University Archives: http://www.aladin.wrlc.org/gsdl/collect/gasw/gasw.shtml

EXHIBITS/ARCHIVES

Clarke School for the Deaf/Smith College Libraries, Northampton, Mass.

Gallaudet University Archives, Washington, D.C.

"History through Deaf Eyes," Washington, D.C.

Volta Bureau Collections, Washington, D.C.

EDUCATIONAL AND DOCUMENTARY FILMS

Deaf Culture Autobiography: MJ Bienvenu. Produced by J. K.Humphrey. Salem, Ore.: Sign Enhancers, 1989.

Deaf Culture Lecture: Cultural Differences—Nathie Marbury. Produced by Nathie Marbury. Salem, Ore.: Sign Enhancers, 1994.

Deaf Minorities. San Francisco, Calif.: San Francisco Public Library, 1984.

Deaf Women: Ambitious Dreams, Emerging Dreams. Rochester, N.Y.: NTID, 1979.

Deaf Women United, produced by C. Bucholz. 1985.

Debbie Rennie—Poetry in Motion. Produced by D. Rennie. Burtonsville, Md.: Sign Media, 1990.

Famous Deaf Americans. Produced by R. Panara. Rochester, N.Y.: NTID, 1981.

Juliana: A Portrait. [S.l.]: Ulano/Mierzwa, 1984.

Linda Bove at NTID. Rochester, N.Y.: NTID, 1988.

Meeting of the Minds. Rochester, N.Y.: NTID, 1989.

Positive Images: Portraits of Women with Disabilities. Produced by J. Harrison and H. Rousso. New York: Women Make Movies, 1989.

Shades of Gray: Black and Deaf. Produced by W. Miller. Rochester, N.Y.: WOKR Partners, 1991.

Signs of Victory. Produced by Special Materials Project, 1981.

Summer's Story: Coming of Age with the Cochlear Implant. Written by Summer Crider. Alachua, Fl.: Munroe MultiMedia, 2002.

When the Mind Hears: Concerning Women. Burtonsville, Md.: Sign Media, 1993.

Contributors

Emily K. Abel is a professor of public health and women's studies at the University of California Los Angeles. Her most recent book is *Hearts of Wisdom: American Women Caring for Kin, 1850–1940* (Harvard University Press, 2000). She currently is writing a history of tuberculosis in Los Angeles.

Sharon Barnartt is a professor in the Department of Sociology at Gallaudet University. She is coauthor (with John Christiansen) of *Deaf President Now: The 1988 Revolution at Gallaudet University* (Gallaudet University Press, 1995), and coauthor (with Richard Scotch) of *Disability Protests: Contentious Politics, 1970–1999* (Gallaudet University Press, 2001). She is the cofounder and co-editor, with Barbara Altman, of the journal *Research in Social Science and Disability*. Her research relates to social movements in the deaf and disability communities, socioeconomic status issues for deaf and disabled men and women, and disability laws and policies.

Brenda Jo Brueggemann is an associate professor at Ohio State University (OSU) where she teaches in the English and Women's Studies departments. She coordinates the Disability Studies minor program and the American Sign Language program at OSU. She has published books, articles, essays, and edited collections in rhetoric, Disability Studies, and Deaf Studies.

Susan Burch is an associate professor of history at Gallaudet University. Her research primarily has focused on Deaf cultural histories in America and Russia. She is currently completing a book project in Deaf history with Hannah Joyner and is the editor of the *Encyclopedia of American Disability History* with Facts on File.

Kristen Harmon is an associate professor of English at Gallaudet University. In addition to articles in the fields of Deaf Studies and Ethnography, she has also published short fiction.

Arlene Blumenthal Kelly is an associate professor in the Department of ASL and Deaf Studies at Gallaudet University. She has published articles in various books and journals, including *Sociolinguistics of Deaf Communities, Disability Studies Quarterly,* and the *American Annals of the Deaf.* Her interests include historical linguistics, fingerspelling, and Deaf history.

Jessica Lee completed her MA in Deaf Studies at Gallaudet University and is currently pursuing a PhD in Cultural Anthropology. She is interested in historical and anthropological study of disability, Deaf studies, identity, and gender.

Linda Risser Lytle is a professor in the Department of Counseling at Gallaudet University. Her research interests include mental health counseling with deaf people, issues in identity development of deaf women, and issues related to health education and deaf people. She also maintains a private practice.

Jennifer Nelson is a professor of English at Gallaudet University. Her interests are in art, English literature, women's literature, and Disability Studies.

Kim E. Nielsen is an associate professor at the University of Wisconsin-Green Bay, where she teaches courses in women's studies and history. She has written extensively on women, politics, and disability in United States history. Her books include *The Radical Lives of Helen Keller* (New York University Press, 2004) and *Helen Keller: Selected Writings* (New York University Press, 2005).

Gina A. Oliva is a professor in the Department of Physical Education and Recreation at Gallaudet University and the author of *Alone in the Mainstream: A Deaf Woman Remembers Public School* (Gallaudet University Press, 2004).

Susan Plann is a professor of Spanish and Portuguese at the University of California Los Angeles and the author of *A Silent Minority: Deaf Education in Spain, 1550–1835* (University of California Press, 1997). She has also published numerous articles on Spanish Deaf history.

Sara Robinson earned a BA in History and an MA in Deaf Studies with a concentration in Deaf History from Gallaudet University. She is currently a PhD student in the Department of History at the Ohio State University.

Margret Winzer is a professor in the Faculty of Education at the University of Lethbridge in Alberta, Canada. She teaches in the areas of special education and early childhood education. She has published widely in the field of special education, particularly on policy studies, comparative studies, and the history of special education.

Index